Adobe® FrameMaker® 7.0

Classroom in a Book®

SO-ABB-314

Adobe

www.adobe.com/adobepress

© 2003 Adobe Systems Incorporated. All rights reserved.

Adobe ® FrameMaker 7.0 Classroom in a Book ® for Windows ®, Macintosh, and UNIX

This manual, as well as the software described in it, is furnished under license and may be used or copied only in accordance with the terms of such license. The content of this manual is furnished for informational use only, is subject to change without notice, and should not be construed as a commitment by Adobe Systems Incorporated. Adobe Systems Incorporated assumes no responsibility or liability for any errors or inaccuracies that may appear in this documentation.

Except as permitted by such license, no part of this publication may be reproduced, stored in a retrieval system, or transmitted, in any form or by any means, electronic, mechanical, recording, or otherwise, without the prior written permission of Adobe Systems Incorporated.

Please remember that existing artwork or images that you may want to include in your project may be protected under copyright law. The unauthorized incorporation of such material into your new work could be a violation of the rights of the copyright owner. Please be sure to obtain any permission required from the copyright owner.

Any references to company names in sample templates are for demonstration purposes only and are not intended to refer to any actual organization.

Adobe, the Adobe logo, the Adobe Press logo, Adobe Type Manager, ATM, Acrobat, the Acrobat logo, Acrobat Capture, Acrobat Catalog, Acrobat Distiller, Acrobat Exchange, Acrobat Reader, Classroom in a Book, FrameMaker, Illustrator, PageMaker, and PostScript are either registered trademarks or trademarks of Adobe Systems Incorporated in the United States and/or other countries. Microsoft, and Windows are either registered trademarks or trademarks of Microsoft Corporation in the United States and/or other countries. Apple, Mac, Macintosh Power Macintosh, QuickTime, and TrueType are trademarks of Apple Computer, Inc., registered in the United States and other countries. Solaris is a trademark of Sun Microsystems, Inc. Indy is a trademark of Silicon Graphics, Inc. UNIX is a registered trademark in the United States and other countries, licensed exclusively through X/Open Company, Ltd. Pentium is a registered trademark of Intel Corporation. All other trademarks are the property of their respective owners.

Adobe Systems Incorporated, 345 Park Avenue, San Jose, California 95110, USA.

Adobe Press books are published by Peachpit Press, Berkeley, CA.
To report errors, please send a note to errata@peachpit.com.

Notice to U.S. Government End Users. The Software and Documentation are "Commercial Items," as that term is defined at 48 C.F.R. §2.101, consisting of "Commercial Computer Software" and "Commercial Computer Software Documentation," as such terms are used in 48 C.F.R. §12.212 or 48 C.F.R. §227.7202, as applicable. Consistent with 48 C.F.R. §12.212 or 48 C.F.R. §§227.7202-1 through 227.7202-4, as applicable, the Commercial Computer Software and Commercial Computer Software Documentation are being licensed to U.S. Government end users (a) only as Commercial Items and (b) with only those rights as are granted to all other end users pursuant to the terms and conditions herein. Unpublished-rights reserved under the copyright laws of the United States. Adobe Systems Incorporated, 345 Park Avenue, San Jose, CA 95110-2704, USA. For U.S. Government End Users, Adobe agrees to comply with all applicable equal opportunity laws including, if appropriate, the provisions of Executive Order 11246, as amended, Section 402 of the Vietnam Era Veterans Readjustment Assistance Act of 1974 (38 USC 4212), and Section 503 of the Rehabilitation Act of 1973, as amended, and the regulations at 41 CFR Parts 60-1 through 60-60, 60-250, and 60-741. The affirmative action clause and regulations contained in the preceding sentence shall be incorporated by reference in this Agreement.

ISBN 0-321-13168-1

Printed in the U.S.A.

9 8 7 6 5 4 3 2 1

Contents

Lesson 3   **Defining Colors and Character Formats**

Lesson 4   **Page Layout**

Lesson 5   **Graphics**

Lesson 13   **Conditional Text**

Lesson 14   **Hypertext and PDF**

Lesson 15   **HTML and Web Publishing**

Part Two

Structured Adobe FrameMaker 7.0

Part One:

FrameMaker 7.0

Getting Started

Welcome to Adobe® FrameMaker 7.0®—the complete publishing system that provides all the tools you need for word processing, page design, graphics, and book building. Combined with all of this is an easy-to-use environment for preparing and authoring documents for storage in or output to valid structured FrameMaker formats.

Whether you're writing simple one-page memos or complex multichapter documents with imported graphics, this versatile application is ideal for organizations that need to reuse and distribute content on multiple devices and operating systems. For example, a single document created with FrameMaker 7.0 can be used for an eBook document, an HTML document for the Web, or an XML document.

The power and flexibility of FrameMaker 7.0

With support for both the Standard Generalized Markup Language (SGML) and the Extended Markup Language (XML), FrameMaker 7.0 allows you to easily import, open and work with existing structured documents and then save them back to SGML or XML when you're finished.

Adobe FrameMaker 7.0 is a robust tool for organizations that need to quickly and efficiently publish complex documents to multiple channels, including XML, HTML, Adobe PDF (Portable Document Format), print, and SGML.

Additional key features include WYSIWYG (what you see is what you get)-based context-sensitive guided editing and authoring for structured documents; automated generation and updating of indexes, tables of contents, cross-references, and hyperlinks.

About Classroom in a Book

Adobe FrameMaker 7.0 Classroom in a Book® is part of the official training series for Adobe graphics and publishing software developed by experts at Adobe Systems. These lessons are designed to let you learn at your own pace. If you're new to Adobe FrameMaker 7.0, you'll learn the fundamental concepts and features you'll need to master the program. If you've been using it for a while, you'll find this book teaches many advanced features, including tips and techniques for using the latest version of Adobe FrameMaker.

Although each lesson provides step-by-step instructions for creating a specific project, there is room for exploration and experimentation. It is recommended that you follow the book from start to finish, especially if you have never used FrameMaker before; but you can, if you wish, do only the lessons that correspond to your interests and needs. Screen illustrations vary among the Windows, Mac OS, and UNIX platforms. Platform, or operating system, differences are mentioned only when they are substantial.

Prerequisites

Before using *Adobe FrameMaker 7.0 Classroom in a Book*, you should have a working knowledge of your computer and its operating system. You should know how to use a mouse and standard menus and commands. You should also know how to copy, open, save, print, and close files. If you need to review these techniques, see your Microsoft® Windows®, Macintosh® (Mac™ OS), or UNIX® documentation. Adobe Acrobat® 5.05 Distiller is provided on the main installation disk, so that you can perform the exercises involving PDF file preparation, but you will need the Acrobat program for viewing them (see "Installing Adobe Acrobat Distiller 5.05 and Internet browsers" on the next page).

Installing the FrameMaker 7.0 program

Before you begin using *Adobe FrameMaker 7.0 Classroom in a Book,* make sure that your system is set up correctly and that you've installed the required software and hardware. You must purchase the Adobe FrameMaker 7.0 software separately. For system requirements and complete instructions on installing the software, see the *InstallReadMe* file on the Adobe FrameMaker 7.0 Application CD.

You must install the application from the Adobe FrameMaker CD onto your hard disk; you cannot run the program from the CD. Follow the on-screen installation instructions. Make sure your serial number is available before installing the application; you can find the serial number on the registration card or CD sleeve.

If you're upgrading from an earlier version of FrameMaker, be sure to save a copy of your user dictionaries before installing the application.

Installing Adobe Acrobat Distiller 5.05 and Internet browsers

You must install Adobe Acrobat Distiller 5.05, which comes on the installation disk, in order to complete the later lessons in this book. You also need to have Adobe Acrobat Reader® 4.0 or later or the Adobe Acrobat® 4.0 or later to view files. You should have Netscape® Navigator 4.7 or later or Microsoft® Internet Explorer 5.5. or later.

Installing WebWorks and XML Cookbook

WebWorks® by Quadralay Corporation and the XML Cookbook are covered in late lessons of this Classroom in a Book (CIB). For system requirements and complete instructions on installing the software, see the *InstallReadMe* file on the Adobe FrameMaker 7.0 Application CD.

Installing the Classroom in a Book fonts

To ensure that the lesson files appear on your system with the correct fonts, you may need to install the Classroom in a Book font files. The fonts for the lessons are located in the Fonts folder on the *FrameMaker 7.0 Classroom in a Book* CD. If you already have these on your system, you do not need to install them. If you have ATM® (Adobe Type Manager®), its documentation describes installation of fonts. Or, ATM Light is available from the Adobe web site (www.adobe.com). If you require additional fonts, installing ATM from the CIB CD will automatically install the necessary fonts.

Note: Windows XP/2000 has built-in support for both TrueType and Type1 fonts. Windows 95/98/ME has built-in support for TrueType fonts, but requires Adobe Type Manager (ATM) to use Type1 fonts.

In some instances, a lesson might require fonts that are not installed on your system. If necessary, FrameMaker will automatically substitute similar fonts, and will display a font substitution dialog box. To reformat the document using available fonts, click OK.

(UNIX) The UNIX-compatible fonts are in the tar archive (unixcib.tar) located in the Unix folder on the *FrameMaker 7.0 Classroom in a Book* CD. For instructions on how to install fonts for FrameMaker 7.0 UNIX, consult the online manual *Working With Fonts in FrameMaker for UNIX* installed with the FrameMaker application. For your convenience, the online manual is also included in the Unix folder as the file Fonts_UNIX.pdf.

Installing fonts from the Adobe FrameMaker 7.0 Classroom in a Book CD

Use the following procedure to install the fonts on your hard drive.

1 Insert the Adobe FrameMaker 7.0 Classroom in a Book CD in your CD-ROM drive.

2 Install the font files using the procedure for the version of your operating system:

• Windows (other than Windows XP or 2000). Open the ATM installer files on the CD, which are located in the Fonts/ATM folder. Double-click the installer file (Setup), and follow the on-screen instructions for installing ATM and the fonts.

• Windows XP and 2000. Do not use the ATM font installer to install the fonts. Instead, simply drag the fonts from the CD to your hard disk and place them in your Adobe common fonts folder (typically in C:\Program Files\Common Files\Adobe\Fonts).

• Mac OS 9. Open the Fonts folder on the CD. Double-click the ATM 4.6.1 + Fonts Installer to install the fonts.

• Mac OS X. Open the Fonts folder on the CD. Select all of the fonts in the Fonts folder and drag them into the Library/Fonts folder on your hard disk. You can select and drag multiple fonts to install them, but you cannot drag the entire folder to install the fonts.

♀ *(Windows and Mac OS) You should also install the Classroom in a Book fonts by copying all the files in the fonts folder on the Adobe FrameMaker 7.0 Classroom in a Book CD to the fonts folder within the folder where you installed FrameMaker 7.0 on your hard disk. Doing so makes the fonts available to FrameMaker 7.0 but not to other applications. (If there is no fonts folder in the same folder where the program is installed, add a folder named* fonts *(all lower case), and then copy the fonts into it. (Unix) Copy the fonts into the (Frame_path)/fminit/fmfonts directory.*

Note: *If you encounter a missing fonts message, you can force FrameMaker to permanently substitute fonts by going to File > Preferences and turning off the "Remember Missing Font Names" option. When you open any files with unavailable fonts in a FrameMaker session, the unavailable fonts will be permanently substituted with available fonts once the file is re-saved with the File > Save As command.*

Copying the Classroom in a Book files

The Classroom in a Book CD includes folders containing all the electronic files for the lessons. Each lesson has its own folder, and you must copy the folders to your hard drive to do the lessons. To save room on your drive, you can choose to install only the folder for each lesson as you need it, and remove it when you're done.

To install the Classroom in a Book files:

1 Make sure the *Adobe FrameMaker 7.0 Classroom in a Book* CD is in your CD-ROM drive.

2 Create a folder named FM_CIB on your hard drive.

3 Copy the lessons you want to the hard drive:

• To copy all of the lessons, drag the Lessons folder from the CD into the FM_CIB folder.

• To copy a single lesson, drag the individual lesson folder from the CD into the FM_CIB folder.

Note: If you are installing the files in UNIX, follow the instructions in Appendix D, "Copying the Sample Files (UNIX)."

Note: If you are installing the files in Windows, you need to unlock them before using them. You don't need to unlock the files if you are installing them in Mac OS.

4 In Windows, unlock the files you copied:

• If you copied all of the lessons, double-click the unlock.bat file in the Lessons folder within the FM_CIB folder.

• If you copied a single lesson, drag the unlock.bat file from the Lessons folder on the CD into the FM_CIB folder. Then double-click the unlock.bat file in the FM_CIB folder.

Starting the FrameMaker 7.0 program

When you start FrameMaker 7.0 for the first time, you are prompted to choose between two interfaces: the standard FrameMaker mode and Structured FrameMaker. Lessons specific to using Structured FrameMaker begin at Lesson 14.

To start Adobe FrameMaker in Windows:

Do one of the following:

• Choose Start > Programs > Adobe > FrameMaker 7.0.

• Choose Start > Run, and then enter the full pathname of the program executable file, enclosed in double quotation marks (optionally followed by the name of a file to open): "C:\Program Files\Adobe\FrameMaker 7.0\FrameMaker.exe".

To start Adobe FrameMaker in Mac OS:

Open the FrameMaker folder, and double-click the FrameMaker program icon. (If you installed the program in a folder other than Adobe FrameMaker, open that folder.)

To start Adobe FrameMaker in UNIX:

In a UNIX window, do one of the following:

• To start the U.S. Edition, enter **maker.**

• To start the International Edition, enter **maker -l** (lowercase L) and the name of the language you want to use (for example, ukenglish, japanese, francais, or deutsch). For example, to start the French version of FrameMaker, you would enter **maker -l francais.**

Unstructured and Structured FrameMaker 7.0

FrameMaker 7.0 combines the power and flexibility of regular FrameMaker and FrameMaker+SGML to provide users with a robust set of stable, mission-critical tools for XML and SGML authoring. You can work with documents in two distinct ways: unstructured and structured.

Unstructured mode, referred to as standard FrameMaker, will be most familiar to users of word processing software and supports a WYSIWYG template-based authoring and publishing workflow.

In structured mode, FrameMaker extends its WYSIWYG authoring environment to support the structuring of content into a hierarchy of elements and attributes using Document Type Definitions (DTDs). It includes a styling language, known as Element Definition Document, or EDD, that enables sophisticated context-sensitive formatting and layout. Structured FrameMaker supports users working with and creating valid SGML and XML. Users choose their preferred mode at first program launch and through the Preferences dialog box, so that those who are not currently working in structured authoring can work with a simpler interface.

The Element Catalog and the Structure View provide context-sensitive guided editing. The Element Catalog quickly shows you which elements are valid; the Structure View window displays any validity errors as they occur in real time. Structured FrameMaker supports round tripping XML, so you can open, edit, and save XML files and DTDs. After authoring and tagging tasks are complete, you can easily save standards-compliant XML files for further processing. FrameMaker 7.0 also includes support for namespaces and Unicode (UTF-8/UTF-16).

Adobe FrameMaker 7.0 and Microsoft® Word®

Adobe FrameMaker 7.0 is especially compatible with Microsoft® Word® and Microsoft Excel®. This user-friendly capability makes it easy to import Word and Excel files into FrameMaker 7.0 and allows you to quickly utilize all its advanced authoring and document management tools. FrameMaker is a significant word processing application in its own right. As your comfort level grows with its many powerful aspects, you will be able to do all of your document creation, starting with the original input, directly in FrameMaker 7.0 itself.

Additional Resources

Adobe FrameMaker 7.0 Classroom in a Book is not intended to replace documentation that comes with the FrameMaker 7.0 program. Only the commands and options used in the lessons are explained in this book. For comprehensive information about program features, refer to these resources:

• The *Adobe FrameMaker 7.0 User Guide,* which is included with the Adobe FrameMaker 7.0 software, contains a complete description of all features, tools, and commands in the software. It is designed to be used as a reference tool, and provides instructions for using FrameMaker on the Windows, Mac OS, and UNIX platforms.

• The *Adobe FrameMaker Quick Reference Card* contains basic information about FrameMaker tools and palettes, and shortcuts for using them.

• Online Help, an online version of the *User Guide*, is accessible by choosing Help > Contents. (For more information, see Lesson 1, "Getting to Know the Work Area.")

• The *Installing FrameMaker Products* (UNIX) guide contains information for system administrators for setting up, licensing, and maintaining FrameMaker on a UNIX network.

• The Adobe Web site (www.adobe.com), which you can view by choosing Help > Adobe Online if you have a connection to the World Wide Web.

Adobe Certification

The Adobe Training and Certification Programs are designed to help Adobe customers improve and promote their product proficiency skills. The Adobe Certified Expert (ACE) program is designed to recognize the high-level skills of expert users. Adobe Certified Training Providers (ACTP) use only Adobe Certified Experts to teach Adobe software classes. Available in either ACTP classrooms or on site, the ACE program is the best way to master Adobe products. For Adobe Certified Training Programs information, visit the Partnering with Adobe Web site at http://partners.adobe.com.

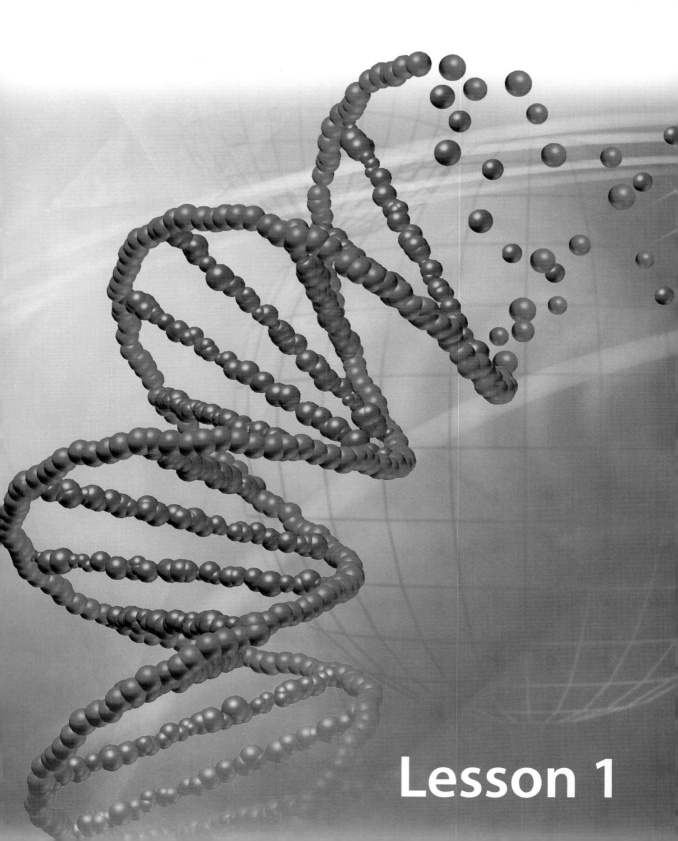

Lesson 1

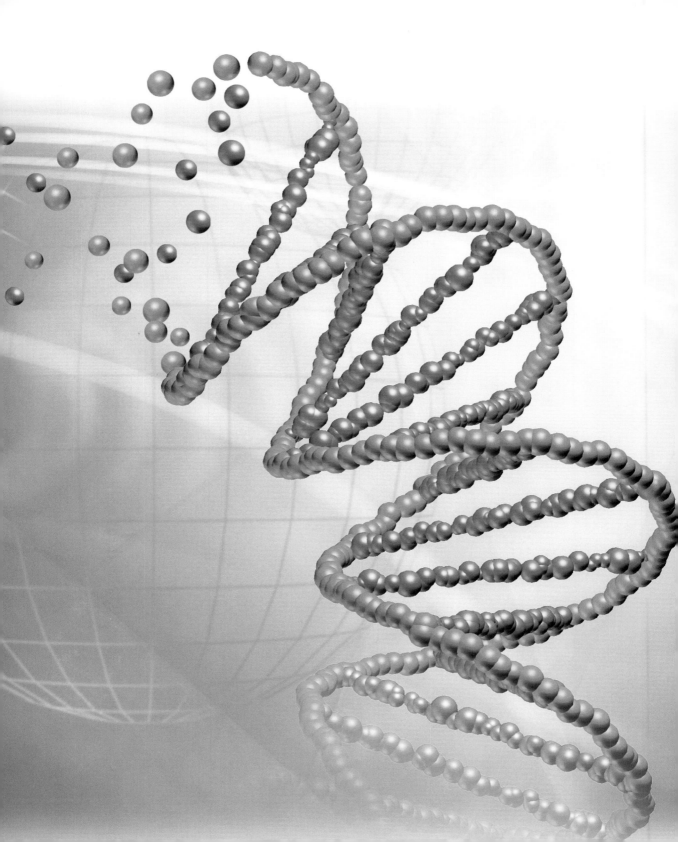

1 Working with FrameMaker 7.0 Documents

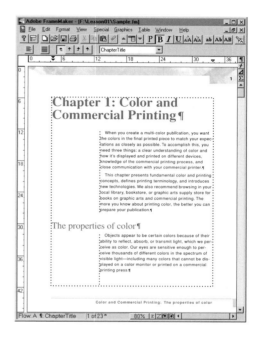

The FrameMaker 7.0 document window contains aids for writing, illustrating, viewing, and navigating within a document. The look of a document is determined by its template, which provides page layouts and predefined formats for paragraphs and selected text.

In this lesson, you'll learn how to do the following:

• Set up the work area.

• Show and hide document window guides.

• Display pages and zoom in on them.

• Format paragraphs by applying formats from a document's Paragraph Catalog.

• Format words and phrases by applying formats from a document's Character Catalog.

• Create a document from a standard template.

Getting started

During this lesson, you'll save documents as you work on them. If you haven't already done so, you should copy the folder containing the sample documents, and then start FrameMaker 7.0.

1 Copy the lessons folders as described in "Installing the Classroom in a Book fonts" on page 3.

2 If FrameMaker 7.0 isn't already running, do one of the following to start it:

• (Windows) Double-click the FrameMaker 7.0 icon, if it is visible, or choose Start > Programs > Adobe > FrameMaker 7.0 > Adobe FrameMaker 7.0. (If you installed FrameMaker 7.0 in a folder other than Adobe, choose that folder from the Start > Programs menu.) After a few moments, the FrameMaker 7.0 application window appears.

• (Mac OS) Double-click the FrameMaker 7.0 icon. After a few moments, the FrameMaker 7.0 menus appear.

(UNIX) In a UNIX window, change to your home directory. Enter **maker** to start the U.S. Edition, or **maker-l** (lowercase *L*) **ukenglish** to start the UK English language version of FrameMaker. After a few moments, the main FrameMaker 7.0 window appears.

Setting up the work area preference

When you first launch FrameMaker 7.0, the program gives you the choice of working in standard FrameMaker or Structured FrameMaker.

1 The FrameMaker 7.0 application opens with the Choose Interface dialog box.

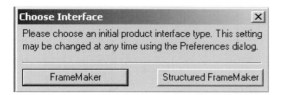

2 Click **FrameMaker** to select the standard FrameMaker application interface.

Note: You will use the (unstructured or standard) FrameMaker interface for the first 15 lessons in this Classroom in a Book; and Structured FrameMaker for lessons 16, 17, and 18.

3 If this is your first use of FrameMaker 7.0 since installation, you may be prompted to register the program. Follow the instructions as appropriate.

The Adobe FrameMaker Document window now appears with work area and commands defined for (unstructured) word processing and document production.

Changing the interface preference

If you have been operating or exploring Structured FrameMaker prior to starting this lesson, you may have noticed that the main menu options are different from standard FrameMaker.

Main menu bar in standard FrameMaker 7.0.

Main menu bar in Structured FrameMaker. Note the menu title Element *is an added feature in this mode.*

To properly set up for Part One, the first 13 lessons of this book, please be sure you are in standard FrameMaker 7.0 by doing the following:

1 From the main menu choose File > Preferences > General (Windows and Mac OS) or File > Preferences (UNIX). The Preferences dialog box appears.

Note: *If the last entry already reads* FrameMaker *or you can tell from the configuration of the main menu title bar that you are already in standard mode, skip steps 2–5; you are properly set up for Part One, the first 13 lessons.*

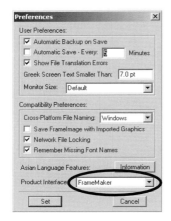

2 In the Product Interface area at the bottom of the dialog box, select *FrameMaker*.

3 Click Set. The application will tell you to Quit and then to Restart the program.

4 Quit FrameMaker. Choose File > Quit.

5 Restart the FrameMaker 7.0 application. After it opens, you will note from the main menu that you are operating in the standard mode.

Exploring the document window

Before you begin work on a document of your own, you'll take a quick look at the FrameMaker 7.0 document window, which appears when you create or open a document.

Opening a document

First, you'll open a sample document.

1 Do one of the following:

- (Windows and Mac OS) Choose File > Open.

- (UNIX) In the main FrameMaker 7.0 window, click Open.

2 Locate and open the Lesson01 folder that you copied to your hard drive. Select Sample.fm in the Lesson01 folder and click Open. The document appears in a document window.

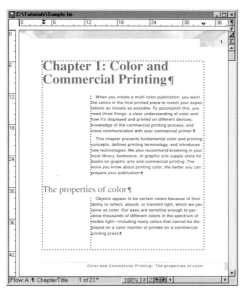

Document window

Saving a document

FrameMaker 7.0 allows you to save files in a variety of formats. For this lesson, you will save files as .fm, which will save them as standard FrameMaker 7.0 formatted files.

To save the file, choose File > Save As, enter the filename **Sample1.fm,** and click Save.

You'll rename and save the documents you use in the lessons so that you can return to the unchanged originals, if you wish, without recopying them from the CD-ROM. It's good practice to save new documents when you create them, and to save frequently when you're editing documents.

You may want to specify a different file type. Choose File > Save As. The Format pop-up menu allows you to save a file in the following formats, among others:

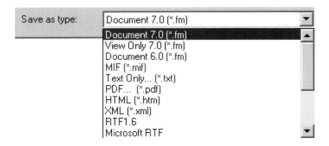

• (FrameMaker 6.0) Saves the FrameMaker 7.0 document as a 6.0 document that you can open and edit in FrameMaker 6.0.

• (MIF) Creates a text file containing FrameMaker statements that describe all text and graphics. It is a good idea to save the MIF file under a different name. (For example, add a .mif extension to the name.)

• (XML) Creates an Extensible Markup Language (XML) document that can be used for data exchange and viewed on the World Wide Web.

• (PDF) Creates a Portable Document Format (PDF) file that can be viewed in Adobe Acrobat and other applications that support PDF files.

Adjusting your view

Several controls and guides appear around the edge of the document window. The window also contains text symbols, such as the end-of-paragraph symbol (¶), and a dotted border around the editable part of the document.

You can use the top ruler to set paragraph indents and tabs.

Top ruler

You can use the formatting bar to format text. When the formatting bar is visible, it appears below the menu bar (Windows) or below the document window's title bar (Mac OS and UNIX).

Formatting bar in Windows

You can also display the QuickAccess bar by choosing View > QuickAccess Bar. This contains shortcuts to commonly used commands.

QuickAccess bar

The status bar at the bottom of the window contains information about the document and controls for zooming and for moving through the document.

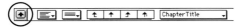

Status bar

Right now, you're just looking at the document, so you'll hide the formatting bar, the rulers, and the QuickAccess bar (if it's visible). You'll also adjust the window size and use a command in a context-sensitive pop-up menu to turn off the text symbols.

1 If the formatting bar is visible, do one of the following to hide it:

• (Windows) Choose View > Formatting Bar.

• (Mac OS and UNIX) Click the formatting bar toggle on the left side of the format-ting bar.

Formatting bar toggle

2 Choose View > Rulers to hide the rulers.

3 If the QuickAccess bar is visible, do one of the following to hide it:

• (Windows) Choose View > QuickAccess Bar.

• (Mac OS) Click the close box.

• (UNIX) Put the pointer on the bar and press Control+c.

Because you hid the rulers, the document window may now be larger than the page. If so, you'll change the window size to fit the page dimensions.

4 If the document window is wider or taller than the page it contains (that is, if you see a gray or black area at the right side of the window, or the top of page 2 at the bottom of the window), choose Fit Window to Page from the Zoom pop-up menu (100%) in the status bar.

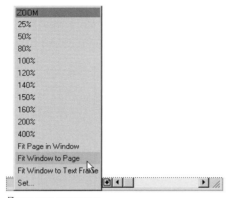

Zoom pop-up menu

To see how the document looks without the text symbols, turn them off. You could do this by using the Text Symbols command on the View menu, but instead you'll use the same command on a *context menu* (a pop-up menu that contains commands that depend on the location of the pointer).

5 In the page margin (away from text), do one of the following:

• (Windows and UNIX) Right-click and choose Text Symbols from the pop-up menu.

- (Mac OS) Control-click and choose Text Symbols from the pop-up menu.

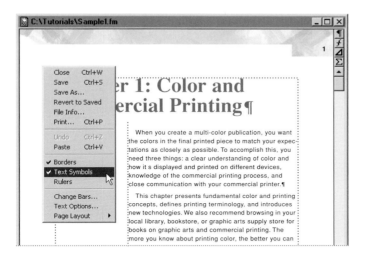

When the pointer is in the page margin, the context menu contains commands that can apply to the document as a whole. Different commands appear when the pointer is over text, a graphic, a table, and so on.

Looking at the pages

FrameMaker 7.0 documents are WYSIWYG, so they appear the same on-screen as in print. You work on pages whose page numbers, margins, headers, and footers are always visible. You add or edit contents in a *text frame,* marked by a rectangular dotted border in the document window. You don't need to edit the headers and footers as you work; the headers and footers—and the entire page design—are usually set up in a template. FrameMaker 7.0 adds pages and adjusts the header and footer text for you as you work.

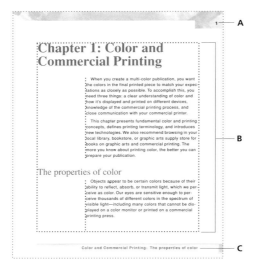

A. *Page number in header* B. *Text frame*
C. *Page footer*

Next, you'll take a quick look at a few pages of the document.

1 In the status bar, click the Next Page button (⬇) to display page 2 of the document.

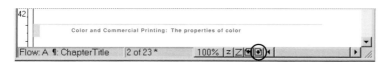

Notice that the page number, which was at the top right of page 1, appears at the top left of this page. (You may need to scroll up to see the page number.)

2 Click the Next Page button three more times to display page 5. Notice that the text in the page footer changes to reflect the first-level heading on the page (the heading *Printing terminology*). You may need to scroll down to see the page footer.

Note: *If the page footer is "greeked" and appears as a gray bar rather than as text, click the Zoom In button (⬚) in the status bar until the footer appears as text.*

The text frame is split into two areas:

• The area on the left is set up for *side heads*—headings that stand to one side of the body text.

• The area on the right is for body text.

The first-level headings straddle both areas.

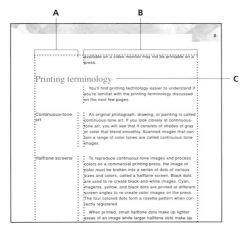

A. *Side-head area* **B.** *Body-text area* **C.** *First-level heading straddles both areas*

Even though the headings and the body text appear in different areas, they're all part of a single *text flow* that begins on page 1 and continues to the end of the document. You can create a document that contains several independent text flows (such as a newsletter), but most FrameMaker 7.0 documents have just one main flow.

Next, you'll select some text to see how the text flows through the document.

3 Place the pointer on the text in the first paragraph on page 5. (If you had to scroll down to see the footer, you may need to scroll up to see the first paragraph.) Then press the mouse button and drag slowly downward without releasing it.

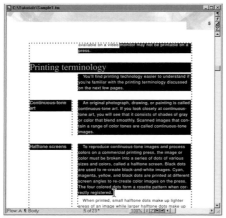

Text is selected as you drag.

4 Continue dragging downward until the pointer moves into the status bar. The document scrolls downward to page 6, and the text continues to be selected. The graphic at the top of the text frame is also selected.

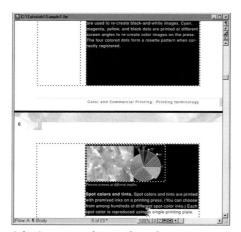

Selection crosses the page boundary.

5 Release the mouse button.

6 Click anywhere on the page to deselect everything.

7 To return to page 1, click the Page Status area in the status bar.

8 Enter **1** in the Page Number text box and click Go.

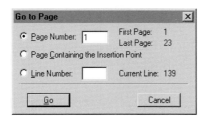

💡 *You can also click the Previous Page button (⬆) repeatedly to get back to page 1, or just Shift-click the Previous Page button to go directly to page 1.*

Now you'll adjust your view again.

9 Click the Zoom In button (☑) in the status bar to zoom the document to 120%.

Note: *If you earlier zoomed to 120% to read the page footer, you do not need to zoom now. If you zoomed to a higher percentage, click the Zoom Out button (☑)to zoom out to 120%.*

10 To save space on the screen, choose Fit Window to Text Frame from the Zoom pop-up menu (120%).

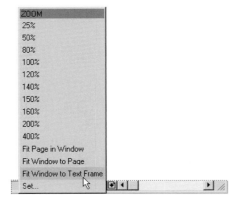

11 Choose View > Borders to hide the borders of the text frame.

Applying predefined paragraph formats

Each FrameMaker 7.0 document contains paragraph formats (styles) in a Paragraph Catalog. Each format consists of many properties—such as line and paragraph spacing, indents, alignment, tab stops, and font properties—and each format has a name, or *tag*. You can change the appearance of paragraphs one property at a time, but you'll find it easier to use the formats in the catalog so that you can change many properties at once.

Looking at paragraph formats

Now you'll display the Paragraph Catalog and look at some of the formats used in the document.

1 At the upper right of the document window, click the Paragraph Catalog button (¶).

Paragraph Catalog button

The Paragraph Catalog appears in a palette. The initial size of the palette depends on your system; you can drag a corner to resize it as needed (for example, to display more format tags).

Paragraph Catalog

The Paragraph Catalog for this document includes paragraph formats for headings (for example, ChapterTitle, Heading1, and Heading2), bulleted and numbered lists (Bullet, Step, and Step1), and ordinary paragraphs of text (Body).

2 If the catalog blocks your view of the document, drag it out of the way. (You can move any FrameMaker 7.0 catalog or dialog box as needed.)

3 Click in the chapter title *Color and Commercial Printing* on page 1 of the document. The insertion point appears in the title, and the tag of the current paragraph appears in the Tag area of the status bar.

Paragraph tag in the Tag area of the status bar

4 Try to click in the word *Chapter* at the beginning of the title paragraph. Notice that the insertion point appears to the right of the chapter number and colon.

This is because the word *Chapter,* the chapter number, and the colon are inserted automatically as part of the chapter title's paragraph format. You can't place the insertion point in automatically inserted text or edit that text in the document window. (You'll learn more about automatically inserted text and automatic numbering in the next lesson.)

5 Click in a paragraph of ordinary (body) text. The tag *Body* appears in the Tag area of the status bar.

6 If you like, click elsewhere in the document to see the tags of other formats used by different paragraphs. When you're finished, return to page 1 of the document.

Applying formats to paragraphs

Next, you'll apply some of the formats to paragraphs. It's usually easier to work with text when text symbols and borders are visible, so you'll display them again.

1 Choose View > Text Symbols and then View > Borders.

2 Click to place the insertion point at the end of the first body paragraph, between the period and the end-of-paragraph symbol.

> need three things: a clear understanding of color and
> how it's displayed and printed on different devices,
> knowledge of the commercial printing process, and
> close communication with your commercial printer.¶

3 Press the Return key (which may be labeled Enter on a PC keyboard) to insert an empty paragraph. The new paragraph's tag is Body.

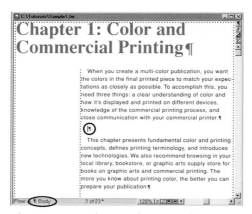

The new paragraph is a Body paragraph.

4 In the Paragraph Catalog, click Heading1. This *tags* the empty paragraph as a Heading1 paragraph. The properties of the Heading1 format are applied to the paragraph, and *Heading1* appears in the Tag area of the status bar.

5 In the document window, type **Introduction**. The text appears at the insertion point.

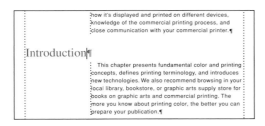

6 Choose Fit Window to Page from the Zoom pop-up menu to display as much of the document as possible at the current zoom setting. Notice that the page footer now contains the text of the new first-level heading, *Introduction*. (You may need to scroll down to see the page footer.)

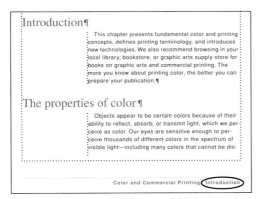

The page footer contains the text of the first Heading1 paragraph on the page.

7 Close the Paragraph Catalog.

Applying predefined character formats

Along with a Paragraph Catalog that contains formats for entire paragraphs of text, a document contains a Character Catalog with formats you can apply to selected text, such as words or phrases. A single character format can specify several font properties, such as the font family, size, weight, angle, and color.

You can change the appearance of words or phrases one property at a time, but you'll usually find it easier to use the formats in the Character Catalog.

1 Display page 4 of the sample document. The words in color and italics at the top and bottom of the page are technical terms. They're formatted using a character format in the Character Catalog.

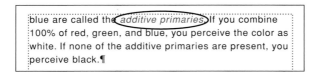

blue are called the *additive primaries*. If you combine
100% of red, green, and blue, you perceive the color as
white. If none of the additive primaries are present, you
perceive black.¶

2 Click to put the insertion point in the phrase *additive primaries* that appears in color at the top of the page. Notice that the Tag area now contains the name of the character format—the *character tag*—in addition to the paragraph tag.

Flow: A ¶: Body f: FirstUse   4 of 23 *

          A   B

A. Paragraph tag B. Character tag

3 At the upper right of the document window, click the Character Catalog button (*f*).

Character Catalog button

The Character Catalog appears in a palette. The initial size of the palette depends on your system; you can drag to resize it as needed (for example, to display more tags for formats).

f Catalog
Default ¶ Font
Emphasis
EquationVariables
FirstUse
Numbers

Delete...

Character Catalog

4 Double-click the word *visible* (at the beginning of the last paragraph on the page), and then Shift-click the word *spectrum* to select both words. (You can also drag to select both words.)

| Color gamuts¶ | | The visible spectrum contains millions of colors; each device used in commercial printing can reproduce a unique subset of this range known as its *color gamut* or |

5 Click FirstUse in the Character Catalog, and then click anywhere else on the page to deselect the text so you can see that it now appears in color and italics.

| Color gamuts¶ | | The *visible spectrum* contains millions of colors; each device used in commercial printing can reproduce a unique subset of this range known as its *color gamut* or |

6 Close the Character Catalog.

You're finished with the sample document.

7 Choose File > Save and then choose File > Close.

Writing a short memo

To finish this lesson, you'll use one of the standard templates that come with FrameMaker 7.0 to write a short memo for a sales report. When you create a new document from a standard template, that document is an untitled copy of the template. The template itself doesn't change when you modify and save the new document.

Creating the memo from a template

First you'll create a blank memo from a template.

1 Do one of the following:

• (Windows and Mac OS) Choose File > New > Document.

• (UNIX) In the main FrameMaker 7.0 window, click New.

The contents of the Templates folder appear in the dialog box.

2 If the contents of the Templates folder don't appear in the dialog box, do one of the following:

• (Windows and Mac OS) Navigate to the Templates folder in the FrameMaker 7.0 folder.

• (UNIX) Click Cancel, click Exit in the main FrameMaker 7.0 window, restart FrameMaker 7.0, and then repeat step 1.

You'll use the Memo template in the Business folder.

3 Double-click Business and then double-click Memo.fm.

Untitled memo

The memo appears as an untitled new document.

4 Choose File > Save, make sure you are in the Lesson01 folder, and then enter the filename **SalesMemo.fm** and click Save.

Entering text and applying formats

The memo contains two text frames. You'll use the small text frame at the top of the page for your name and address, and the large text frame for the body of your memo.

Near the top of the page is the date on which this memo was last modified. (Because you're creating the memo now, today's date appears there.) The date, the word *memo,* and the gray image of a world map were placed on a master page (a special page that controls a page design for the document) when the Memo template was created.

To make it easier to enter text, you'll turn on borders and text symbols.

1 Choose View > Borders and then View > Text Symbols.

2 Click in the small text frame at the upper right of the page. The paragraph in the text frame uses the CompanyName paragraph format, as shown in the status bar.

3 Choose Edit > Select All in Flow to select all the text in the frame.

4 Type your name and press Return/Enter. Your name replaces the selected text.

5 Type your address, pressing Return/Enter to start a new line as needed.

6 To redisplay the page, press Control+l (lowercase *L*). A FrameMaker 7.0 *variable* on the master page causes your name to appear in large bold type along the left side of the page. (You may need to scroll down the page to see your name along the side.)

7 Click to the right of the word *To* in the large text frame.

The word *To*—like the word *Chapter* and the chapter number in the sample document you looked at earlier—is inserted automatically as part of the paragraph's format (MemoTo).

8 Type **Sales Department Staff** and press Return/Enter.

The next paragraph uses the MemoFrom format, as shown in the status bar. This format begins with the word *From*.

9 Type your name and press Return/Enter.

The next paragraph uses the MemoSubject format, which begins with the word *Re*.

10 Type **September Sales** and press Return/Enter.

The next paragraph uses the MemoCc format. This format begins with the text *Cc* and is followed by a thin line. The line, like the text *Cc*, is automatically inserted as part of the paragraph format.

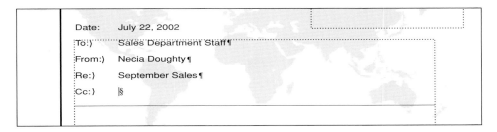

11 To leave the Cc line blank, press Return again.

The next paragraph begins the body of the memo, and it uses the Body paragraph format.

12 Type **Sales for September should exceed expectations for several reasons:** and press Return.

Next you'll type a short bulleted list.

13 At the right side of the document window, click the Paragraph Catalog button (¶) to display the Paragraph Catalog again.

FrameMaker 7.0 is a powerful program that enables you to create and edit an extensive variety of documentation types; later lessons will explore many of these other types of documents.

14 In the catalog, click the Bulleted format.

The Body paragraph changes to Bulleted.

15 Type **Strong sales of existing products** and press Return.

16 Type **Rapid acceptance of our new products** and press Return.

17 Type **Favorable exchange rates**. The memo is finished.

18 Close the Paragraph Catalog. Save and close the document.

Moving on

You've completed this lesson. For in-depth information about the work area, document window, entering and editing text, and applying paragraph and character formats, see Chapter 1, "Work area"; Chapter 2, "Working with FrameMaker 7.0 Documents"; Chapter 3, "Word Processing"; and Chapter 4, "Text Formatting," in the *Adobe FrameMaker User Guide*.

Review questions

1 How do you set the standard FrameMaker work area?

2 How do you show and hide rulers, borders, and text symbols?

3 How do you zoom in for a closer look at a document's contents?

4 What is the primary difference between paragraph formats and character formats?

5 How do you open the Paragraph Catalog and the Character Catalog?

6 How do you apply a paragraph format from the catalog?

7 How do you apply a character format from the catalog?

8 What happens when you create a document from a template?

Answers

1 When you initially launch the program, click on FrameMaker in the Choose Interface dialog box. After initial use, go to the main menu and choose File > Preferences > General and then select FrameMaker from the Product Interface pop-up menu.

2 Choose View > Rulers, View > Borders, and View > Text Symbols. (You can also choose these commands from the context menu when the pointer is in the page margin.)

3 In the status bar, click the Zoom In button or choose a setting from the Zoom pop-up menu.

4 Paragraph formats apply to entire paragraphs; character formats apply to selected text, such as words and phrases.

5 Click the Paragraph Catalog button in the upper right corner of the document window; click the Character Catalog button in the upper right corner of the document window.

6 Click to put the insertion point in the paragraph, then click the format's tag in the Paragraph Catalog.

7 Select the text to which you want to apply the format, then click the format's tag in the Character Catalog.

8 FrameMaker 7.0 creates an untitled copy of the template, leaving the template unchanged. You can give the copy a different filename by using the Save As command.

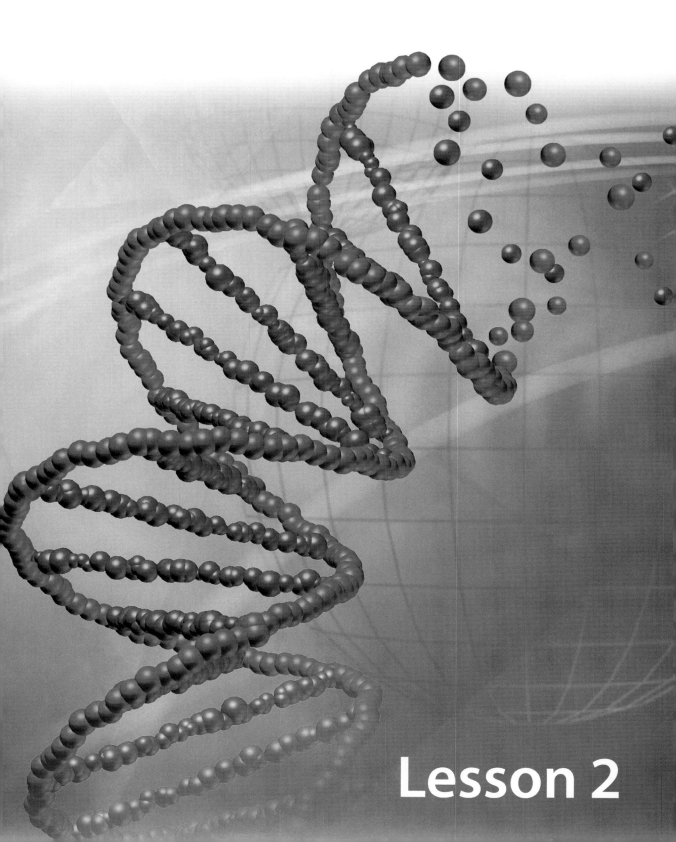

Lesson 2

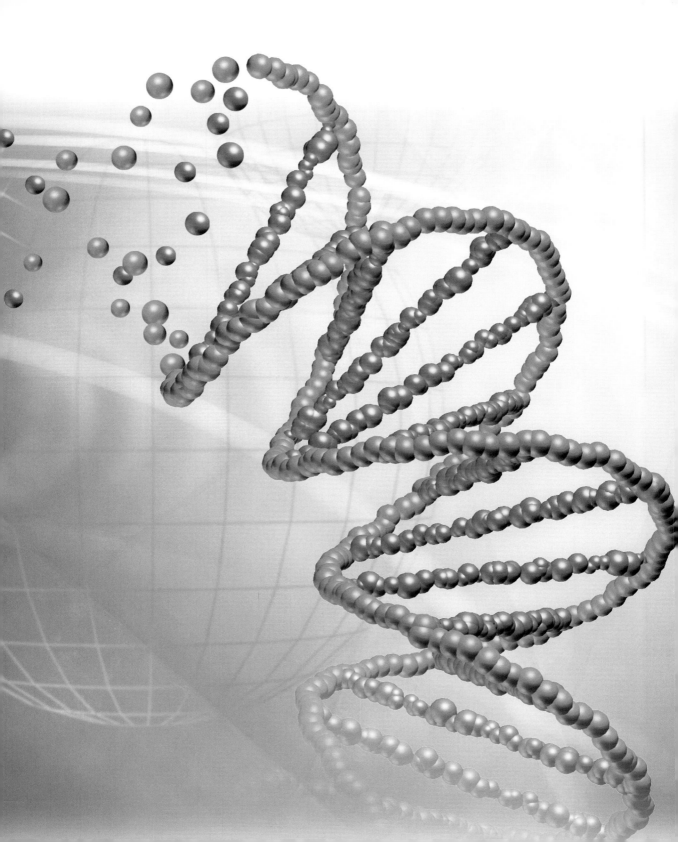

2 | Defining Paragraph Formats

Create your publication
: Define the colors you will use and decide if they will be process or spot colors. Create or gather the content, vector art, and bitmap images for your publication. Review the design to determine how the page elements interact and overlap. Determine if you will use a CMS. Discuss printing issues with your commercial printer as your design evolves.

Proof and hand off your les
: Print proof copies of your publication on a black-and-white or color PostScript desktop printer. Consult your printer about what proofing methods he or she recommends to check color quality and to safeguard against production problems. Decide what type of file to give to your service provider. Gather your files, the final laser proofs, your report listing details about your document, and any additional files, such as bitmap images and vector artwork.

Check and print your publication
: Examine the film separations for quality and accuracy. Check that objects appear on the correct separation. Check proofs made from separations for correct trapping and smooth and consistent tints. Meet with your printer to review press proofs for final color quality. After you approve the press proof, the publication is printed and assembled.

Defining project requirements

Every printed project requires you to balance cost, schedule, and quality. Another key factor in

The templates that come with FrameMaker 7.0 include paragraph formats for changing the appearance of entire paragraphs of text. When you're setting up your own templates or creating custom documents, you'll modify these formats and create some of your own.

In this lesson, you'll learn how to do the following:

- Create a custom document.
- Set ruler and grid spacing.
- Set up a side-head area.
- Create and modify paragraph formats for headings, body text, and bulleted and numbered lists.
- Delete formats from the Paragraph Catalog.

Creating a custom document

In this lesson, you'll set up the paragraph formats for the chapters of a small book. You'll start by creating a custom document.

1 If necessary, copy the Lesson02 folder and start FrameMaker 7.0.

2 If FrameMaker 7.0 is not in standard mode, choose File > Preferences > General, and then select FrameMaker from the Product Interface pop-up menu.

3 If you want to see how your document will look at the end of this lesson, open Finished.fm in the Lesson02 folder. When you're ready to continue, close Finished.fm.

4 Do one of the following:

- (Windows and Mac OS) Choose File > New > Document.
- (UNIX) In the main FrameMaker 7.0 window, click New.

5 Click Custom.

Notice that the values in the text boxes are in inches (for the U.S. Edition) or centimeters (for the International Edition). You'll change the default units for the document, so that measurements in dialog boxes will appear in points.

6 Choose Point from the Units pop-up menu at the lower right. The values in the text boxes are converted to points.

7 In the Pagination area, select Double-Sided. Notice that in the Margins area, the text boxes formerly labeled Left and Right are now labeled Inside and Outside.

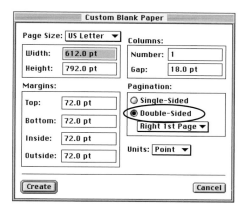

8 In the Page Size area, change the Width to 460 points and the Height to 560 points.

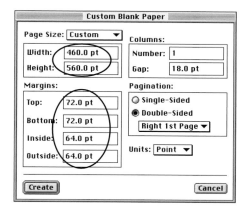

💡 *You can enter just the number (for example, **460** rather than **460 pt**), because you already specified points as the units for the document.*

9 The Top and Bottom margins remain at 72 points, but change the Inside and Outside margins to 64 points.

10 Click Create.

An untitled, blank document appears. Because borders and text symbols are on, you see a dotted text frame border with an end-of-flow symbol (§) in the upper left corner. This is the only text symbol you see because the document doesn't contain any text yet.

If borders and text symbols are not visible, choose View > Borders and View > Text Symbols to see them.

11 Choose File > Save, make sure you are in the Lesson02 folder, and then enter the filename **Formats.fm** and click Save.

Next, you'll turn on a typing aid that will help you work more efficiently.

12 Choose Format > Document > Text Options.

In the Text Options dialog box, Smart Quotes is already selected. This tells FrameMaker 7.0 to insert the appropriate left or right curved quotation mark ("or") when you type a quotation mark.

13 Select Smart Spaces and click Apply.

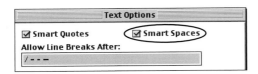

Smart Spaces prevents you from typing more than one standard (proportional) space in a row. This helps you keep spacing between words and sentences consistent. (Smart Spaces does not affect special fixed-width spaces, such as em spaces.)

Finally, you'll look at the Paragraph Catalog for the document.

14 Click the Paragraph Catalog button (¶) at the top right side of the document window. Notice that even new custom documents contain a basic set of predefined paragraph formats for headings, body text, numbered and bulleted lists, and other items.

Paragraph Catalog for a new custom document

Later, you'll change these formats for your document.

15 Close the Paragraph Catalog.

Copying text

It's easier to see whether text formats look the way you want when you have text in a document, so you'll paste some text into your blank document.

1 Choose File > Open.

Note: In some instances, a lesson might require fonts that are not installed on your system. If necessary, FrameMaker will automatically substitute similar fonts, and will display a font substitution dialog box. To reformat the document using available fonts, click OK.

2 Select Text.fm in the Lesson 02 folder and click Open. The text in this document already uses the paragraph tags that appear in the blank document.

3 Click anywhere in the text and then choose Edit > Select All in Flow to select all the text in Text.fm.

4 Choose Edit > Copy.

5 Choose File > Close to close Text.fm.

6 In Formats.fm, click inside the text frame and choose Edit > Paste. The text from Text.fm is pasted into Formats.fm, and the last page of text appears in the document window.

7 Shift-click the Previous Page button ( ) in the status bar to display the first page of the document.

8 Choose File > Save.

For a complete list of keyboard shortcuts, see the Quick Reference section of Help.

Setting up rulers and the grid

Later in this lesson, you'll use the formatting bar and the top ruler to set indents and tabs for the text. To make your work easier, you'll now change the ruler units to picas—the appropriate setting for a document that uses points as display units (each pica contains 12 points).

You'll also set up the invisible *snap grid*. Items in the top ruler (such as controls for tabs and indents) and objects on a page snap to this grid as you move them. This helps you place tabs, indents, and objects at regular intervals.

Now, you'll set up the rulers.

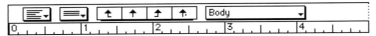

Top ruler

1 If the formatting bar doesn't appear under the menu bar in Windows, choose View > Formatting Bar. (The formatting bar will already appear below the document's title bar on the Mac OS and on UNIX systems.)

2 Choose View > Options.

3 Choose Pica from the Rulers pop-up menu to change the ruler markings.

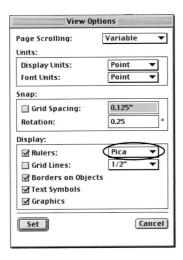

4 Enter **6** (for 6 points) in the Grid Spacing text box in the Snap area of the View Options dialog box and click Set.

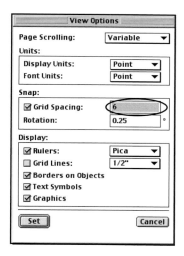

5 Click the Graphics menu. If a check mark or filled in box appears next to the Snap menu item, it indicates that the Snap command is on. If there is no check mark or filled in box, then the Snap command is not on.

6 If Snap is not on, choose Graphics > Snap.

Creating a side-head area

The formats you create for your document will place second-level headings at the left edge of the text frame (indicated by the dotted border); other text will appear to the right of these headings. To achieve this effect, you'll set up a *side-head area*—an area on one side of the text frame that will contain headings.

1 Click anywhere in the first paragraph on page 1 to place an insertion point in the text.

2 Choose Format > Page Layout > Column Layout.

3 Select Room for Side Heads.

4 In the Room for Side Heads area, change Width to 92 and Gap to 14.

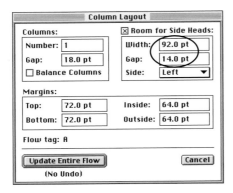

5 Click Update Entire Flow. All the text moves into the right side of the text frame. The side-head area appears to the left, but it's empty. Next, you'll change the format of the headings so that they extend across or move into the side-head area.

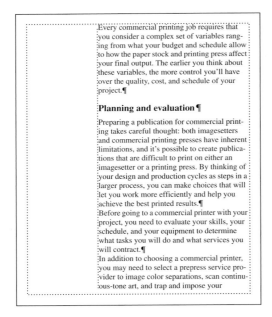

Displaying the Paragraph Designer

You use the Paragraph Designer to create and change the paragraph formats in your document. You'll display the designer and look at the properties it contains.

1 Choose Format > Paragraphs > Designer. The Paragraph Designer appears.

If you plan to use the Paragraph Designer many times, drag it to a position that doesn't obstruct your document and keep the palette open until you've made all of your changes.

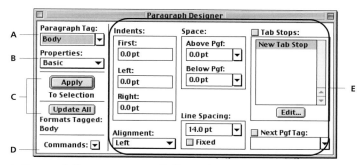

A. Paragraph Tag pop-up menu *B.* Properties pop-up menu
C. Controls for applying and updating properties *D.* Commands
pop-up menu *E.* Current group of properties

On the left are the Paragraph Tag pop-up menu, showing the tag of the paragraph containing the insertion point, and the Properties pop-up menu, showing the name of the current group of properties (initially, these are the Basic properties). The properties themselves appear on the right side of the Paragraph Designer.

Below the Properties pop-up menu are controls for applying the properties to a selection (or to the paragraph containing the insertion point) and for updating a paragraph format and all the paragraphs that use it.

2 Choose Default Font from the Properties pop-up menu. (In Windows, you can just click the Default Font tab at the top of the designer.) The Default Font properties appear at the right side of the designer.

3 If you like, display any of the other groups of properties.

Formatting headings

Now you'll use the Paragraph Designer to redefine the formats for two levels of headings.

Formatting first-level headings

The first-level headings in the document are all tagged Heading1. You'll modify their paragraph format next.

1 Click anywhere in the heading *Planning and evaluation*.

You'll make first-level headings span the side-head area and the body-text area.

2 In the Paragraph Designer, choose Pagination from the Properties pop-up menu. (In Windows, you can just click the Pagination tab.)

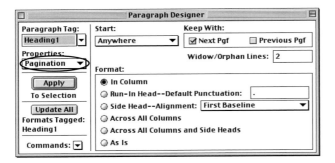

On the right side of the Paragraph Designer, Next Pgf is selected in the Keep With area. This forces the heading to stay on the same page as the first lines of the paragraph that follows the heading.

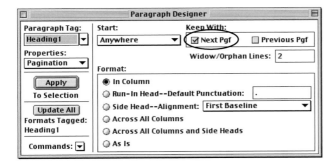

3 In the Format area, select Across All Columns and Side Heads. This allows first-level headings to span both areas of the text frame.

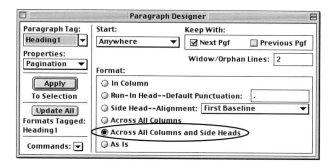

4 On the left side of the Paragraph Designer, click Update All. (If FrameMaker 7.0 notifies you that some paragraphs use format overrides, click Remove Overrides.) This changes all paragraphs tagged Heading1 and also changes the Heading1 format in the Paragraph Catalog.

Heading moves to the left edge of the text frame.

Next you'll change the font properties of Heading1 paragraphs.

5 In the Paragraph Designer, choose Default Font from the Properties pop-up menu.

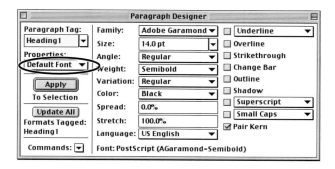

6 Change the Size to 20. Make sure the Weight is Regular. The value 20 does not appear in the pop-up menu, so you must enter it in the Size text box.

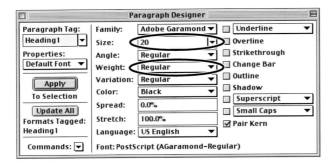

7 Click Update All.

Finally, you'll change the paragraph spacing and line spacing to reduce the space between the heading and the body text that follows it.

8 Choose Basic from the Properties pop-up menu.

9 Change the Space Below to 0 and the Line Spacing to 20, and click Update All.

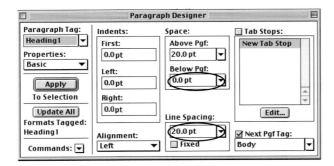

Formatting second-level headings

The second-level headings in the document are all tagged Heading2. You'll modify their paragraph format.

1 Click the Next Page button ( ) in the status bar twice to display page 3.

2 Click in the second-level heading *Define project and quality requirements.*

3 In the Paragraph Designer, display the Pagination properties.

4 In the Format area, select Side Head Alignment and click Update All. (If FrameMaker 7.0 notifies you that some paragraphs use format overrides, click Remove Overrides.)

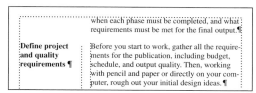

Heading2 paragraphs move into the side-head area.

5 Display the Default Font properties.

6 Change the Family to Myriad-Roman (Windows) or Myriad (Mac OS and UNIX) and the Size to 10, and click Update All.

Finally, you'll add some space between the Heading2 paragraphs and the preceding body text.

7 Display the Basic properties.

8 Change the Space Above to 20 and the Space Below to 0, and click Update All.

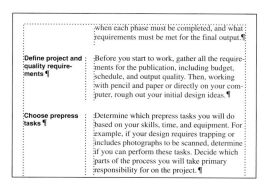

9 If you need to update your display or refresh your screen view, press Control+l (lowercase *L*).

Formatting body text

Next you'll change the format of ordinary paragraphs in the document, which are tagged Body. You'll change the font, make the body text smaller, and add space between the lines.

1 Click in a paragraph of body text on page 3.

2 In the Paragraph Designer, display the Default Font properties.

3 Change the Family to Myriad-Roman (Windows) or Myriad (Mac OS and UNIX), the Size to 9, and the Spread to 5. Spread (sometimes called tracking) adds or subtracts space between characters for a looser or tighter look.

4 Click Update All. (If FrameMaker 7.0 notifies you that some paragraphs use format overrides, click Remove Overrides.)

Next you'll change the paragraph and line spacing.

5 Display the Basic properties.

6 Change the Space Above to 5 and the Line Spacing to 13, and then click Update All.

Finally, you'll indent the first line of the paragraph. The indent symbols appear in the top ruler.

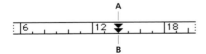

A. *First-line indent* **B.** *Left indent*

7 Drag the first-line indent symbol to the right, to the next ruler marking. Because you turned on Snap earlier in this lesson, the indent symbol snaps to the next ruler marking.

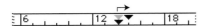

The First Indent setting in the Paragraph Designer changes to 10.0 pt. (In a paragraph format, indents and tabs are measured from the edge of the text frame margin, not the edge of the page.)

Notice that the indent changed only in the paragraph that contains the insertion point. You need to apply the change to all the Body paragraphs.

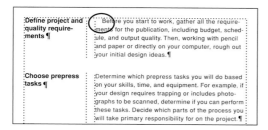

8 In the Paragraph Designer, click Update All. All Body paragraphs are indented.

Formatting numbered lists

Next you'll create two paragraph formats for numbered lists. The first format, for the first item in a list, will number the paragraph with a 1. The second format, for subsequent items in the list, will increment the number by 1.

All numbered steps will use a *hanging indent*. That is, the number will appear at the left margin, and the text will be indented from the left margin.

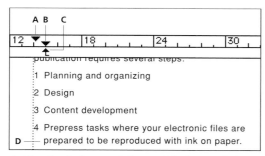

*A. First-line indent symbol **B.** Left indent symbol
C. Left-aligned tab stop **D.** Hanging indent*

Creating a format for the first item in a list

Rather than modify an existing format, you'll create a new format. The items you want to number are already formatted as body paragraphs.

1 Click the Previous Page button (🔼) in the status bar to display page 2.

2 Click in the paragraph *Planning and organizing* (the second paragraph under the heading).

3 In the bottom-left corner of the Paragraph Designer, choose New Format from the Commands pop-up menu.

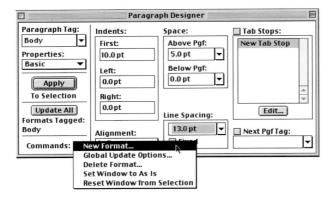

4 Enter **Step1** in the Tag text box.

5 Make sure that the options Store in Catalog and Apply to Selection are selected and click Create.

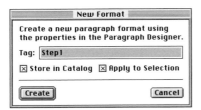

The tag of the current paragraph changes to Step1, and the Step1 format is added to the Paragraph Catalog.

Next you'll use the rulers and formatting bar to set up indents and a tab stop.

6 In the ruler, drag the first-line indent symbol back as far to the left as it will go.

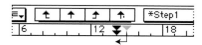

7 Drag the left indent symbol to the next ruler marking to the right.

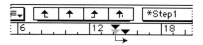

You'll use a tab stop to set the space between the item number and the text that follows. The *tab well* in the formatting bar contains symbols for left-aligned, center-aligned, right-aligned, and decimal-aligned tab stops.

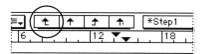

Left-aligned tab stop

8 Drag a left-aligned tab stop from the tab well to just under the left indent.

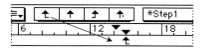

Notice that the settings for the tab stop appear in the Paragraph Designer.

9 In the Paragraph Designer, click Update All. The appearance of the paragraph doesn't change because you haven't added a tab character. You'll do that when you set up automatic numbering.

Setting up numbering for the first item

A document can use automatic numbering for different types of items (for example, numbered steps and numbered chapters and sections). An autonumber format may include a *series label* that specifies an independently numbered series and *building blocks* that serve as placeholders for numbers or letters. An autonumber format may also include tabs, text, and punctuation.

You'll finish the Step1 paragraph format definition by setting up its autonumber format.

1 In the Paragraph Designer, display the Numbering properties.

2 Enter **S:** (the uppercase letter *S* followed by a colon) in the Autonumber Format text box. This is the series label you'll use for items in a numbered list.

3 Select <n=1> in the Building Blocks scroll list. This building block, which will insert the number 1 in the paragraph, appears in the text box.

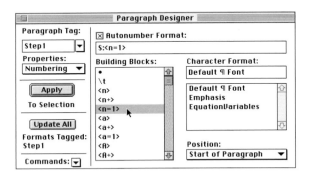

4 Select \t in the scroll list to add a tab character to the autonumber format.

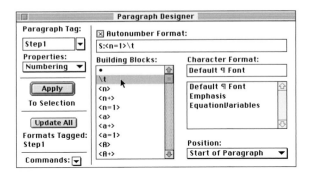

5 Click Update All. The autonumber appears at the beginning of the paragraph. The tab character is represented by the tab symbol (**)**).

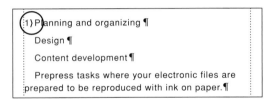

6 Choose File > Save.

Formatting subsequent numbered items

Now you'll create a paragraph format for the subsequent numbered items in a list. (This format will increase the step number of each successive item by 1.) You'll begin by applying the Step1 format to the other paragraphs in the numbered list, because that format is very close to the format you want. Then you'll create a new paragraph format for the paragraphs and change the autonumber format.

1 Drag to select the three paragraphs below the numbered step.

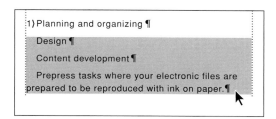

2 Choose Step1 from the Paragraph Formats pop-up menu in the formatting bar. This pop-up menu contains all the formats in the Paragraph Catalog. You can apply formats from this menu just as you apply them from the catalog.

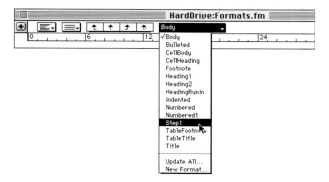

All the selected paragraphs now begin with the number 1, but you'll fix that next.

3 In the Paragraph Designer, choose New Format from the Commands pop-up menu.

4 Enter **Step** in the Tag text box.

5 Make sure that the options Store in Catalog and Apply to Selection are selected and click Create.

6 Delete everything after the colon in the Autonumber Format text box.

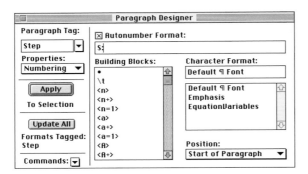

7 Select <n+> in the Building Blocks scroll list. This building block will increment by 1 the number of the previous paragraph in the series.

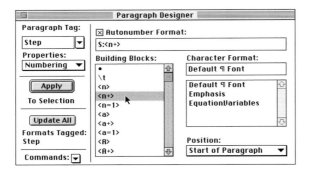

8 Select \t in the Building Blocks scroll list to add a tab character, and then click Update All.

9 Click anywhere in the document to deselect the text.

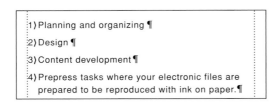

10 To see how the document looks without the text symbols, choose View > Text Symbols.

Formatting bulleted lists

Next you'll create a format for items in a bulleted list. You'll work with the Step1 format as a base, because it's very close to the format you want.

1 Go to page 12 (or page 11 on some Windows systems) of the document by clicking in the page number area of the status bar. Then type "12" in the Go to Page dialog box and press Go.

2 Select the paragraph beginning with *What experience do they have* and drag to select the paragraphs that follow it. The last paragraph in the selection should be *What color matching systems are supported?*

3 Choose Step1 from the Paragraph Formats pop-up menu in the formatting bar.

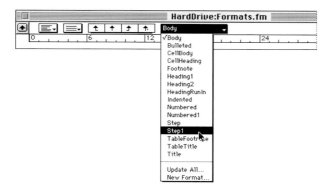

All the selected paragraphs are numbered 1.

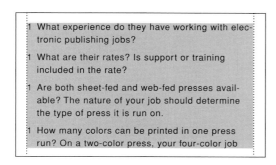

4 In the Paragraph Designer, choose New Format from the Commands pop-up menu.

5 Enter **Bullet** in the Tag text box.

6 Make sure the options Store in Catalog and Apply to Selection are selected and click Create.

7 Delete the contents of the Autonumber Format text box.

8 In the Building Blocks scroll list, do one of the following:

- (Windows and UNIX) Select \b.

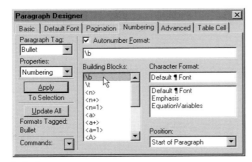

Windows

- (Mac OS) Select the bullet symbol (•).

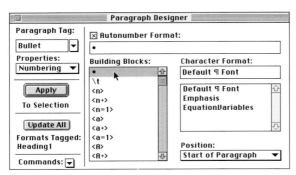

Mac OS

This building block inserts a round bullet symbol at the beginning of each Bullet paragraph.

9 Select \t in the Building Blocks scroll list to insert a tab, and then click Update All.

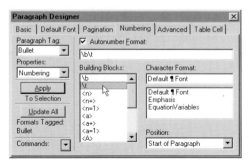

Windows

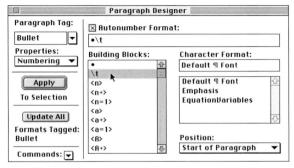

Mac OS

10 Click anywhere on the page to deselect the paragraphs.

Next you'll change the left indent of the bulleted paragraphs.

11 Click in the first bulleted paragraph.

12 In the ruler, drag the left indent symbol as far to the left as it will go (to the left margin).

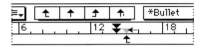

The paragraph no longer uses a hanging indent.

> Modify the following questions to match the requirements of your own project.
>
> • What experience do they have working with electronic publishing jobs?
>
> • What are their rates? Is support or training included in the rate?
>
> • Are both sheet-fed and web-fed presses available? The nature of your job should determine the type of press it is run on.

13 In the Paragraph Designer, click Update All to update the other bulleted items and the Bullet format in the catalog.

14 If you like, apply the Bullet paragraph format to the items under the next heading (on pages 12 and 13).

Creating a chapter title

All that's missing now is the chapter title. You'll add the title and create a new chapter title format.

1 Go to page 1.

2 Choose View > Text Symbols.

3 Click at the beginning of the first paragraph on the page and press Return/Enter to create an empty paragraph.

4 Click in the empty paragraph and type **Planning for Commercial Printing** (the text of the title).

The paragraph format for the chapter title will be similar to the Heading1 format, so you'll start with that format.

5 In the formatting bar, choose Heading1 from the Paragraph Formats pop-up menu.

6 In the Paragraph Designer, choose New Format from the Commands pop-up menu.

7 Enter **ChapterTitle** in the Tag text box.

Note: *Paragraph tags must be all one word.*

8 Make sure the options Store in Catalog and Apply to Selection are selected and click Create.

9 Display the Default Font properties.

10 Change the Size to 30. This value does not appear in the pop-up menu, so you must enter it in the Size text box.

11 Change the Weight to Semibold and then click Update All.

12 Display the Basic properties.

13 Change the Space Below to 18 and click Update All.

14 Display the Numbering properties.

15 Enter **C:Chapter** **<n+>** in the Autonumber Format text box. Be sure to enter a space before the <n+> building block. (You can enter the building block by typing it or selecting it from the scroll list.)

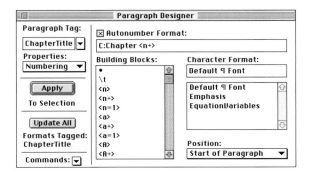

This autonumber format tells FrameMaker 7.0 to number chapters in a different sequence than steps (the series label is C: rather than S:) and to begin the paragraph with the word *Chapter* followed by a space and the chapter number.

16 Add a colon and a space at the end of the text in the Autonumber Format text box, and click Update All.

When you assemble the chapters into a book, they will be numbered sequentially.

17 Close the Paragraph Designer.

Deleting formats

When you created the document, its Paragraph Catalog already contained some paragraph formats that you won't use. You'll delete the unused formats.

1 Click the Paragraph Catalog button (¶) on the right side of the document window to display the Paragraph Catalog.

2 At the bottom of the catalog, click Delete.

3 Select Bulleted (not Bullet) in the scroll list and then click Delete.

4 Select HeadingRunIn and Click Delete again.

5 Delete the Indented, Numbered, Numbered1, and Title (not ChapterTitle) formats.

6 Click Done. Notice that the formats you deleted no longer appear in the Paragraph Catalog.

7 Close the Paragraph Catalog.

8 Save and close the document.

Moving on

FrameMaker 7.0 comes with a variety of templates, such as memos, letters, reports, newsletters, and books. To see a list of available templates, choose File > New > Document, click Explore Standard Templates, and select a template from the list. Click Show Sample to see how a document using the selected template looks.

You've completed this lesson. For in-depth information about formatting text, see Chapter 5, "Text Formatting," in the *Adobe FrameMaker 7.0 User Guide*.

Review questions

1 How do you create a custom new document?

2 What is the effect of turning on the invisible snap grid?

3 List three options for positioning headings and other paragraphs in a document that has a side-head area.

4 How do you change a paragraph format?

5 How do you create a new paragraph format?

6 What items can you include in an autonumber format?

Answers

1 Choose File > New > Document (Windows and Macintosh) or choose New from the main FrameMaker 7.0 window (UNIX). Click Custom, set the options for the document, and click Create.

2 Items in the ruler and objects in the document snap to the invisible grid when you move them. This helps you position tab stops, indents, and objects at regular intervals.

3 The paragraphs may appear in the side-head area, in the body-text area, or across both area

4 In the Paragraph Designer, change properties of the format and click Update All.

5 In the Paragraph Designer, choose New Format from the Commands pop-up menu. Enter a tag for the format, specify whether the format is stored in the catalog and applied to the selection, and click Create.

6 An autonumber format may include a series label, a building block for an automatically inserted number or a bullet, a building block for a tab, and text and other items.

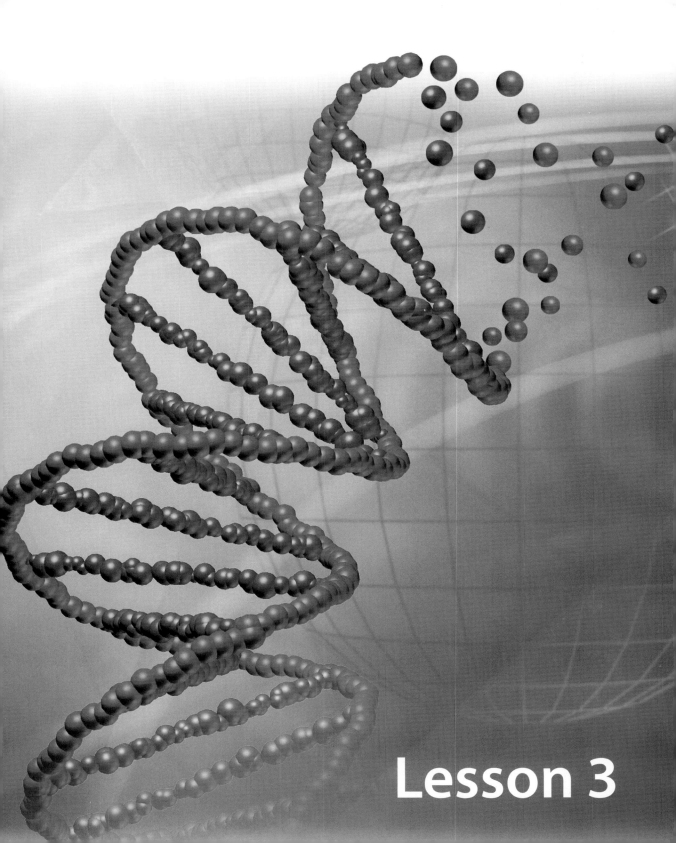

Lesson 3

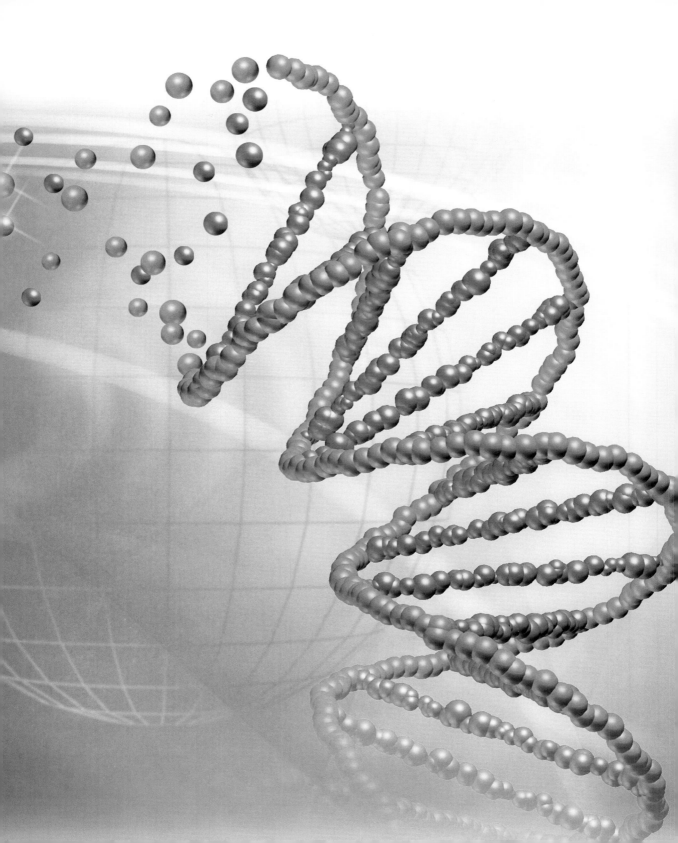

3 | Defining Colors and Character Formats

Chapter 1: Planning for Commercial Printing

Every commercial printing job requires that you consider a complex set of variables ranging from what your budget and schedule allow to how the paper stock and printing press affect your final output. The earlier you think about these variables, the more control you'll have over the quality, cost, and schedule of your project.

Planning and evaluation

Preparing a publication for commercial printing takes careful thought: both imagesetters and commercial printing presses have inherent limitations, and it's possible to create publications that are difficult to print on either an imagesetter or a printing press. By thinking of your design and production cycles as steps in a larger process, you can make choices that will let you work more efficiently and help you achieve the best printed results.

Before going to a commercial printer with your project, you need to evaluate your skills, your schedule, and your equipment to determine what tasks you will do and what services you will contract.

All FrameMaker 7.0 documents include some basic color definitions, and the standard templates also provide character formats for changing the appearance of words and phrases. When you're setting up templates or creating custom documents, you can define other colors and create your own character formats.

In this lesson, you'll learn how to do the following:

• Define custom colors and tints.

• Use color in paragraph formats.

• Create character formats.

• Use a character format in paragraph autonumbers.

• Apply a character format to words and phrases.

Defining custom colors and tints

Color is an effective way to draw the eye to text and objects you want to emphasize. Every FrameMaker 7.0 document includes definitions for several standard colors.

In this lesson, you'll define a color to use for autonumbers and for selected words and phrases. Then you'll create a lighter tint of that color to use for headings.

1 If necessary, copy the Lesson03 folder from the *FrameMaker 7.0 Classroom in a Book* CD and start FrameMaker 7.0.

2 If FrameMaker 7.0 is not in standard mode, choose File > Preferences > General, and then select FrameMaker from the Product Interface pop-up menu. You'll be prompted to restart the application.

3 Open Color.fm in the Lesson03 folder.

4 Choose File > Save As, enter the filename **Color1.fm**, and click Save.

5 Choose View > Color > Definitions.

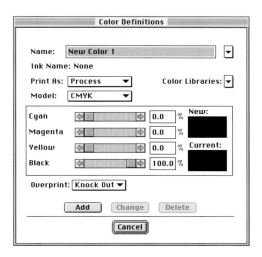

You can define a color by specifying exact color values. In this case, however, you'll use a predefined color from one of the color libraries that come with FrameMaker 7.0. These libraries contain colors that can be matched precisely by commercial printers.

6 Choose PANTONE® Uncoated from the Color Libraries pop-up menu.

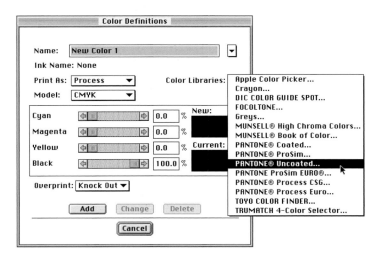

7 At the top of the PANTONE Uncoated dialog box, enter **194** in the Find text box. The contents of the dialog box scroll to show you the PANTONE color you specified.

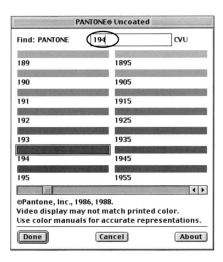

8 Click Done. FrameMaker 7.0 displays a swatch of the color in the New area and inserts the corresponding color values—percentages of cyan, magenta, yellow, and black—in the dialog box. These four colors can combine to represent most of the visible colors.

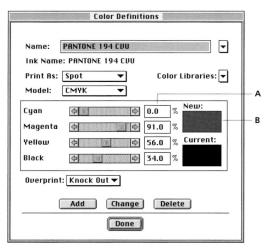

A. Color values ***B.*** *Color swatch*

You'll leave the color values unchanged and give the color a name that describes how it's used (to highlight technical terms when they first appear).

Note: Naming a color to indicate its use can help you remember when to use it. However, if the document will be printed by a commercial printer, you should change the color name back to the original (ink) name before creating a PostScript® file or sending the file to the printer.

9 Enter **FirstUseColor** in the Name text box and click Add.

For the chapter title and headings, you'll use a lighter shade of the color you just defined. You can do this by creating a *tint* of the color. A tint is always displayed and printed in the same manner and on the same plate as its base color.

Note: Using tints prevents oversaturation during printing and allows a wide range of colors without increasing the number of inks required for printing.

10 Enter **HeadingColor** in the Name text box. Choose Tint from the Print As pop-up menu.

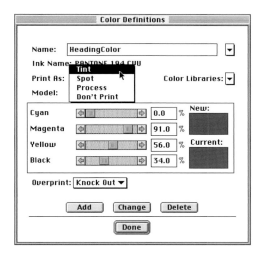

The contents of the dialog box change so you can specify the base color for the tint.

11 Make sure that FirstUseColor is selected from the Base Color pop-up menu and enter **90** in the Tint text box.

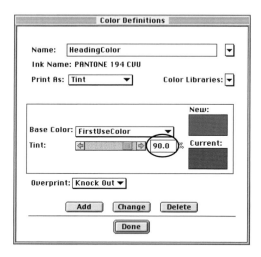

12 Click Add and then click Done. Save the document. The document now contains definitions for the two custom colors you'll use.

Adding color to paragraph formats

The chapter title and headings appear in black. You'll change their paragraph formats so they appear in the custom color you just defined for them.

1 Click in the chapter title. Choose Format > Paragraphs > Designer to display the Paragraph Designer.

2 On the left side of the Paragraph Designer, choose Default Font from the Properties pop-up menu. (In Windows, you can click the Default Font tab at the top of the designer.)

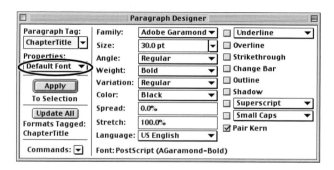

3 Choose HeadingColor from the Color pop-up menu and click Update All. The chapter title appears in color.

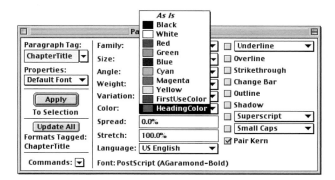

Now you'll add color to the headings.

4 Click in the heading *Planning and evaluation*.

5 In the Paragraph Designer, choose HeadingColor from the Color pop-up menu and click Update All.

6 Go to page 3 and click in any Heading2 paragraph. (The Heading2 paragraphs are in the side-head area.)

7 In the Paragraph Designer, choose HeadingColor from the Color pop-up menu and click Update All.

8 Save the document.

Adding color to autonumbers

In numbered lists, the automatically inserted numbers currently appear in black, but you'll make them appear in color.

Creating a character format

To add color to the autonumbers, you'll create a *character format*—a format that you use for characters, words, or phrases rather than for whole paragraphs. A character format can change one or more text properties.

1 Go to page 2 and click in the first numbered paragraph.

2 Choose Format > Characters > Designer to display the Character Designer. The Character Designer works in the same way as the Paragraph Designer, but it contains only one group of properties.

3 In the Character Designer, choose FirstUseColor from the Color pop-up menu.

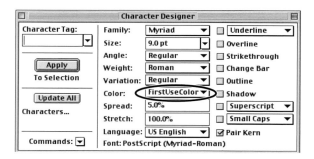

4 At the bottom left of the Character Designer, choose New Format from the Commands pop-up menu.

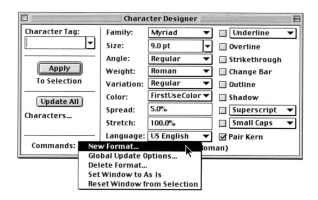

5 In the Tag text box, enter **Numbers**.

6 Turn off Apply to Selection and click Create to store the character format in the Character Catalog.

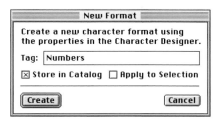

Using the character format for autonumbers

Now that you've defined the character format, you can use it to add color to automatically inserted numbers. Your document uses two paragraph formats for numbered paragraphs (one for the first, and the other for the rest of them), so you'll change both paragraph formats.

1 Make sure the insertion point is still in the first numbered paragraph.

2 In the Paragraph Designer, choose Numbering from the Properties pop-up menu.

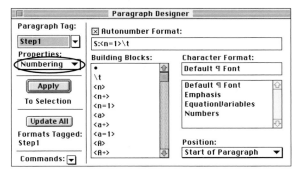

3 Select Number in the Character Format scroll list and click Update All.

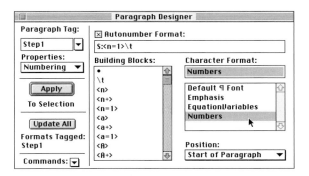

The autonumber of the first numbered paragraph now appears in color. You'll make the same change to the paragraph format for the other numbered paragraphs.

4 Click in the second numbered item.

5 In the Paragraph Designer, select Numbers in the Character Format scroll list and click Update All. All the numbers are now in color.

6 Save the file.

Emphasizing words and phrases

You'll emphasize technical terms by displaying them in a different character format. First, you'll create the format.

1 Go to page 10 of Color1.fm.

2 In the third body paragraph (or second paragraph on some Windows systems) double-click the word *PostScript*.

3 Double-click the word *description,* then shift-click the word *Postscript* to select the three words *PostScript printer description.*

> Files should be checked for correct print settings and that the correct PostScript printer description (PPD) file was used. Verify that colors are named, defined, and applied correctly. Document files must be linked to the most current bitmap images and graphics. Missing fonts should be located so that the files print correctly from another computer.

You'll emphasize technical terms by displaying them in italics and in color. Because the character format you need hasn't been created yet, you'll use the Character Designer to create it. After you store it in the document's Character Catalog, you can use it wherever you need it.

4 In the Character Designer, choose Set Window to As Is from the Commands pop-up menu.

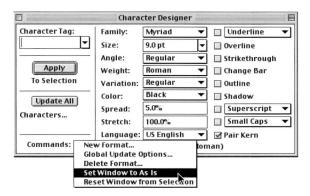

When a property of a character format is set to As Is, FrameMaker 7.0 doesn't change that property when you apply the character format. Be sure to set properties you don't want to change to As Is when you define a character format, so you can apply the format without making unintended changes. (For example, if Size is set to As Is in a character format, you can apply the format to text in paragraphs with different font sizes without changing those sizes.)

In this case, the character format will affect only two properties (Angle and Color), so you'll specify only those two.

5 Choose Italic from the Angle pop-up menu and FirstUseColor from the Color pop-up menu.

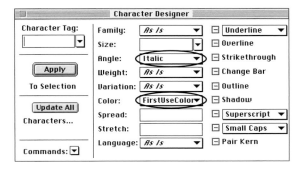

6 Choose New Format from the Commands pop-up menu.

7 Enter **FirstUse** in the Tag text box.

8 Select Apply to Selection (leave Store in Catalog selected) and click Create. The selected text is reformatted, and the new character format is stored in the Character Catalog.

9 Click away from the selected text to deselect it, so you can better see the effect of the character format.

10 Close the Character Designer.

Now you can use the new character format whenever you need it.

11 Go to the Scanning and color correction section at the bottom of page 9 or the top of page 10 and select the words *continuous-tone art*.

12 Click the Character Catalog button (*f*) at the right side of the document window.

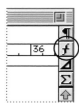

The Character Catalog appears.

13 In the Character Catalog, click FirstUse to apply the format to the selected text.

14 Save the document.

15 If you want, experiment with applying a character format to other text. When you're finished, close the Character Catalog.

Moving on

You've completed this lesson. For in-depth information on formatting text, see Chapter 5, "Text Formatting," in the *Adobe FrameMaker 7.0 User Guide*. For in-depth information on using color, see Chapter 11, "Color," in the *Adobe FrameMaker 7.0 User Guide.*

Review questions

1 What kinds of color definitions can you use for a document?

2 How can you make all paragraphs with a particular format (such as chapter titles) appear in color?

3 What is a tint?

4 How do you define a character format?

5 Which properties do you set to As Is when you create a character format?

6 How do you display the Character Designer? How do you display the Character Catalog?

Answers

1 All FrameMaker 7.0 documents include some basic color definitions. You can add custom color definitions by specifying color values or by choosing the colors from a library.

2 Add color to the paragraph format. To do this, display the Default Font properties of the Paragraph Designer, choose a color from the Color pop-up menu, and click Update All.

3 A tint is a lighter shade of another color in the document, defined as a percentage of that color. The tint is displayed and printed in the same manner as the base color, on the same plate.

4 Display the Character Designer, choose Set Window to As Is from the Commands pop-up menu, and set any properties you want to change. Then choose New Format from the Commands pop-up menu, enter a tag, and click Create.

5 You set to As Is the properties that you don't want to change when you apply the character format.

6 To display the Character Designer choose Format > Characters > Designer. To display the Character Catalog choose Format > Characters > Catalog.

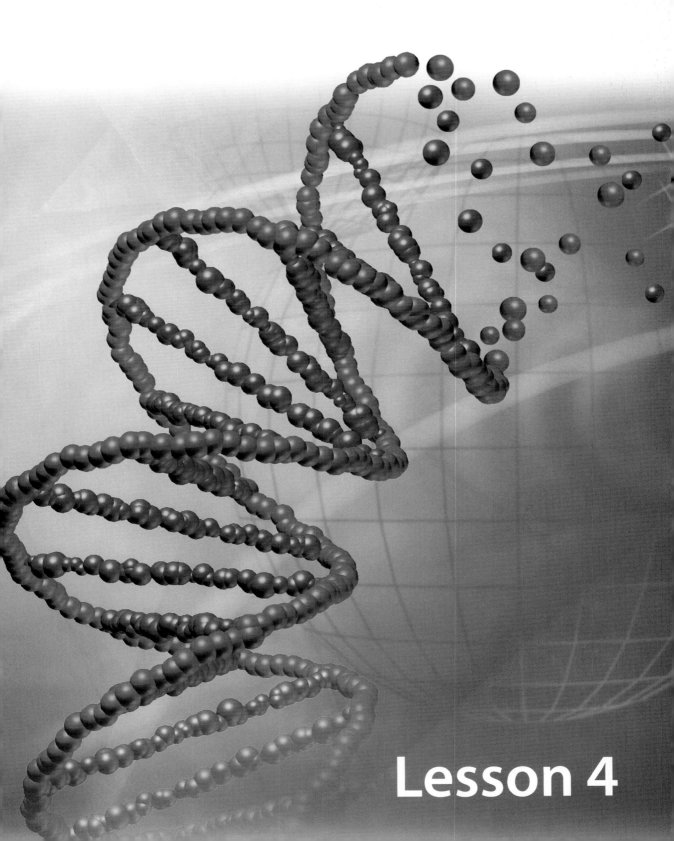

Lesson 4

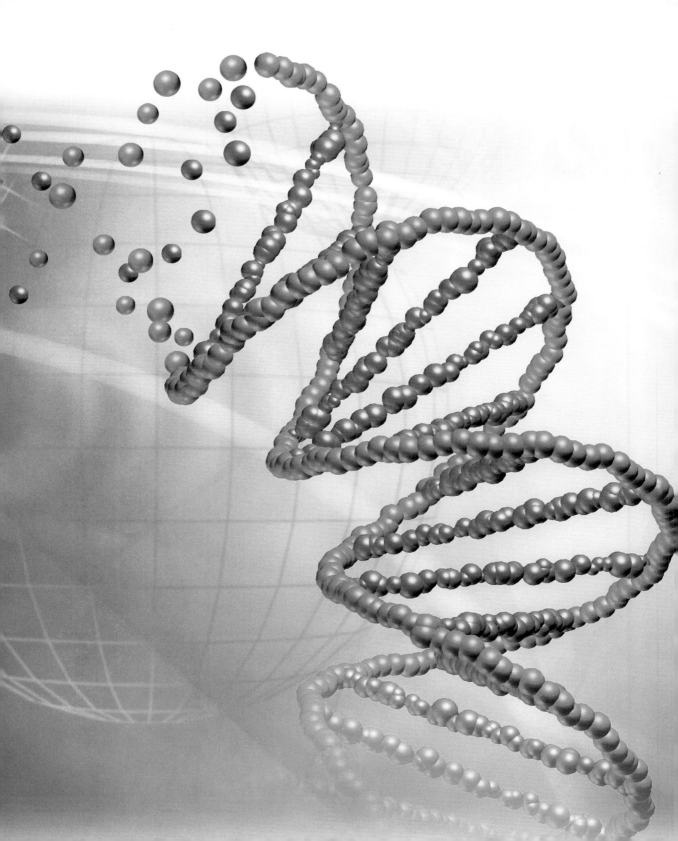

4 | **Page Layout**

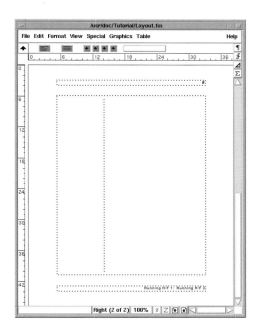

Page layouts for FrameMaker 7.0 documents are stored on special master pages—one master page for each layout used in a document. The master pages define column layouts for text and the contents and placement of headers and footers. The master pages also may contain background text or graphics that appear on the corresponding body pages.

In this lesson, you'll learn how to do the following:

- Change the column layout.
- Display master pages.
- Create and position page headers and footers.
- Use system variables for numbering pages and for creating running headers and footers.
- Create custom master pages

Changing column layout

To learn how page design works in FrameMaker 7.0, you'll set up the page layout for the chapters of a small book. The sample document already contains the paragraph and character formats that you'll use for document text.

You'll begin by narrowing the page margins so more text will fit on each page.

1 If necessary, copy the Lesson04 folder from the *FrameMaker 7.0 Classroom in a Book* CD and start FrameMaker 7.0.

2 If FrameMaker 7.0 is not in standard mode, choose File > Preferences > General, and then select FrameMaker from the Product Interface pop-up menu. You'll be prompted to restart the application.

3 Open Layout.fm in the Lesson04 folder.

4 Choose File > Save As, enter the filename **Layout1.fm**, and click Save.

5 Choose Format > Page Layout > Column Layout.

6 In the Margins area, set the Bottom to 62 and the Inside and Outside margins to 54.

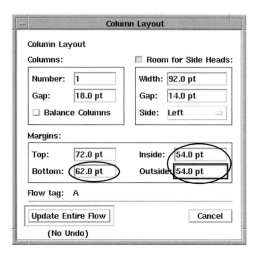

7 Click Update Entire Flow. When the margins decrease, the text frame becomes taller and wider. The width of the side-head area stays the same, but the width of the body column increases.

Displaying master pages

A document's *master pages* contain the layouts for the *body pages* that contain the document's contents. The master pages also contain the header and footer information that appears on each body page, and they may contain text or graphics that repeat from page to page.

Every FrameMaker 7.0 document has at least one master page. Layout1.fm has two master pages because it's a double-sided document. One master page is used for all the left pages, and another is used for all the right pages.

1 Choose View > Master Pages to display the master page that determines the layout of the current body page.

The name of the master page (Right) appears in the Page Status area of the status bar. The Page Status area also tells you that this is the second of two master pages.

The master page name appears in the Page Status area.

The Right master page contains three text frames.

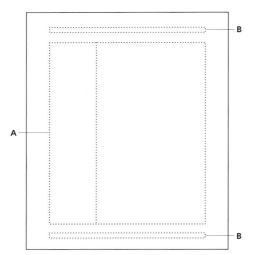

A. *Template text frame* **B.** *Background text frames*

2 Click in the large text frame. This is a *template text frame,* which provides the layout for the text frames in which you type on body pages.

The left side of the Tag area in the status bar shows you the *flow tag*—the name of the text flow that the text frame belongs to.

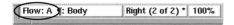

The flow tag is A.

Most documents contain one main text flow that runs from the first page to the last. The flow is usually tagged A. When text fills a body page, FrameMaker 7.0 adds a page automatically, copies the template text frame to the body page from the appropriate master page, and continues the text on the new page.

3 Click in the small text frame at the top of the page. This text frame and the small text frame at the bottom of the page are used for the headers and footers that appear on body pages.

The status bar doesn't contain a flow tag, indicating that the text flow for this text frame is *untagged*.

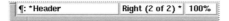

As you'll see, the contents of untagged text frames appear on body pages as *background text*—text that can only be edited on the master pages. Background text frames aren't copied to the body pages.

4 Type your name in the header text frame at the top of the page. If your name appears as a gray bar, click the Zoom In button (⧉) in the status bar until your name appears.

5 Choose View > Body Pages to display the body page. Your name appears at the top of the page, but the background text frame's borders are not displayed.

Background text appears without a text frame border.

6 Click on your name. The pointer doesn't change to an I-beam (I) as it usually does over text, and no insertion point appears, because the text isn't editable on the body page.

The pointer remains an arrow.

7 Click the Next Page button (⬇) in the status bar to display page 2. Your name doesn't appear at the top of page 2 because this is a left-hand page. It uses the Left master page, whose untagged text frames are still empty.

8 Click the Next Page button (⬇) again. Your name appears on page 3 because it's a right-hand page and, like page 1, it gets its page design from the Right master page.

9 Choose View > Master Pages to display the Right master page again.

10 Select your name in the header text frame and press Delete.

Numbering pages

You'll add the page number at the top of every page. This number will appear on the left side of left-hand pages and on the right side of right-hand pages.

You make page numbers appear on the pages of your document by inserting a page number *system variable* on the master pages. System variables are placeholders for system information such as the page number, page count, date, and filename.

The paragraphs in the header and footer text frames are tagged Header and Footer. The Header and Footer formats aren't stored in the Paragraph Catalog because you usually don't need to apply these formats to any other paragraphs.

Note: *The asterisk in the status bar indicates that the Header paragraph format doesn't match a format in the catalog.*

The paragraph format for the paragraph in the header text frame contains center-aligned and right-aligned tab stops (shown in the top ruler).

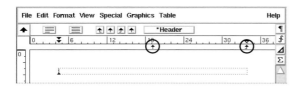

Now you'll change the font used in the header paragraph. The Header paragraph format is used on the Left and Right master pages, so you can update both header paragraphs at the same time.

1 Choose Format > Paragraphs > Designer to display the Paragraph Designer.

2 Choose Default Font from the Properties pop-up menu. (In Windows, you can just click the Default Font tab at the top of the designer.)

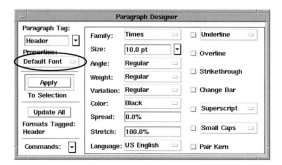

3 Choose Myriad-Roman (Windows) or Myriad (Mac OS and Unix) from the Family pop-up menu and Bold from the Weight pop-up menu, and click Update All. You won't see any change, because the text frame doesn't contain any text yet. But when you add a variable to the text frame, the variable will appear in Myriad Bold.

4 Close the Paragraph Designer.

You'll set up page numbering so that the numbers appear on the right side of right-hand pages and on the left side of left-hand pages. You're on the Right master page now, so you'll use the right-aligned tab stop to right-align the page numbers.

5 Press Tab twice. The insertion point moves to the far right of the header text frame.

Next, you'll insert a variable representing the current page number.

6 Choose Format > Headers & Footers > Insert Page #.

A number sign (#) appears at the right side of the header text frame. It will be replaced by the page number on the body pages.

Next, you'll insert the page number variable in the header of the Left master page.

7 Click the Previous Page button ( ) in the status bar to display the Left master page. The name of the master page appears in the Page Status area of the status bar.

8 Click in the header text frame and choose Format > Headers & Footers > Insert Page #. The number sign appears at the left margin. This is where you want page numbers to appear on left-hand pages.

9 Choose View > Body Pages to display the body pages again. The page number now appears on each page. If you want, scroll through the document to see how the page number alternates between the left and right sides.

Page number displayed

10 Save the document.

Creating a running footer

If you want the same text to appear in the footer of every page, you can simply type the text in the footer text frames on the master pages. However, for this document you'll create a *running footer*—a footer whose text depends on the contents of the page.

For example, a running footer based on Heading1 paragraphs contains the text of the first Heading1 paragraph on the page. If the page doesn't contain a Heading1 paragraph, the footer contains the text of the most recent Heading1 paragraph on preceding pages. (You can also create *running headers* with text that changes depending on the contents of the page.)

Like a page number, a running header or footer is created by inserting a system variable on a master page rather than by typing text. The running footers for this document will contain the chapter title and a first-level heading.

1 Choose View > Master Pages to display a master page.

2 Check the Page Status area of the status bar for the name of the current master page. If you are on the Left master page, click the Next Page button (⬇) to display the Right master page.

3 Click in the footer text frame. (You may need to scroll down to see this text frame.)

The footer will appear on the right side of right-hand pages and on the left side of left-hand pages. You're on the Right master page, so you'll use a tab stop to right-align the footer.

4 Press Tab. The insertion point moves to the right margin of the footer text frame.

Next, you'll insert a variable that displays the chapter title.

5 Choose Format > Headers & Footers > Insert Other.

6 Scroll the Variables scroll list until you see *Running H/F 1* in the list. This is one of twelve system variables provided especially for running headers and footers.

7 Select Running H/F 1. The definition of the variable appears under the scroll list.

The definition uses the <$paratext> *building block,* which tells FrameMaker 7.0 to use the text of a paragraph with the tag that follows in square brackets. The definition specifies the Title paragraph format. Your chapter title uses the ChapterTitle format, so you'll change the definition.

8 Click Edit Definition.

9 Enter **Chapter** in front of *Title* in the Definition text box and click Edit. The variable definition is now <$paratext[ChapterTitle]>. (Capitalization is significant, so be sure to match the capitalization style of the paragraph tag you're using, as shown here.)

10 Click Insert. *Running H/F 1* appears in the footer, but the actual chapter title will appear on body pages.

You'll separate the chapter title from the text of the first-level heading with a colon and an en space (a wide space).

11 Type a colon (:) in the footer at the insertion point.

12 To type an en space, press and release the Escape key, then the spacebar, and then the lowercase letter *n*.

Now you'll add another running footer variable, to display the text of first-level headings.

13 Choose Format > Headers & Footers > Insert Other.

14 Select Running H/F 2 in the Variables scroll list. The variable is defined to display the text of a paragraph with the tag Heading1. This is the definition you want; your first-level headings use the Heading1 format.

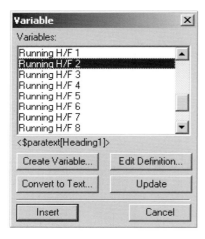

15 Click Insert.

Finishing the footers

To finish the footers, you'll change their paragraph format and then copy the footer variables to the left master page.

1 Choose Format > Paragraphs > Designer to display the Paragraph Designer.

2 In the Default Font properties, change the Family to Myriad-Roman (Windows) or Myriad (Mac OS and Unix), the Size to 8 (points), the Weight to Bold, and the Spread to 10.

3 Click Update All and close the Paragraph Designer.

Now you'll copy the footer variables to the left master page.

4 Click Running H/F 1 in the footer once to select it. (If you double-click it by mistake, the Variables dialog box appears. Click Cancel and try again.)

5 Shift-click Running H/F 2 in the footer to extend the selection.

6 Choose Edit > Copy.

7 Click the Previous Page button (◆) in the status bar to display the Left master page.

8 Click in the footer text frame and choose Edit > Paste. (You may need to scroll down to see the footer text frame.) Because you did not press Tab, the variables appear at the left side of the text frame.

9 Choose View > Body Pages to display the body pages again, and scroll through the document. The running footer now appears on each page.

10 Save the document.

Note: FrameMaker 7.0 allows you to define and use as many as twelve different running headers and footers in a document. This can be very useful if you want different headers and footers on different page layouts, such as the first page of a document.

Custom master pages

Many types of documents can be created using custom master pages as well as left and right master pages. For instance, the first page of each lesson in *Adobe FrameMaker 7.0 Classroom in a Book* uses a custom master page.

Note: Although a FrameMaker document can contain up to 100 different master pages, most often you'll use only a few.

Creating a custom master page

1 Go to page 1 of Layout1.fm and click anywhere inside the text frame.

2 Choose View > Master Page to display the master page currently applied to page 1.

3 Choose Special > Add Master Page and enter **Start** in the Name text box.

4 Select Right from the Copy from Master Page pop-up menu and click Add.

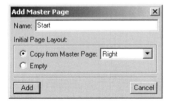

The final exercise in this lesson will address the Start master page. Now you'll create a second custom master page that won't be based on the Right or Left master pages.

1 Choose Special > Add Master Page and enter **Last** in the Name text box.

2 In the Initial Page Layout area, select Empty and click Add.

3 Save the document.

Modifying a custom master page

You can define different headers and footers, change margins, and change the column layout in custom master pages.

1 Go to the master page called Start.

2 Click the Display the Tools Palette button ( ) at the upper right corner of the document window to access the Tools palette.

The Tools palette appears.

A. *Selection tools* **B.** *Drawing tools*
C. *Drawing properties*

3 Select the Select Object cursor (▶)from the top right corner of the Tools palette. You will discover more contents of the Tools palette in Lesson 5.

4 Click anywhere in the header of the Start master page to select its background text frame.

5 Delete the header text frame by pressing Delete.

6 Delete the footer in the same way. You'll modify this master page more later.

Now you'll customize the Last master page by creating a second text frame in which you can type your own notes separately from the rest of the document text flow.

7 Go to the master page called Last.

8 Select the Place a Text Frame tool (▤)from the Tools palette to add a new text frame.

9 Draw a moderate size box as shown below.

10 After you've finished drawing the box, the Add New Text Frame dialog box appears. Choose Template for Body Page Text Frame and Flow Tag **A**. Click Add.

11 Draw a smaller text box near the bottom of the Last master page, as shown below.

12 When the Add New Text Frame dialog box appears, type **B** for the Flow Tag and then click Add.

13 Select the Select Object tool (➤)from the upper right corner of the Tools palette and click on the larger text frame. Choose Graphics > Object Properties.

14 Change the Width to 352 and change the Height to 320. In the Offset From area, change the Top offset to 72 and the Left offset to 54. Make sure the Tag is A. Make sure Autoconnect and Room for Side Heads are selected and click Set.

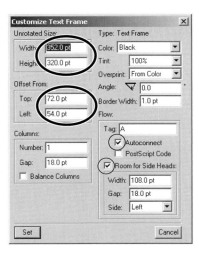

15 Make sure the Select Object tool (▶) is still selected from the Tools palette and click on the smaller text frame.

16 Choose Graphics > Object Properties.

17 Change the Width to 162 and change the Height to 78. In the Offset From area, change the Top offset to 408 and the Left offset to144.

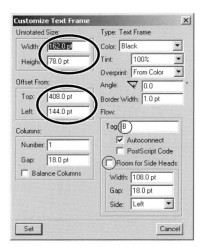

18 Make sure **B** is entered in the Tag area and deselect Room for Side Heads. Click Set.

19 Select the Smart Select tool (▶I) from the top left of the tool bar.

Assigning a different master page to a body page

Once you have created a custom master page, you then assign it to one or more body pages in your document. Assigning the custom master page to a body page changes the layout of the body page to the layout that you customized in the master page.

1 Choose View > Body Pages.

2 Go to the first page of Layout1.fm and click inside the text frame.

3 Choose Format > Page Layout > Master Page Usage.

4 In the Use Master Page area, choose Start from the Custom pop-up menu.

5 In the Apply area of the dialog box, make sure Current is selected to apply the changes to the body page you have currently selected.

6 Click Apply. Notice that the first page of Layout1.fm no longer has a footer or page number in the header.

7 Go to the last page of Layout1.fm and click inside the text frame.

8 Choose Format > Page Layout > Master Page Usage.

9 In the Use Master Page area, choose Last from the Custom pop-up menu.

10 In the Apply area of the dialog box, make sure Current is selected to apply the changes to the body page you have currently selected.

11 Click Apply. Notice that the last page of Layout1.fm contains a small text frame. This is a convenient way to add your own notes to a newsletter or any other document that requires multiple text flows.

12 Click on the smaller text frame and type **Notes:**. You can experiment by typing more text into the text frame. Notice how the text in this text frame is disconnected from the rest of the text flow.

Reordering custom master pages

When you are in the master page view of the document, the Left and Right master pages always occur on pages one and two in the list of master pages. The custom master pages you create can occur in any sequence after the Left and Right master pages. You can reorder the custom master pages. This is useful if you have created many master pages. Since you have only created two custom master pages you won't need to reorder them, but you'll see how it's done.

1 Choose View > Master Pages from any page in Layout1.fm.

2 Choose Format > Page Layout > Reorder Custom Master Pages.

3 Select a master page in the Custom Master Pages list and click Move Up or Move Down to move the page accordingly.

4 Repeat step 3 as often as necessary to obtain the order you want.

5 Click Set to reorder the pages and close the dialog box.

6 Save the document.

You may find it convenient to order the custom master pages alphabetically or by the sequence in which they will be used in the document.

Note: *If you create multiple custom pages and do not reorder them, FrameMaker simply adds the most recent to the end of the sequence.*

Assigning master pages to paragraph tags

You can assign master pages to body pages containing specified paragraph tags. In this exercise, you'll set the HighlightText paragraph tag to be assigned the custom master page called Start.

Modify the master page to be assigned

Begin by reconstructing the master page called Start. In similar fashion to that of the master page called Last, you'll resize the main text frame, but all resulting frames will be kept in "*Flow Tag A.*"

1 You'll still be in the master page layouts. Go to the master page called Start.

2 Redesign the Start page further, by resizing the text frame. Using the Select Object tool (➤) to make the frame active, choose Graphics > Object Properties.

3 Change the height to **136**.

4 Click Set.

5 Choose > Edit > Copy, then Edit > Paste.

6 When the Add New text Frame appears this time, leave it in Flow Tag A and click Add. A message appears telling you it has been accepted. Click OK.

7 Choose > Graphics > Object Properties.

8 Change the Top to **220.5** and change the Left to **54**. Click Set.

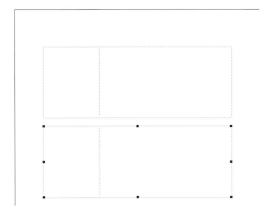

9 Copy and paste again, and, after accepting Flow Tag A Again, change the third frame's Object Properties to Top **370** and Left **54**. Click Set.

10 Save the document.

You now have divided Start into three equally sized frames.

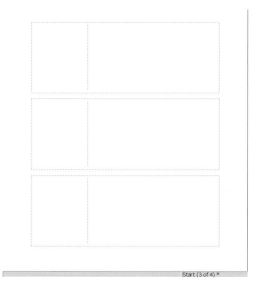

Start (3 of 4) *

Map the master page to be applied

You'll map a paragraph tag to the master pages using a mapping table found in the Reference Pages. When you choose the Apply Master Pages command, the master page will be applied to the body page or body pages on which the referenced paragraph tag appears. If more than one referenced paragraph tag appears on a body page, the first referenced paragraph tag on the page determines which master page is applied.

To assign a master page to body pages on which a paragraph tag appears:

1 Choose View > Reference Pages.

2 Click the Next Page button until the six-column UnstructMasterPageMaps page appears. In your file it should be reference page 2.

3 Edit the mapping table. Under the Paragraph Tag Name column heading, type **HighlightText**, which is the name of the paragraph tag to which you want the master page to be applied. You'll create the HighlightText paragraph format later, but be sure to use the same capitalization as shown above (capital H and T, all one word).

4 Under the Right-Handed Master Page column heading, type **Start**, which is the name of the master page you want to apply. The specified master page will be applied to all body pages, including left-handed pages in double-sided documents, on which the HighlightText paragraph tag appears, unless you specify a different master page under the Left-Handed Master Page column.

5 Under the Left-Handed Master Page column heading, type **Start**, which is the name of the master page that you want to apply to the left-handed body pages on which the paragraph tag HighlightText appears in double-sided documents.

6 Under the Range Indicator heading, type **Single** to apply the master page only to the body page on which each paragraph tag appears. If this cell is blank, master pages are applied to single pages.

7 Under the Comments heading, type **Show good work**.

8 Save the document.

▢ *For a more complete knowledge of this and other features of applying master pages, see* Chapter 12, "Page Layouts," in the *Adobe FrameMaker 7.0 User Guide*.

Create a new paragraph format

Now you'll complete the steps necessary to assign the Start master page to the HighlightText paragraph tag.

1 Choose > View > Body Pages of Layout1.fm.

2 Go to the last page in the file and insert the cursor in a new paragraph below the last bulleted line of text.

3 Type **Beautiful Printing Results!** and press return.

4 In the second new paragraph, type **More Great Examples**.

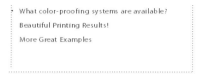

In order to link up the Start master page and a format called HighlightText through the reference page table of assignments, you'll create the new paragraph tag.

1 Select both of these new paragraphs at the end of the document.

2 Choose > Format > Paragraphs > Designer. In the Properties pop-up menu choose Basic.

3 Assign the Paragraph Tag as Body. Click apply. The bullets are removed from the two lines of text.

What color-proofing systems are available?
Beautiful Printing Results!
More Great Examples

4 In the Paragraph Designer, choose Commands > New Format.

5 Name the new format **HighlightText**. Be sure both check boxes are selected and press Create.

6 In the Paragraph Designer, press Update All.

The two new lines of text are tagged with the paragraph format HighlightText.

7 In the Paragraph Designer Properties > Basic, make the Alignment Center.

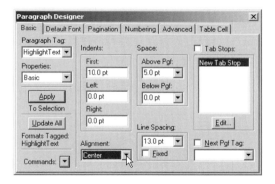

8 In the Paragraph Designer, press Update All.

9 In the Paragraph Designer, choose Properties > Default Font.

10 In the Family pop-up menu, select:

• (Windows) AGaramond-SemiboldItalic, Weight Regular.

• (Mac OS and UNIX) Adobe Garamond, Weight Semibold, Angle Italic.

11 Make the Size **24** pt. Select HeadingColor for Color. Type **0.0%** for Spread.

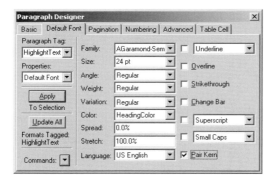

12 In the Paragraph Designer, press Update All. If there is not room for the paragraphs on one page, a new page may be created for one or both of them.

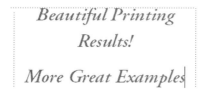

Beautiful Printing Results!

More Great Examples

13 In the Paragraph Designer, choose Properties > Pagination.

14 Under Start, select Top of Column. In Format, click Across All Columns and Side Heads.

15 In the Paragraph Designer, press Update All.

The two HighlightText paragraphs are now centered at the top of two new pages.

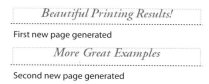

First new page generated

More Great Examples

Second new page generated

16 Save the document and click anywhere in the document to begin the final steps.

Assign the master page to a paragraph tag

The goal of these exercises is to produce a page of samples of good printing, using the Start master page layout. Each Frame from the Start master page layout has been set up to have samples imported into them while maintaining Flow Tag A.

1 In the main menu title bar, choose Format > Page Layout > Apply Master Pages. A FrameMaker interface box will appear.

2 Click OK.

The two HighlightText paragraphs are now at the top of the first two boxes of the first added new page.

The master page usage for it has been changed to Start through the Apply Master Pages command.

3 Save and close the document.

You have completed the lesson on page layout, working with some of the powerful tools of *Adobe FrameMaker 7.0.*

Moving on

You've completed this lesson. For in-depth information about variables, page layout, and templates see Chapter 8, "Variables," Chapter 12, "Page Layout," and Chapter 13, "Templates," in the *Adobe FrameMaker 7.0 User Guide.*

Review questions

1 How do you change the page margins of a document?

2 What are master pages?

3 What are the main differences between the template text frames and background text frames that appear on master pages?

4 How do you insert a page number in a header or footer?

5 What is a running header or footer?

6 How do you create a running header or footer?

7 When is it useful to define multiple running headers and footers?

8 What are the benefits of tying a master page layout to a specific paragraph format?

Answers

1 Choose Format > Page Layout > Column Layout, specify new margins, and click Update Entire Flow.

2 Master pages are pages that contain layouts for body pages. Master pages also contain header and footer information, and they may contain background text or graphics that appear on the corresponding body pages.

3 Template text frames provide layouts for the text frames on body pages. The template text frames have flow tags and are copied to body pages. Background text frames, such as those for headers and footers, have no flow tags and are not copied to body pages. The contents of background text frames appear on body pages, but the contents can be edited only on master pages.

4 To insert a page number go to a master page, click in a header or footer text frame and choose Format > Headers & Footers > Insert Page #. The actual page number will appear on the body pages that use that master page.

5 A running header or footer contains information that depends on the contents of the page (for example, the text of the first Heading1 paragraph on the page).

6 On a master page, click in a header or footer text frame and choose Format > Headers & Footers > Insert Other. Select one of the four variables for running headers and footers, change its definition if necessary, and click Insert.

7 When you have a complex document with many different master pages, and you want different content in their headers and footers.

8 Tying a master page layout to a paragraph format saves time and assures consistency of layout in a complex document.

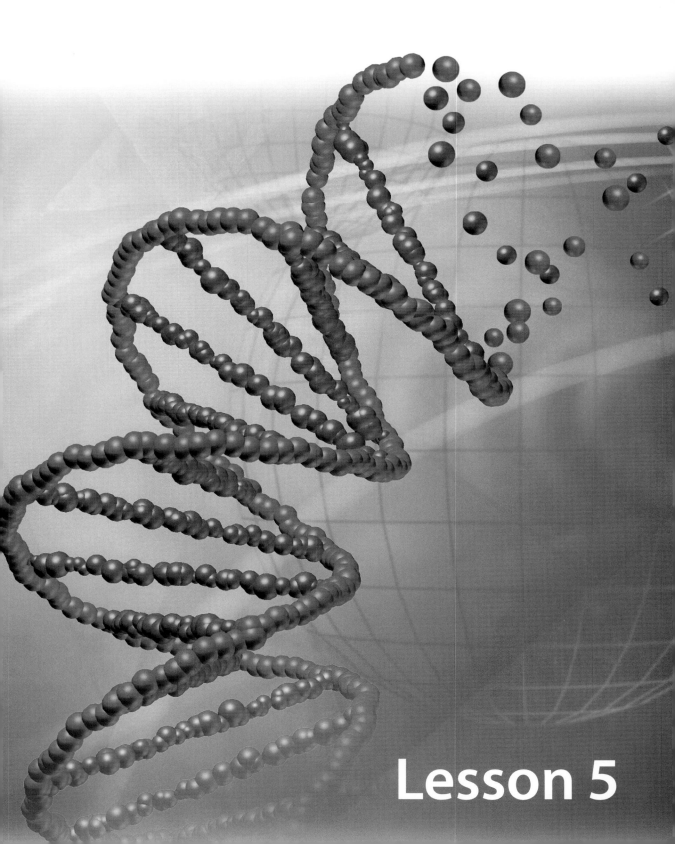

Lesson 5

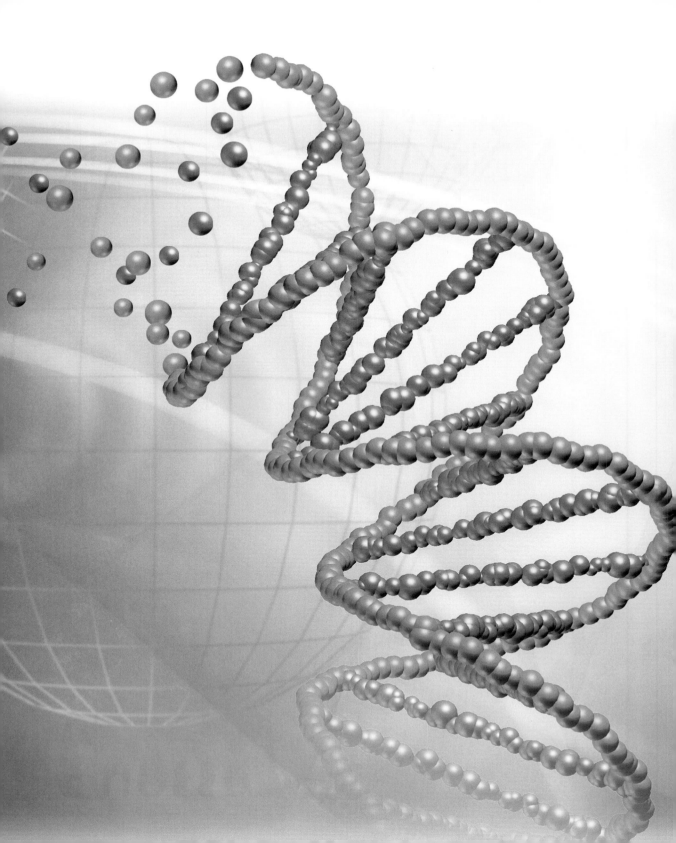

5 | Graphics

Chapter 1: Planning for Commercial Printing

Every commercial printing job requires that you consider a complex set of variables ranging from what your budget and schedule allow to how the paper stock and printing press affect your final output. The earlier you think about these variables, the more control you'll have over the quality, cost, and schedule of your project.

Planning and evaluation

Preparing a publication for commercial printing takes careful thought: both imagesetters and commercial printing presses have inherent limitations, and it's possible to create publications that are difficult to print on either an imagesetter or a printing press. By thinking of your design and production cycles as steps in a larger process, you can make choices that will let you work more efficiently and help you achieve the best printed results.

Before going to a commercial printer with your project, you need to evaluate your skills, your schedule, and your equipment to determine what tasks you will do and what services you will contract.

In addition to choosing a commercial printer, you may need to select a prepress service provider to image color separations, scan continuous-tone art, and trap

Planning for Commercial Printing: Planning and evaluation

You can draw or import graphics to add graphic interest to a page design or to illustrate your document. You can also specify graphic properties such as fill pattern, pen pattern, line width, and color, and you can resize, reshape, rotate, and rearrange graphics.

In this lesson, you'll add master page graphics to complete the page design of the sample chapter you've been working on. You'll import one graphic and draw the rest. When you're finished, the graphics you add to the master pages will appear on each body page.

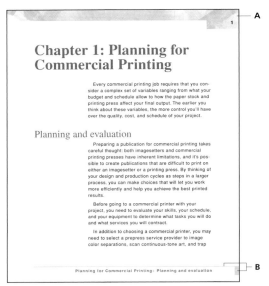

A. Imported graphic *B. Drawn graphics*

You'll learn how to do the following:

- Adjust frames for graphics.

- Import a graphic.

- Mask part of an imported graphic.

- Draw lines and rectangles.

- Change drawing and graphic properties.

- Move, resize, align, distribute, and group graphic objects.

Adjusting header and footer frames for graphics

Before adding graphics to them, you'll reposition the header and footer frames on each master page.

1 If necessary, copy the Lesson05 folder from the *FrameMaker 7.0 Classroom in a Book* CD and start FrameMaker 7.0.

2 If FrameMaker 7.0 is not in standard mode, choose File > Preferences > General, and then select FrameMaker from the Product Interface pop-up menu.

3 Open Graphics.fm in the Lesson05 folder.

4 Choose File > Save As, enter the filename **Graphics1.fm**, and click Save.

The Graphics1.fm file uses the page design you created in the previous lesson. It also contains definitions for two additional colors (FooterColor and PageRule). One of these colors has already been applied to the page footers.

The document is set to 100% zoom. Don't change it for now. If the header and footer appear as gray bars rather than as text, don't worry. The text is just *greeked* —that is, it's represented by a substitute for the real text at this magnification. You'll zoom in later.

Note: In this lesson, the graphics are added to background frames on master pages, which determine their fixed position and appearance on body pages. Lesson 9 provides information on placing graphics in anchored or unanchored frames directly on body pages.

Changing the Right master page

The header and footer text frames on the master pages were positioned automatically by FrameMaker 7.0 when the document was created. You'll reposition the header and footer on the Right master page.

First you'll move the page header closer to the edge of the page. You'll use the rulers at the top and left side of the document window to help you position the header text frame. The ruler markings are in picas. (Six picas equal one inch or 12 points. There are 72 points in an inch.)

1 Choose View > Master Pages. FrameMaker 7.0 displays the master page of the body page you were on. In this case, the Right master page is displayed.

Before you reposition objects, you'll make sure that the snap grid is on. (Objects snap to the grid as you drag or resize them.)

2 Click the Graphics menu and choose Snap, if it is not already turned on. A check mark or filled-in check box next to the Snap menu item indicates the Snap command is on.

3 Do one of the following to select the header text frame:

- (Windows and UNIX) Control-click the header text frame.

- (Mac OS) Option-click the header text frame.

Handles appear around the header text frame.

4 Place the pointer inside the header text frame (not on a handle). The pointer changes to a hollow arrow.

5 Shift-drag the header text frame to the right until the right edge of the text frame is at the 36-pica mark on the top ruler. Holding down Shift as you drag constrains the movement to horizontal or vertical.

Vertical lines appear below the ruler as you drag, to indicate the left side, center, and right side of the frame.

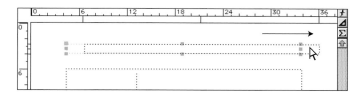

The header text frame still needs to move a little more to the right, so you'll adjust its position slightly.

6 Do one of the following to move the header text frame four points to the right:

• (Windows) Press Alt-Right Arrow four times (using the arrow key to the left of the numeric keypad).

• (Mac OS) Press Option-Right Arrow four times.

• (UNIX) Press Control-Right Arrow four times.

Next you'll move the header text frame closer to the top of the page.

7 With the header text frame still selected, Shift-drag it upward until the top of the text frame is 2 picas below the top of the page. Here you can use the horizontal lines next to the ruler to line up the frame as you drag it.

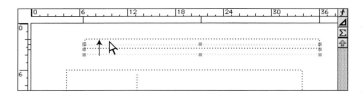

8 Click in the page margin to deselect the header text frame.

Finally, you'll reposition the footer text frame.

9 If necessary, scroll down until you see the footer text frame.

10 Do one of the following to select the footer text frame:

• (Windows and UNIX) Control-click the footer text frame.

• (Mac OS) Option-click the footer text frame.

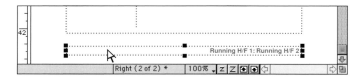

You'll move the footer text frame a total of 12 points, so you'll use a key combination that moves the text frame 6 points at a time.

11 Do one of the following to move the footer text frame down 12 points:

• (Windows) Press Alt-Shift-Down Arrow twice (using the arrow key to the left of the numeric keypad).

• (Mac OS) Press Option-Shift-Down Arrow twice.

• (UNIX) Press Control-Shift-Down Arrow twice.

12 Save the document.

 *The actual distance moved depends on the current zoom setting, so that you can do finer work when you're zoomed in closer. For example, at 200% magnification, using the keyboard shortcut moves an object 6 points. At 100% magnification, the object would move 12 points. And at 50% zoom, the object would move 24 points.*

Changing the Left master page

Now you'll reposition the header and footer text frames on the Left master page to make the left and right pages symmetrical.

1 Click the Previous Page button ( ) in the status bar to display the Left master page.

Left (1 of 2) *   100% ⌄ z Z 🔲 🔳 ⟡

2 Do one of the following to select the header text frame:

• (Windows and UNIX) Control-click the header text frame.

• (Mac OS) Option-click the header text frame.

3 Shift-drag the header text frame to the left until the left edge of the frame is at the 2-pica mark on the top ruler.

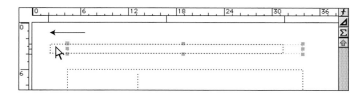

4 With the header text frame still selected, Shift-drag it upward until the top of the frame is 2 picas below the top of the page.

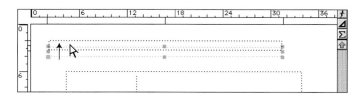

5 Click in the page margin to deselect the header text frame.

6 Select the footer text frame, scrolling down the page if necessary.

You could use the arrow keys to move the footer text frame as you did on the Right master page. This time, though, you'll use a dialog box to position it.

7 Choose Graphics > Object Properties.

8 In the Offset From area, change the Top offset to 533 and click Set.

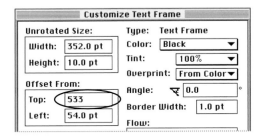

9 Save the document.

Importing a graphic

The page design used with this document calls for a graphic to appear at the top of each page. The graphic was created in another application and saved in TIFF format. You'll import the graphic and position it on the page.

Two ways to import graphics

There are two ways to import a graphic: by copying it into the document or by creating a reference to it.

When you import a graphic by copying, a copy of the original graphic is stored in the document. There are two advantages to this method:

• If you move the document—for example, to bring it to a print shop—the graphics are already contained in the document.

• You don't have to depend on the original graphic file. The original graphic can be changed, moved to a different directory, or deleted without affecting the copies in your document.

When you import by reference, the graphic file isn't stored in the document. Instead, the document contains a pointer to the original graphic file. There are two advantages to this method:

• When you import by reference, the document doesn't contain any image; instead, it contains only a pointer to the stored graphic file on the disk. This can greatly reduce the size of a file. (If you import by copying on both the Left and Right master pages, the document contains the same image twice, increasing the file size.)

• When you import by reference, the graphic in the document will be updated automatically whenever the stored graphics file is changed. (If you import by copying and then change the graphic file, you need to reimport the graphic to update the image stored in the document.)

In this lesson, you'll import the graphic by reference.

1 If necessary, scroll up until you see the top of the Left master page.

2 Click in the page margin to make sure that nothing is selected on the page and that there's no insertion point.

3 Choose File > Import > File.

4 Open the Art folder in the Lesson05 folder.

5 Select Import by Reference, then select Banner.tif in the scroll list.

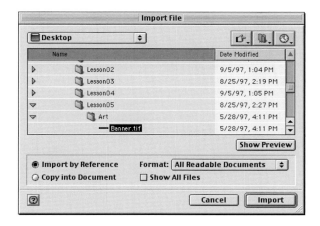

6 Click Import. The Imported Graphic Scaling dialog box appears.

7 Select 72 dpi (dots per inch) to set the scaling for the graphic, and click Set.

The best printed results are obtained if you choose a dpi value that divides evenly (or with a small remainder) into the resolution of your printer. The best screen representations are achieved with a dpi value that divides evenly into your monitor's screen resolution.

The graphic is centered on the page.

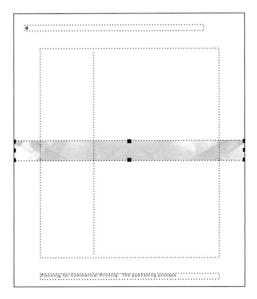

Note: *If the graphic is cropped by a text frame, appears in an anchored frame, or doesn't appear at all, you probably had an insertion point when you chose File > Import > File. Choose Edit > Undo, click outside the text frames, and try again.*

Next, you'll reposition the graphic at the top of the page.

8 With the graphic still selected, choose Graphics > Object Properties.

9 In the Offset From area, change the Top offset to 0 (zero) and click Set. The graphic moves to the top of the page.

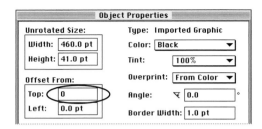

10 Save the document.

Masking part of a graphic

Next, you'll mask part of the graphic at the top of the page by placing a white rectangle over part of the graphic.

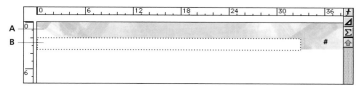

A. *Imported graphic* **B.** *White rectangle masking part of graphic*

First you'll draw the rectangle.

1 At the right side of the document window, click the Tools button (◢) to display the Tools palette.

The Tools palette contains the following items:

- Selection tools that control how you select text and objects.
- Drawing tools for drawing various objects.

• Pop-up menus for changing an object's drawing properties.

2 Click the rectangle tool (▭) on the Tools palette.

3 Click the Fill pop-up menu and choose White.

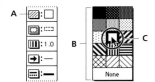

A. Fill pop-up menu button B. Fill pop-up menu C. Selected fill

4 Click the Pen pop-up menu and choose Solid.

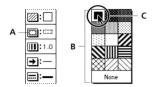

A. Pen pop-up menu button B. Pen pop-up menu C. Selected fill

You'll change the pen pattern to white later, but for now it's handy to be able to see the rectangle's border.

5 Move the pointer to the document window. The pointer changes to a cross hair (+).

6 Drag from the left side of the document window to draw a rectangle 396 points wide and 18 points high. The width and height appear in the status bar as you drag. (If you don't get it exactly the right size by dragging, in the next steps you'll have a chance to enter the specific width and height in a dialog box.)

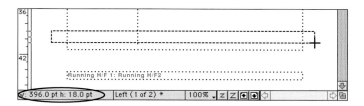

Now you'll position the rectangle.

7 With the rectangle still selected, choose Graphics > Object Properties.

8 In the Offset From area, change the Top offset to 24 and the Left offset to 64. (If you didn't get the width and height you wanted by dragging, change the Width to 396 and the Height to 18 in the Offset From area.) Click Set.

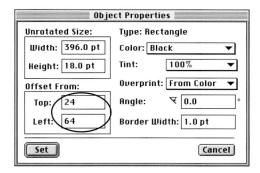

9 On the Tools palette, choose White from the Pen pop-up menu. The rectangle remains selected, but its border disappears.

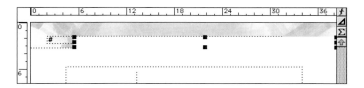

Last, you'll *group* the imported graphic and the rectangle, so you can manipulate them as a single object.

10 With the rectangle still selected, Shift-click the imported graphic to add it to the selection. Handles now appear around both the rectangle and the imported graphic.

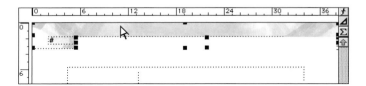

11 Choose Graphics > Group. One set of handles now appears around the grouped set of objects.

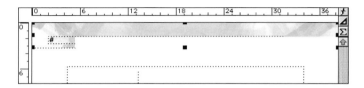

It's a good habit to group graphic objects that you want to treat as a single object. This ensures that moving and copying will be consistent.

12 Save the document.

Copying the graphics

You'll use the same graphic at the top of every page, so you'll copy the grouped graphics to the Right master page. However, you'll flip the graphic for a symmetrical look.

1 With the grouped objects still selected, choose Edit > Copy.

2 Click the Next Page button ( ) in the status bar to display the Right master page. Don't click anywhere on the page, because if you click inside a text frame, the graphic will be pasted inside the frame instead of at the top of the page.

3 Choose Edit > Paste. The graphic appears at the top of the page, in the same position as on the Left master page.

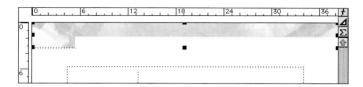

The page header disappeared, because the graphic was pasted in front of the header text frame.

4 With the graphic still selected, choose Graphics > Send to Back. The header text frame reappears.

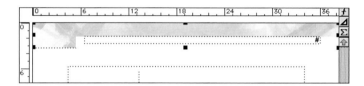

To make the notch in the graphic (created by the white rectangle you drew in the previous section) appear on the left, you'll flip the graphic.

5 With the graphic still selected, choose Graphics > Flip Left/Right.

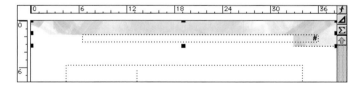

6 If you want, choose View > Body Pages to display the first page of the document, and then scroll through the document to see the modified headers and footers. When you're finished, choose View > Master Pages and make sure the Right master page is displayed.

7 Save the document.

Drawing lines and rectangles

The last part of the page design involves creating a line and a rectangle that will appear at the bottom of each page.

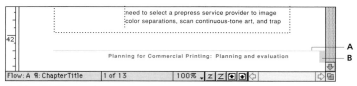

A. *Line* B. *Rectangle*

Because the Snap grid is on and is set to 6 points, when you draw an object, it will "jump" in size in 6-point increments. For finer control, you'll turn off the Snap command now.

1 Choose Graphics > Snap to turn off Snap.

Now you'll draw the line.

2 If necessary, scroll down until you can see the footer on the Right master page.

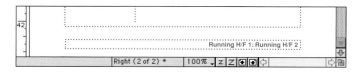

3 Click the line tool (╲) on the Tools palette.

4 Choose Solid from the Pen pop-up menu.

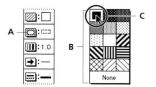

A. *Pen pop-up menu button* B. *Pen pop-up menu* C. *Selected fill*

5 Choose the second line width from the Line Width pop-up menu.

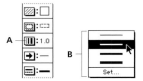

A. Line Width pop-up menu button B. Line Width pop-up menu

The default value for the second line width is 1.0 point.

Note: *If the line is thicker than 1 point, choose Set on the Line Width pop-up menu, click Get Defaults, and choose the second line width from the Line Width pop-up menu again.*

6 On the Tools palette, make sure that the line end is set to no arrows, the line style is set to solid, the color is set to PageRule, and the tint is set to 100%.

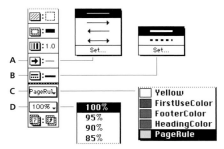

A. Line end: no arrows B. Line style: solid
C. Color: PageRule D. Tint: 100%

7 Move the pointer to the document window. The pointer changes to a cross hair (+).

8 Shift-drag from just above the left side of the page footer to draw a horizontal line that extends to the right edge of the page. (Don't drag beyond the edge of the page.)

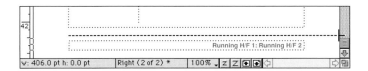

The line appears a few points above the text frame.

9 If you want to adjust the vertical position of the line, do one of the following to move the line 1 point at a time:

- (Windows) Press Alt+Up Arrow or Alt+Down Arrow (using the arrow keys to the left of the numeric keypad).

- (Mac OS) Press Option+Up Arrow or Option+Down Arrow.

- (UNIX) Press Control+Up Arrow or Control+Down Arrow.

♀ *You can set drawing properties before you draw the object or select the object after it is drawn and change its properties. Whatever property you select remains the current property until you change it.*

Now you'll draw the rectangle.

10 Click the rectangle tool (☐) on the Tools palette.

11 Choose Solid from the Fill pop-up menu.

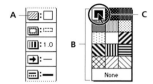

A. *Fill pop-up menu button* B. *Fill pop-up menu* C. *Selected fill*

12 In the document window, drag to draw a rectangle below the right side of the horizontal line. The rectangle should be approximately 8 points wide and 18 points high. (The dimensions appear in the status bar as you drag.) Don't worry about the exact placement of the rectangle. You'll fix that next.

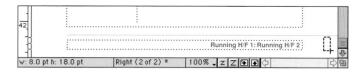

13 Close the Tools palette.

Aligning and distributing objects

You have the graphics you need (the line and the rectangle), and the line is in the position you want. Now you need to place the rectangle correctly in relation to the line. FrameMaker 7.0 provides two commands, Align and Distribute, that change the positions of objects with respect to each other. You'll use these commands now.

1 With the small rectangle you created in the previous section still selected, Shift-click the horizontal line to add it to the selection.

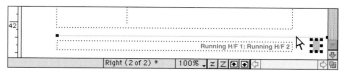

Rectangle and line selected

2 Choose Graphics > Align.

You'll align the right sides of the rectangle and line.

3 In the Top/Bottom area, select As Is to leave the vertical alignment unchanged.

4 In the Left/Right area, select Right Sides and click Align.

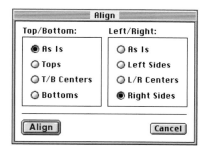

The right side of the rectangle is aligned with the right endpoint of the line. (The last object selected—the line—doesn't move. Other selected objects—in this case, the rectangle—move until the objects are aligned with the last-selected object.)

5 Make sure the rectangle and line are both selected, choose Graphics > Distribute.

6 In the Horizontal Spacing area, select As Is, so that you don't change the horizontal spacing.

7 In the Vertical Spacing area, select Edge Gap and make sure the edge gap is set to 0.

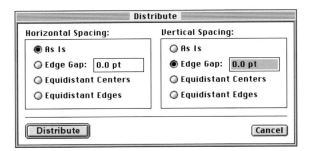

8 Click Distribute. The rectangle moves up until it touches the line (that is, the gap between them is 0).

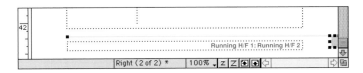

9 Choose Graphics > Group to group the two objects. A single set of handles appears around the grouped set of objects.

10 Save the document.

Copying the graphics

To complete the page design, you'll copy the line and rectangle to the Left master page.

1 With the grouped objects still selected, choose Edit > Copy.

2 Click the Previous Page button (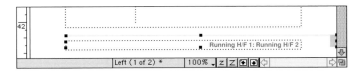) in the status bar to display the Left master page. As before, don't click anywhere on the page. (If you click inside a text frame, the graphic will be pasted inside the frame instead of at the bottom of the page.)

3 Choose Edit > Paste. The graphic appears at the bottom of the page, in the same position as on the Right master page.

Next, you'll flip and move the graphic to position it correctly.

4 With the grouped objects still selected, choose Graphics > Flip Left/Right.

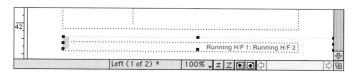

5 Choose Graphics > Object Properties.

6 In the Offset From area, change the Left offset to 0 and click Set.

The page design is finished.

7 If the header and footer appear as gray bars rather than as text, click the Zoom In button (Z) in the status bar until the header and footer appear as text.

8 Choose View > Body Pages to display the first page of the document, and then scroll through the document to see the modified page design.

9 Save and close Graphics1.fm.

Moving on

You've completed this lesson. For in-depth information about graphics, see Chapter 9, "Graphics," chapter 10, "Anchored Frames," and Chapter 18, "Importing, Linking, and Exporting," in the *Adobe FrameMaker 7.0 User Guide*.

Review questions

1 How large is a point? A pica?

2 What does the Snap command do?

3 What is the difference between importing a graphic by copying it into the document and importing a graphic by reference?

4 Name an advantage of each method.

5 What is the function of the Tools palette?

6 What does the Group command do?

Answers

1 There are 72 points—or 6 picas—in an inch. There are 12 points in a pica.

2 The Snap command makes objects snap to an invisible grid as you draw, drag, or resize them.

3 Importing a copy of a graphic places a copy of the original graphic into the document. Importing a graphic by reference links the document to the original graphic.

4 When you import a graphic by copying, you can move the document without regard to the original source graphic. You can also modify, move, or delete the original graphic without affecting the copy in the document. When you import by reference, you can greatly reduce the document's file size compared to importing the graphic by copying. Importing by reference also updates the graphics in the document whenever the original graphics are updated.

5 The Tools palette contains selection tools that control how you select text and objects, drawing tools for drawing various objects, and pop-up menus for changing an object's properties.

6 The Group command groups two or more objects into a single object. This makes it easier to move, modify, and copy the objects together.

Lesson 6

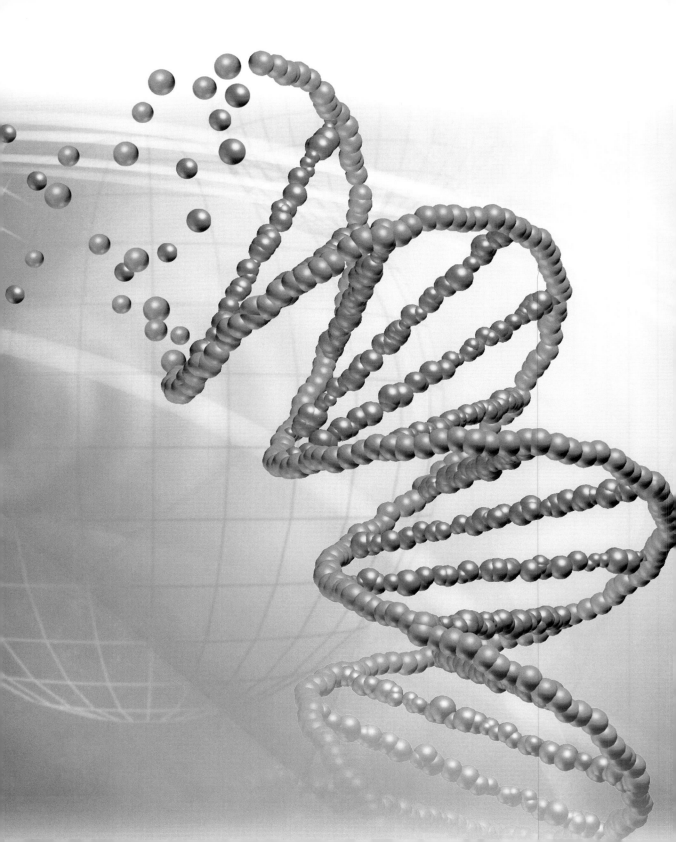

6 | Document Editing

FrameMaker 7.0 includes several powerful editing tools: the Find/Change command (for finding and changing text and other items), a spelling checker (which can find and correct misspelled words and common typing errors), and a thesaurus (which defines words and provides synonyms, antonyms, and related words). To save typing and ensure consistency, you can use variables for words or phrases that appear in multiple places in a document.

In this lesson, you'll learn how to do the following:

• Turn off the display of graphics in a document.

• Define and insert user variables.

• Change variable definitions.

• Use the Find/Change command to find and replace text.

• Use the Thesaurus to replace words with their synonyms.

• Use the Spelling Checker to find and correct spelling and typing errors.

Viewing the document

The text you'll edit is in a veterinary article about Labrador Retrievers. To begin, you'll open and view the article.

1 If necessary, copy the Lesson06 folder from the *FrameMaker 7.0 Classroom in a Book* CD and start FrameMaker 7.0.

2 If FrameMaker 7.0 is not in standard mode, choose File > Preferences > General, and then select FrameMaker from the Product Interface pop-up menu.

3 Open Editing.fm in the Lesson06 folder.

4 Choose File > Save As, enter the filename **Editing1.fm**, and click Save.

5 In the status bar, click the Next Page button (⬇) to page through the document. The last page is page 4.

6 In the status bar, Shift-click the Previous Page button (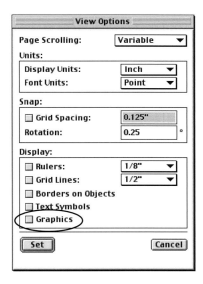) to go back to page 1.

Turning off the display of graphics

Throughout this lesson, you'll select and edit text. To make pages display faster, and to make it easier to see the selected text, you'll turn off the display of graphics.

1 Choose View > Options.

2 Turn off Graphics and click Set.

The graphics temporarily disappear from the document. (They won't appear in print either.) They are not deleted—when you finish editing the text, you'll redisplay the graphics.

3 If you like, page through the document to see how it looks without graphics. When you're finished, go back to page 1.

4 If you find the text too small to read, click the Zoom In button () in the status bar until the text is legible.

Defining a user variable

The name of the dog breed (*Labrador Retriever*) appears often in the article, as does a shorter version of the name (*Labrador*). The long name is already defined as a user variable.

A *user variable* is a placeholder for text, such as a technical term or name, that you can define once and use repeatedly in a document. When you change the definition, FrameMaker 7.0 updates the variable throughout the document. In this way, variables can help save you time and ensure consistency in your documents.

Note: *FrameMaker provides system variables that you can redefine but cannot delete.*

In this part of the lesson, you'll create a user variable.

1 Click once on the heading, *LABRADOR RETRIEVERS.* The entire phrase (except for the *S* at the end) is selected, indicating that you can't edit the variable as you do regular text.

First you'll define a user variable for the short name. Then you'll simply insert the variable rather than type the name yourself.

2 Choose Special > Variable.

3 Click Create Variable.

4 Enter **ShortName** in the Name text box, and enter **Labrador** in the Definition text box.

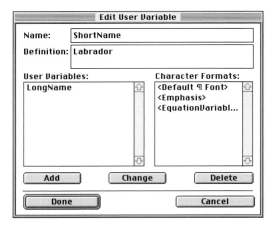

5 Click Add, and then click Done.

The new variable appears in the Variable dialog box.

6 Click Done.

Inserting variables

Now you'll insert variables rather than type the text each time.

1 On page 1, double-click the word *breed* in the fourth line of body text to select the word.

> **LABRADOR RETRIEVERS**
>
> **BACKGROUND**
> The Labrador Retriever first appeared as a
> breed in England in the late 1800's. A
> descendant of working dogs brought to
> Europe from Newfoundland, the breed is
> a relative of other retrievers, such as the
> Golden Retriever, the Flat-Coated
> Retriever, and the Chesapeake Bay
> Retriever. The Labrador's generous temper-

2 Choose Special > Variable.

3 In the Variables scroll list, select ShortName and click Replace. *Labrador* appears in place of *breed*.

> **LABRADOR RETRIEVERS**
>
> **BACKGROUND**
> The Labrador Retriever first appeared as a
> breed in England in the late 1800's. A
> descendant of working dogs brought to
> Europe from Newfoundland, the Labrador
> is a relative of other retrievers, such as
> the Golden Retriever, the Flat-Coated
> Retriever, and the Chesapeake Bay
> Retriever. The Labrador's generous temper-

Now you'll insert another variable. This time, you'll use a keyboard shortcut.

4 In the status bar, click the Next Page button (⬇) to display page 2.

5 Near the bottom of the right-hand column, click just to the left of the word *Few* to place the insertion point.

> look elsewhere, for the Labrador rates low
> on the barking scale and high on amiability.
> Few breeds can match its intelligence,
> energy, sociability, and bravery.
>
> **PUPPIES**
> Any winsome Labrador pup can be the
> epitome of cute and cuddly, but it's a good
> idea to shop around before deciding on the
> puppy to bring home. Spend some time
> observing the temperaments of all the pup-

6 Type **Nevertheless, the** and press the spacebar.

7 Press Control+0 (zero). The status bar changes to prompt you for a variable name. (In Windows and on UNIX systems, the status bar displays the name of the first variable in the Variable scroll list.)

8 Type the letter **S**. Because only the ShortName variable begins with the letter *S*, the prompt changes to indicate that variable.

9 Press Return. The variable is added to the text.

10 Press the spacebar. Type **remains one of the most popular breeds among dog lovers** followed by a period and a space to end the sentence.

Finding and changing text

Because the article was typed before the ShortName variable was defined, the word *Labrador* still appears throughout the article as typed text rather than as a variable. You'll change that by replacing occurrences of *Labrador* throughout the document with the ShortName variable.

First you'll copy the ShortName variable to the Clipboard.

1 Go back to page 1.

2 In the fourth line of body text on page 1, click *Labrador* once to select the variable. (If you double-click by mistake, the Variable dialog box appears. Just click Cancel.)

LABRADOR RETRIEVERS

BACKGROUND
The Labrador Retriever first appeared as a breed in England in the late 1800's. A descendant of working dogs brought to Europe from Newfoundland, the Labrador is a relative of other retrievers, such as the Golden Retriever, the Flat-Coated Retriever, and the Chesapeake Bay Retriever. The Labrador's generous temper-

3 Choose Edit > Copy. The variable is copied to the Clipboard.

4 Choose Edit > Find/Change.

5 Enter **Labrador** in the Find text box.

6 Choose By Pasting from the Change pop-up menu. This option lets you replace by pasting whatever you last copied—in this case, the ShortName variable.

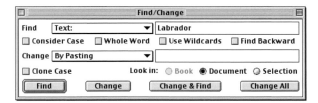

7 Click Find. The next occurrence of *Labrador* on page 1 is selected.

8 Click Change & Find. The selected text is replaced with the variable, and the next occurrence is selected.

The article contains quite a few occurrences of the word *Labrador,* so you'll have FrameMaker 7.0 replace them all at the same time.

9 Make sure that Look in Document is selected near the bottom right of the dialog box, click Change All, then click OK.

All the remaining occurrences of the word *Labrador* in this document are replaced by the ShortName variable. When FrameMaker 7.0 shows you the number of changes made in the document, click OK to dismiss the alert box. Page 4 of the article appears, with the insertion point in the last paragraph, just after the last occurrence of the variable.

> from owning a pet—with com-
> mon sense and a little
> resourcefulness your
> Labrador need not tax
> your pocketbook. And
> in return you'll
> receive years of
> affection, fun,
> and devotion.

10 Close the Find/Change dialog box.

Other ways to use Find/Change

You can use Find/Change and Find/Next commands to find many other items, not just text. For instance, you can choose Variable of Name from the Find pop-up menu and type the name of the variable to find or change. Or, you can specify a paragraph tag and its name to quickly find the next or previous instance of that paragraph format in your document.

Changing a variable definition

You'll change the definition for the ShortName variable from *Labrador* to *Lab*. FrameMaker 7.0 will then make the change throughout the document.

1 Choose Special > Variable.

2 Select ShortName in the Variables scroll list and click Edit Definition.

3 Enter **Lab** in the Definition text box and click Change.

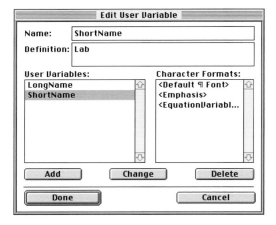

4 Click Done, and then click Done again. FrameMaker 7.0 replaces Labrador with Lab throughout the article.

In addition, your Lab will inevitably run up
certain costs. Your basic (but still real)
costs will include collars, leashes, dishes,
toys, bedding, food, chew bones, and
veterinary fees. Additional costs can
include licensing fees, travel crates,
kennel boarding, car restraints,
and pet tags. But don't let
these expenses deter you
from owning a pet—with common sense and a little resourceful-
ness you Lab need not tax your
pocketbook. And in return
you'll receive years of affec-
tion, fun, and devotion.

*You can also import variable definitions from other FrameMaker documents using the
File > Import > Formats command. This is a useful way to ensure consistency in a family of
documents.*

Using the Thesaurus

The FrameMaker 7.0 Thesaurus provides you with alternate words that have a similar
meaning to the selected word. In this part of the lesson, you'll replace the word *faithfulness*
with a synonym from the Thesaurus.

1 Go back to page 1 of the article and double-click the word *faithfulness* near the middle
of the first paragraph.

Retriever. The Lab's generous temperment
and faithfulness make it a favorite for breed-
ers, who often cross the Lab with other
breeds to produce dogs with a combination
of of desirable traits. One interesting result
of such cross-breeding is the Labradoodle,
the curly-coated product of the Lab and the
Standard Poodle, and sure to attract attention on any dogwalk. Traditional Labs, how-

2 Choose Edit > Thesaurus.

3 The Thesaurus dialog box appears. It contains several definitions for *faithfulness* and a list of synonyms for each definition.

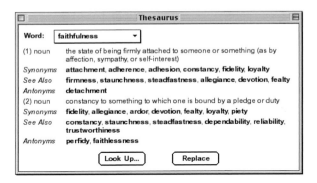

4 Click the word *loyalty* in the first Synonyms list. The Thesaurus dialog box now contains the definition and synonyms for *loyalty*.

Before you decide to use *loyalty*, you'll try a word of your own.

5 Click Look Up. The Thesaurus Look Up dialog box appears.

6 Enter **companionship** in the Word text box and click Look Up.

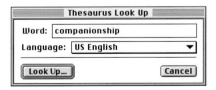

7 The Thesaurus dialog box now contains the definition and synonyms for *companionship*.

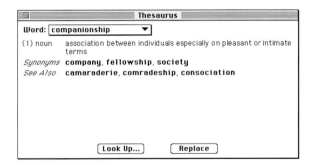

Unfortunately, *companionship* doesn't seem close enough to the meaning you intend, so you'll use *loyalty* instead.

8 In the Thesaurus dialog box, choose loyalty from the Word pop-up menu. (The words you've looked up recently appear in the pop-up menu.)

9 Click Replace.

Now you'll check for other occurrences of *faithfulness* in the article. (Before continuing, you might want to move the Thesaurus dialog box away from the document window.)

10 Choose Edit > Find/Change. Enter **faithfulness** in the Find text box and click Find. The next occurrence is on page 2.

> **CHARACTER**
> Labs are well known for their friendly personalities and gentle faithfulness. People of all ages have found them to be truly enthusiastic and loyal companions, whether in the field, the park, or the family home. A natural retriever, the Lab loves to

You can use *loyalty* here, too, but you'll replace the entire phrase *gentle faithfulness*.

11 Shift-click the word *gentle* to extend the selection.

12 In the Thesaurus dialog box, click Replace.

Note: *If the Thesaurus dialog box is hidden by the document window, choose Edit > Thesaurus.*

13 In the Find/Change dialog box, click Find. There are no more occurrences of *faithfulness* in the article.

Note: *If the Find/Change dialog box is hidden by the document window, choose Edit > Find/Change.*

14 Click OK to dismiss the alert message. Then close the Find/Change dialog box and the Thesaurus dialog box.

Checking spelling

You're almost finished with the article, so you'll check the spelling next.

In this part of the exercise, you'll use three dictionaries:

• The main dictionary contains words found in a standard dictionary. You can't add or delete words in this dictionary.

• A personal dictionary contains words, that aren't in the main dictionary, that you want FrameMaker 7.0 to allow when it checks any document on your computer. You can add and delete words in this dictionary.

• A document dictionary contains words that FrameMaker 7.0 allows in the current document, but aren't found in the main or personal dictionaries. Unlike the other two dictionaries, the document dictionary isn't a separate file; it's part of the document. You can add and delete words in the document dictionary.

1 Go back to page 1.

2 Click in the heading *BACKGROUND* to place the insertion point.

3 Choose Edit > Spelling Checker.

4 Click Start Checking.

Because the first word found is not in any of the dictionaries, FrameMaker 7.0 selects the word *temperment* and suggests that it's a misspelling. FrameMaker 7.0 recommends a spelling of *temperament*, and provides several other choices.

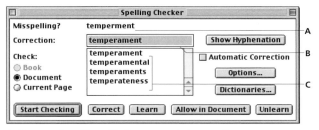

A. *Suspected problem* **B.** *Recommended correction*
C. *Additional choices*

The suggested correction is the right one, so you'll accept it.

5 Click Correct.

Next, FrameMaker 7.0 stops at the repeated words *of of* and suggests that only one of the words is necessary. This is a typing error rather than a spelling error.

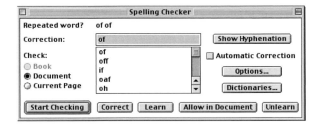

6 Click Correct.

FrameMaker 7.0 now stops at *Labradoodle,* a word that describes a breed that hasn't found it's way into the dictionaries yet.

7 Click Allow in Document. FrameMaker 7.0 adds the word to the document's dictionary. If *Labradoodle* appears elsewhere in this document, FrameMaker 7.0 won't question it again.

This time, FrameMaker 7.0 stops at *dogwalk*. You'll replace this with the two words *dog walk*.

8 Enter **dog walk** in the Correction text box and click Correct.

💡 *You can also click on the word dogwalk to the right of Misspelling to add it to the Corrections text box, and then edit the word to dog walk.*

Now FrameMaker 7.0 stops at *furriness*.

9 Enter **fur** in the Correction text box and click Correct.

10 FrameMaker 7.0 finds two spaces in a row and suggests replacing them with a single space.

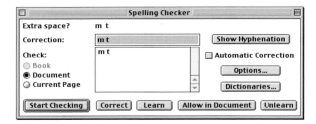

11 Click Correct.

FrameMaker 7.0 next questions the word *dysplasia*. You want to allow this word in the article and in other articles that you're writing.

12 Click Learn. FrameMaker 7.0 adds the word to your personal dictionary and won't question this word in any document you spell-check.

Because FrameMaker 7.0 finds no more words that aren't in its dictionaries, Spelling OK now appears in the Spelling Checker dialog box.

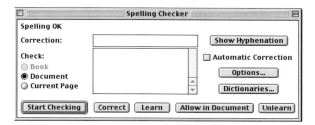

13 Close the Spelling Checker dialog box.

Viewing the finished article with graphics

You've finished editing the article, so now you'll redisplay the graphics.

1 Choose View > Options.

2 Select the Graphics option and click Set. The graphics reappear.

3 Save and close Editing1.fm.

Moving on

You've completed this lesson. For in-depth information on the Find/Change, Spelling Checker, and Thesaurus commands, see Chapter 4, "Word Processing," in the *Adobe FrameMaker 7.0 User Guide*. For in-depth information on variables, see Chapter 8, "Variables," in the *Adobe FrameMaker 7.0 User Guide*.

Review questions

1 Why might you turn off graphics when editing a document? How do you hide and display graphics?

2 What is a user variable? Why should you use one?

3 How do you create a variable?

4 What does the Thesaurus do? How do you open it?

5 Describe three kinds of dictionaries FrameMaker 7.0 provides.

6 How do you open the spelling checker? Name the two types of errors the Spelling Checker detects.

Answers

1 Hiding graphics makes pages display faster, which can make it easier to edit text. To specify whether to display graphics, choose View > Options, select or turn off Graphics, and click Set.

2 A variable is a placeholder for text. Once you define a variable with text—such as with a product name or term—that text appears wherever you insert the variable in your document. If you change the definition later, FrameMaker 7.0 updates all occurrences of that variable in the document with the updated text. By changing the variable's definition, you don't have to retype or find and replace each occurrence of text you want to reuse. You also ensure that the text is used consistently in the document.

3 To create a variable, choose Special > Variable. Click Create Variable. Enter a name for the variable in the Name text box, and enter the variable text and character format(s) in the Definition text box. Click Add, then click Done. When the new variable appears in the Variable dialog box, click Done.

4 You use the Thesaurus to look up words with a similar meaning to the word you specify. To open the Thesaurus, choose Edit > Thesaurus.

5 The main dictionary contains words found in a standard dictionary. You can't add or delete words in this dictionary.

A personal dictionary contains words that aren't in the main dictionary, but that you want FrameMaker 7.0 to allow when it checks a document. You can add and delete words in this dictionary.

A document dictionary contains words that aren't in the main dictionary or personal dictionary, but that you want FrameMaker 7.0 to allow in the current document. You can add and delete words in this dictionary. However, the document dictionary isn't a separate file; it's part of the document.

6 To open the Spelling Checker, Choose Edit > Spelling Checker. The Spelling Checker looks for misspelled words and typographical errors (such as repeated words).

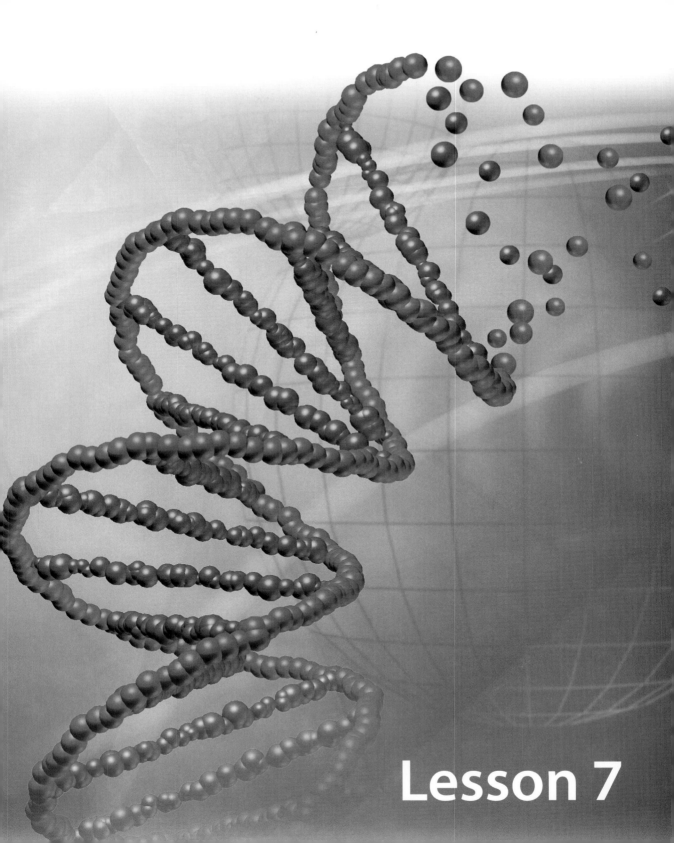

Lesson 7

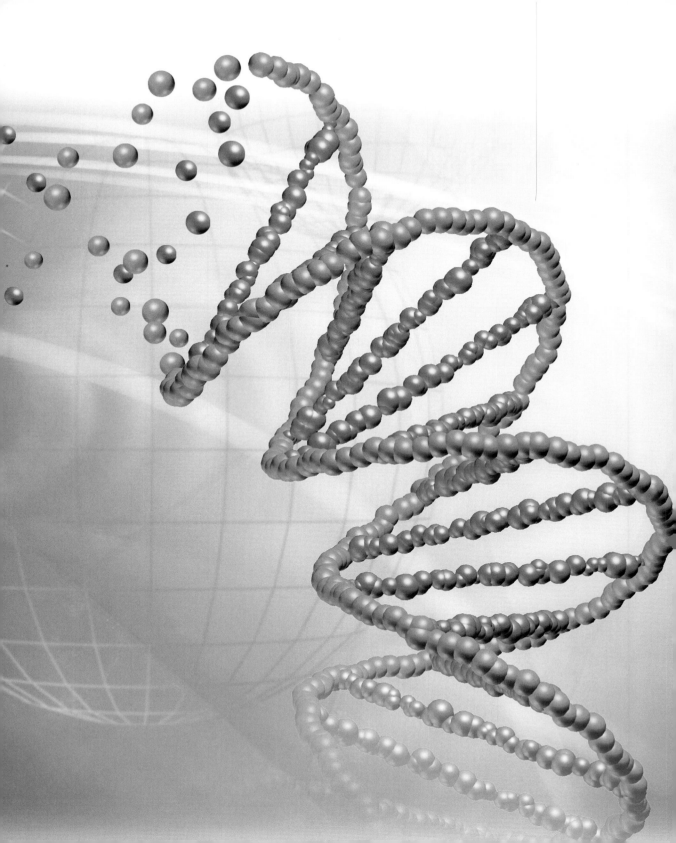

7 | Tables

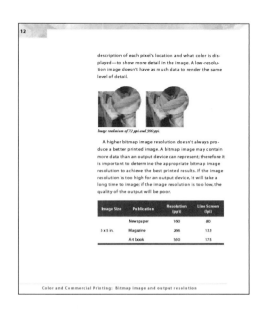

You can use tables to organize information and to make it attractive and easy to understand. FrameMaker 7.0 documents contain table formats that determine the appearance of tables. You can store table formats in a document's Table Catalog and reuse them as needed.

In this lesson, you'll learn how to do the following:

• Insert an empty table.

• Fill in the contents of a table.

• Add rows and columns to a table.

• Resize columns.

• Rearrange rows and columns.

• Change a table format.

• Straddle table cells.

Inserting a table

You'll create a small table that describes recommended print resolutions and line screens for different types of publications.

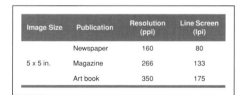

Image Size	Publication	Resolution (ppi)	Line Screen (lpi)
	Newspaper	160	80
5 x 5 in.	Magazine	266	133
	Art book	350	175

Finished table

1 Open Tables.fm in the Lesson07 folder.

2 Choose Save As, enter the filename **Tables1.fm**, and click Save.

3 Click the Page Status area in the status bar.

4 Enter **12** in the Page Number text box and click Go. Page 12 of the document appears.

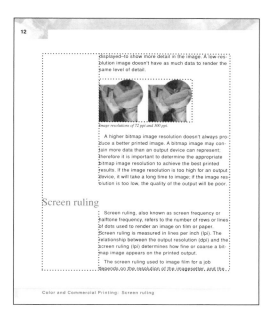

5 Choose View > Text Symbols to display the text symbols.

6 Click at the end of the paragraph just above the heading *Screen ruling*.

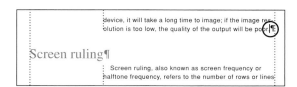

7 Choose Table > Insert Table. Or right-click (Windows and UNIX) or Control-click (Mac OS) to display a context menu for tables.

Like paragraph and character formats, table formats are stored in a catalog (the *Table Catalog*). However, unlike the Paragraph Catalog and the Character Catalog, the Table Catalog appears in the scroll list in the Insert Table dialog box rather than in a palette.

This document contains two table formats, Format A and Format B.

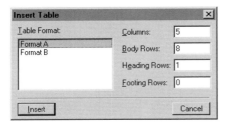

Neither of the table formats exactly meets your needs, so you'll choose one and modify it.

8 Select Format A in the Table Format scroll list.

9 Enter **3** in the Columns text box and **2** in the Body Rows text box. You'll eventually need another column and another row, but you'll add them later.

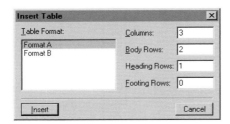

Note: Changing the default properties of a format changes the properties for new, empty tables, but does not change the appearance of existing tables with that format.

10 Click Insert. The table's *anchor symbol* (⊥) appears where the insertion point was, and the new empty table appears below the paragraph. The anchor connects the table to the text, so that when you edit the text, the anchor and the table move with it.

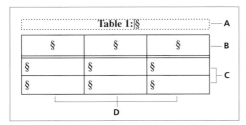

A. Table title *B.* Heading row *C.* Body rows *D.* Columns

Filling in the table

Now you'll fill in the heading row and the body rows. You won't need a title for this table, so you'll remove it later.

1 Click in the first heading cell and type **Image Size**.

Table 1:§		
Image Size|§	§	§
§	§	§
§	§	§

2 Press Tab, type **Publication**, press Tab again, type **Line Screen (lpi)**, and press Tab one more time.

Table 1:§		
Image Size§	Publication§	Line Screen (lpi)§
§	§	§
§	§	§

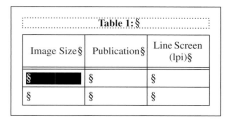 *To move back one cell, press Shift+Tab.*

The heading row is complete, and the first body cell is highlighted.

3 Type **5 x 5 in.**, press Tab, type **Art book**, press Tab, type **175**, and press Tab again to complete the first body row.

Table 1:§		
Image Size§	Publication§	Line Screen (lpi)§
5 x 5 in.§	Art book§	175§
§	§	§

4 Press Tab to skip the first cell in the second row.

💡 *To move ahead or back one row in the same column, do one of the following: press Control+Alt+Tab or Control+Alt+Shift+Tab (Windows); press Control+Tab or Control+Tab+Shift (Mac OS); press Meta+n or Meta+p (UNIX).*

5 Type **Newspaper**, press Tab, and type **80** to complete the second body row.

Table 1: §		
Image Size §	Publication §	Line Screen (lpi) §
5 x 5 in. §	Art book §	175 §
§	Newspaper §	80 §

Adding rows and columns

The table needs another row for the recommended values for magazines and another column for the resolution. First you'll add a row.

1 With the insertion point in the last row of the table, press Control+Return. An empty row is inserted below the insertion point.

Table 1: §		
Image Size §	Publication §	Line Screen (lpi) §
5 x 5 in. §	Art book §	175 §
§	Newspaper §	80 §
§	§	§

2 Press Tab to skip to the second cell in the new row.

3 Type **Magazine**, press Tab, and type **133**.

Table 1: §		
Image Size §	Publication §	Line Screen (lpi) §
5 x 5 in. §	Art book §	175 §
§	Newspaper §	80 §
§	Magazine §	133 §

Now you'll add a column.

4 With the insertion point still in the last column, choose Table > Add Rows or Columns.

5 Select Add 1 Column, choose Right of Selection from the pop-up menu, and click Add.

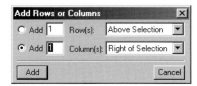

A fourth column appears at the right side of the table, and the table moves into the side-head area because it's too wide to fit entirely in the body column. You'll fix this later; the entire table will eventually appear in the body text area.

Table 1: §			
Image Size §	Publication §	Line Screen (lpi) §	§
5 x 5 in.§	Art book§	175§	§
§	Newspaper§	80§	§
§	Magazine§	133§	§

💡 *The QuickAccess bar contains some commonly used commands for editing tables. To display the QuickAccess bar, choose View > QuickAccess Bar.*

For online help for the table commands, click the question mark on the QuickAccess Bar.

6 Click in the empty heading cell at the top of the new column; type **Resolution (ppi)**.

Table 1: §			
Image Size §	Publication §	Line Screen (lpi) §	Resolution (ppi)§
5 x 5 in.§	Art book§	175§	§
§	Newspaper§	80§	§
§	Magazine§	133§	§

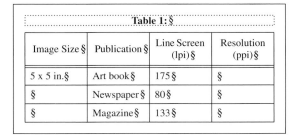

7 Click in the first body cell below the new heading and type **350**.

8 Click in the next empty body cell in the current column and type **160**.

9 Click in the last body cell in the current column and type **266**.

Table 1: §			
Image Size §	Publication §	Line Screen (lpi) §	Resolution (ppi) §
5 x 5 in.§	Art book§	175§	350§
§	Newspaper§	80§	160§
§	Magazine§	133§	266§

10 Save the document.

Rearranging information

In this section, you will rearrange some of the information in the table. You'll move the Line Screen column to the far right, and then move the Art Book row to the bottom of the table.

First, you'll move the column.

1 Drag from the heading *Line Screen* down into the first body row to select the entire column. Whenever you drag from the heading into the body, the entire column is selected.

2 Choose Edit > Cut.

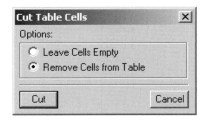

3 In the Cut Table Cells dialog box, select Remove Cells from Table and click Cut.

The column of cells has been removed from the table.

Table 1: §		
Image Size §	Publication §	Resolution (ppi) §
5 x 5 in.§	Art book§	350§
§	Newspaper§	160§
§	Magazine§	266§

Note: If the screen display needs redrawing, press Control+l (lowercase L).

4 Click anywhere in the last column of the table.

5 Choose Edit > Paste.

6 Select Insert Right of Current Columns and click Paste.

Table 1: §			
Image Size §	Publication §	Resolution (ppi) §	Line Screen (lpi) §
5 x 5 in.§	Art book§	350§	175§
§	Newspaper§	160§	80§
§	Magazine§	266§	133§

Third column is pasted to the right.

Now you'll move the row containing art book information.

7 To select the entire Art book row, drag from the first cell in the row to the last.

Table 1: §			
Image Size §	Publication §	Resolution (ppi) §	Line Screen (lpi) §
5 x 5 in.§	Art book§	350§	175§
§	Newspaper§	160§	80§
§	Magazine§	266§	133§

8 Choose Edit > Cut.

9 In the Cut Table Cells dialog box, select Remove Cells from Table and click Cut.

Image Size §	Publication §	Resolution (ppi) §	Line Screen (lpi) §
§	Newspaper §	160 §	80 §
§	Magazine §	266 §	133 §

Table 1: §

10 Click anywhere in the bottom row.

11 Choose Edit > Paste.

12 Select Insert Below Current Rows and click Paste. The Art book row is now at the bottom of the table.

Image Size §	Publication §	Resolution (ppi) §	Line Screen (lpi) §
§	Newspaper §	160 §	80 §
§	Magazine §	266 §	133 §
5 x 5 in. §	Art book §	350 §	175 §

Table 1: §

First row is pasted at bottom.

Finally, you'll move the Image Size information to the first row.

13 Drag from inside the cell that contains the text *5 x 5 in.* through the border of the next cell, and then back again to select just the one cell. The cell is selected once its entire interior is highlighted, rather than just its contents, and a selection handle appears at the right side of the cell. Uncheck View > Borders if the cell selection handle is covered by them.

Image Size §	Publication §	Resolution (ppi) §	Line Screen (lpi) §
§	Newspaper §	160 §	80 §
§	Magazine §	266 §	133 §
5 x 5 in. §	Art book §	350 §	175 §

Table 1: §

Entire cell is selected, displaying a selection handle (circled).

💡 *To select a single cell, you can Control-click the cell (Windows and UNIX) or Option-click it (Mac OS). Notice that the cursor changes into a resizing arrow (◄) when it rolls over the selection handle, which appears on the cell's right edge at its middle vertical point.*

14 Choose Edit > Cut.

15 Click in the top body cell in the column and choose Edit > Paste.

Table 1: §			
Image Size §	Publication §	Resolution (ppi) §	Line Screen (lpi) §
5 x 5 in. §	Newspaper §	160 §	80 §
§	Magazine §	266 §	133 §
§	Art book §	350 §	175 §

16 Save the document.

Formatting text in table cells

When you inserted a new table, its cells used a predetermined paragraph format (as defined in its table format). To change the text properties in the table, you can change the paragraph formats the table uses. You'll begin formatting the table by changing the table text to a smaller font.

1 Click any text in the heading row and choose Format > Paragraphs > Designer. The paragraphs in the heading cells use the CellHeading paragraph format.

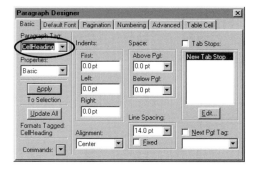

2 Choose Default Font from the Properties pop-up menu. (In Windows, you can just click the Default Font tab at the top of the Paragraph Designer.)

3 Change the Family to Myriad-Roman (Windows) or Myriad (Mac OS and UNIX), the Size to 8, and the Weight to Bold.

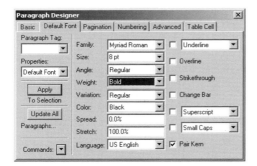

4 Click Update All.

Table 1: §			
Image Size§	**Publication**§	**Resolution (ppi)**§	**Line Screen (lpi)**§
5 x 5 in.§	Newspaper§	160§	80§
§	Magazine§	266§	133§
§	Art book§	350§	175§

5 If the table headings appear as gray bars, click the Zoom In button (⊠) in the status bar until the headings are legible.

You're finished with the heading format for now.

6 Click the text in any body cell. The paragraphs in body cells use the CellBody paragraph format.

7 In the Paragraph Designer, change the Family to Myriad-Roman (Windows) or Myriad (Mac OS and UNIX), the Size to 8, and then click Update All.

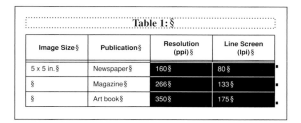

Table 1: §			
Image Size §	Publication §	Resolution (ppi) §	Line Screen (lpi) §
5 x 5 in. §	Newspaper §	160 §	80 §
§	Magazine §	266 §	133 §
§	Art book §	350 §	175 §

Finally, you'll center the numbers in the last two columns of the table. Because you don't want to center the contents of all the body cells, you'll create a new paragraph format just for the centered body cells.

8 Drag to select all the body cells in the Resolution and Line Screen columns.

Table 1: §			
Image Size §	Publication §	Resolution (ppi) §	Line Screen (lpi) §
5 x 5 in. §	Newspaper §	160 §	80 §
§	Magazine §	266 §	133 §
§	Art book §	350 §	175 §

9 In the Paragraph Designer, choose Basic from the Properties pop-up menu.

10 Choose Center from the Alignment pop-up menu and click Apply.

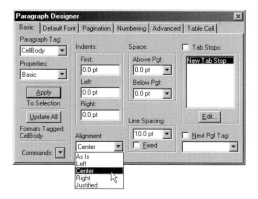

The text in these cells is centered. Now you'll store this style as a new format.

11 Choose New Format from the Commands pop-up menu.

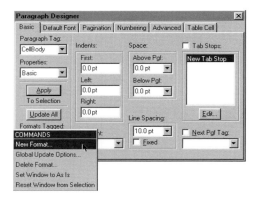

12 Enter **CellBodyCenter** in the Tag text box.

13 Make sure that both options, Store in Catalog and Apply to Selection, are selected and click Create.

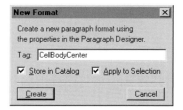

The current paragraph's tag changes to CellBodyCenter, and the CellBodyCenter format is added to the Paragraph Catalog.

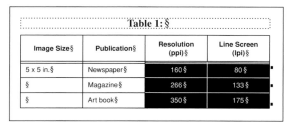

Table 1: §			
Image Size§	**Publication**§	**Resolution (ppi)**§	**Line Screen (lpi)**§
5 x 5 in.§	Newspaper§	160§	80§
§	Magazine§	266§	133§
§	Art book§	350§	175§

Cell contents are centered.

14 Close the Paragraph Designer.

15 Save the document.

Resizing columns

Now that the text formats are finished, you'll resize the columns.

1 Drag from the first cell in any row to the last to select an entire row.

Table 1: §			
Image Size§	Publication§	Resolution (ppi)§	Line Screen (lpi)§
5 x 5 in.§	Newspaper§	160§	80§
§	Magazine§	266§	133§
§	Art book§	350§	175§

2 Drag the cell selection handle to the left by a full column width. All the columns are resized.

Table 1: §			
Image Size§	Publicatio n§	Resolution (ppi)§	Line Screen (lpi)§
5 x 5 in.§	Newspaper§	160§	80§
§	Magazine§	266§	133§
§	Art book§	350§	175§

Now that the table is narrow enough, it moves back into the body text area.

However, the second column is now too narrow, so you'll widen it.

3 Drag down to select one or more cells in the second column.

Table 1: §			
Image Size§	Publicatio n§	Resolution (ppi)§	Line Screen (lpi)§
5 x 5 in.§	Newspaper§	160§	80§
§	Magazine§	266§	133§
§	Art book§	350§	175§

4 Drag a selection handle on the right side of the column to widen the column slightly.

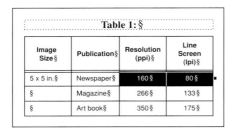

The third and fourth columns are also too narrow. You'll resize them so that the two columns are the same width.

5 Drag from anywhere in the third column into the fourth column to select cells in both columns.

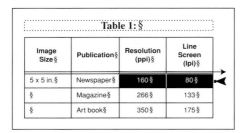

6 Drag a selection handle about halfway to the right edge of the text frame. Both columns are resized.

7 Save the document.

💡 *You can quickly resize a column by placing the insertion point in a cell that has the desired column length of text and pressing Esc +t+w.*

Changing the table format

Like paragraph and character formats, you change table formats in a designer dialog box (the *Table Designer*). Like the Paragraph Designer, the Table Designer contains several groups of properties.

When you inserted the table, you used one of the predefined table formats in the document. The first thing you'll do now is create a format specifically for this type of table.

1 Click anywhere in the table and choose Table > Table Designer.

2 Choose New Format from the Commands pop-up menu.

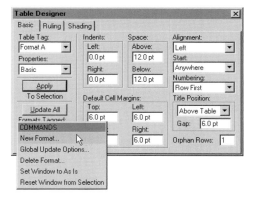

3 In the New Format dialog box, enter **StandardTable** in the Tag text box.

4 Make sure that both options, Store in Catalog and Apply to Selection, are selected and click Create. The next time you insert a table, the StandardTable format will be available.

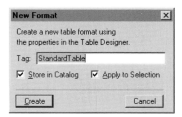

5 If the Basic properties aren't displayed in the Table Designer, choose Basic from the Properties pop-up menu.

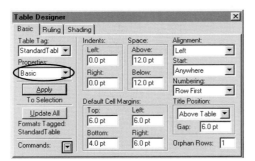

6 In the Title Position area choose No Title from the pop-up menu and click Update All.

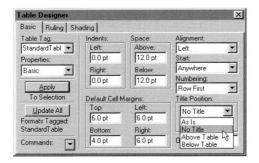

The title is removed from the table.

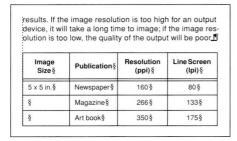

results. If the image resolution is too high for an output device, it will take a long time to image; if the image resolution is too low, the quality of the output will be poor.

Image Size §	Publication§	Resolution (ppi) §	Line Screen (lpi) §
5 x 5 in.§	Newspaper§	160§	80§
§	Magazine§	266§	133§
§	Art book§	350§	175§

Changing table ruling

The table's ruling (currently a thin line around the table and between body rows, and a double line between the heading and the body) is determined by the table format's Ruling properties, which let you choose from a variety of ruling patterns. You'll remove most of the table ruling, but you'll add a thick rule at the bottom of the table to separate it from the text that follows it.

1 In the Table Designer, choose Ruling from the Properties pop-up menu.

2 In every pop-up menu that shows Thin or Double, choose None to remove the table ruling.

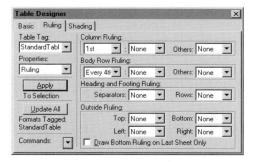

3 Click Update All. All the ruling is removed from the table.

4 Choose Thick from the Bottom pop-up menu and click Update All.

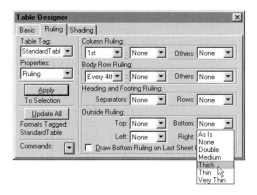

5 Choose View > Borders to hide the dotted cell borders and View > Text Symbols to hide text symbols.

The bottom border is thick enough, but the color is too dark. You'll create your own ruling style that uses a different color.

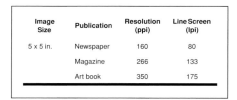

Image Size	Publication	Resolution (ppi)	Line Screen (lpi)
5 x 5 in.	Newspaper	160	80
	Magazine	266	133
	Art book	350	175

6 With the insertion point still in the table, choose Table > Custom Ruling & Shading. The ruling styles available in the document appear in the Apply Ruling Style scroll list.

7 Select Thick in the Apply Ruling Style scroll list, and click Edit Ruling Style.

8 Enter **ThickBrown** in the Name text box. This will be the name of the ruling style.

9 Choose Brown from the Color pop-up menu and click Set.

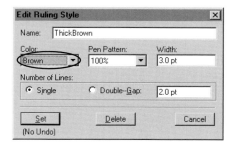

The ThickBrown ruling style is now available for table ruling.

10 Close the Custom Ruling and Shading dialog box.

11 Choose ThickBrown from the Bottom pop-up menu of the Table Designer.

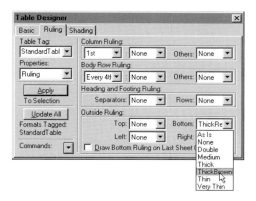

12 Click Update All.

13 Save the document.

Changing table shading

The table's shading is determined by the format's Shading properties. The table doesn't currently use any shading, but you'll shade the heading row in the same color you used for the bottom ruling.

1 Choose Shading from the Properties pop-up menu in the Table Designer.

2 In the Heading and Footing Shading area, choose 100% from the Fill pop-up menu and Brown from the Color pop-up menu.

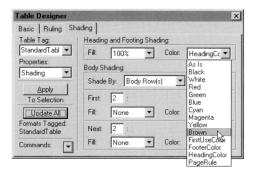

3 Click Update All. The heading row is now shaded.

4 Close the Table Designer.

The black text in the heading is hard to read against the brown background, so you'll change the text to white.

5 Click in any heading cell. Choose Format > Paragraphs > Designer.

6 Choose Default Font from the Properties pop-up menu.

7 Choose White from the Color pop-up menu.

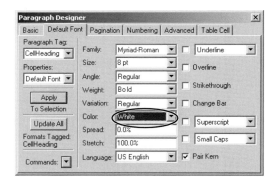

8 Click Update All.

The heading row text is now white against the shaded background.

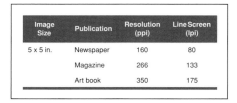

9 Close the Paragraph Designer and save the file.

You've finished modifying the table format.

Straddling table cells

The contents of the first body cell (*5 x 5 in.*) are intended to apply to all the rows, not just the first one. To make this clear, you'll make the first cell in the column straddle all the others.

1 Drag from the cell with the text *5 x 5 in.* down to the last empty cell in the column.

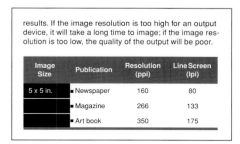

2 Choose Table > Straddle. The cell now spans all the body cells in the column.

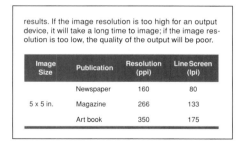

3 Click anywhere on the page to deselect the cells.

Reusing a table format

Now that you've set up the table format, you can reuse it whenever you need to.

1 Go to the last page of the document.

2 Click at the end of the text or right click to access the context menu and choose Table > Insert Table.

3 Select StandardTable in the Table Format scroll list and click Insert. The table that appears uses the format you created in this lesson. Because the straddle cell you created is not part of the format, it does not appear in the table.

4 If you want, experiment by adding information to the table.

5 When you're finished, drag from the first heading cell to any body cell in the last column to select the entire table.

6 Choose Edit > Cut.

7 Select Remove Cells from Table and click Cut. Save and close Tables1.fm.

Moving on

You've completed this lesson. For in-depth information about tables, see Chapter 6, "Tables," in the *Adobe FrameMaker 7.0 User Guide*.

Review questions

1 Where are table formats stored?

2 Name four components that make up a table in FrameMaker 7.0.

3 What two keyboard shortcuts let you move forward and backward between cells?

4 What's the quickest way to insert an empty row below an insertion point?

5 How do you add a row or column?

6 How do you select a cell?

Answers

1 As with paragraph and character formats, table formats are stored in a catalog (the *Table Catalog*). The Table Catalog appears in a scroll list in the Insert Table dialog box.

2 FrameMaker 7.0 tables include such elements as a title, rows, columns, heading rows, heading cells, body rows, body cells, rules, and shading.

3 To move forward one cell using the keyboard, press Tab. To move backward one cell using the keyboard, press Shift+Tab.

4 To insert an empty row below the insertion point, press Control+Return.

5 Click in a cell to set the insertion point. Choose Table > Add Rows or Columns. Specify whether you want to add rows or columns, and how many. Then choose where you want the rows or columns to be located in relation to the insertion point, and click Add.

6 To select a cell using the mouse, drag from inside the cell through the border of the next cell and then back again to select just the one cell. You can also Control-click the cell (Windows and UNIX) or Option-click it (Macintosh).

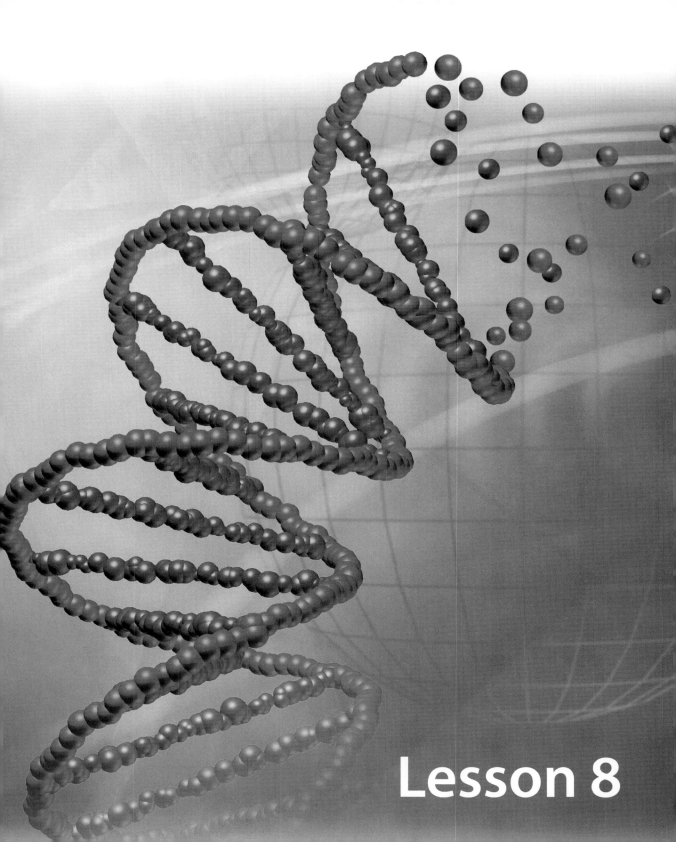

Lesson 8

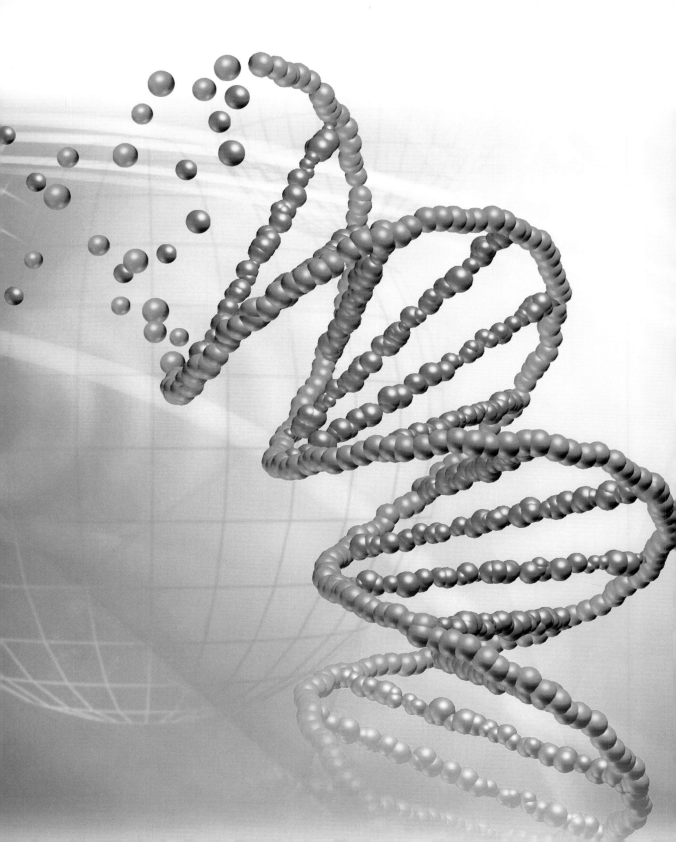

8 | **Customizing Tables**

from $75.9 million to $135.6 million, a gain of 79 percent, and earnings per share rose from $1.07 to $1.80, a gain of 68 percent.

The fourth quarter included a restructuring charge of $31.5 million associated with the Farm Suppliers Outlet Corporation acquisition, and a write-off of $15.0 million for in-process research and development related to the purchase of The Exotic Tradesman, Inc. Exotic flower reve-

nue, which includes whole plants, cut flowers, seedlings and bulbs, grew 12 percent to $578.9 million, compared with $519.0 million in 2001.

During 2002, we expect to expand our flow of products worldwide, including flora optimized for previously inhospitable regions, through hybrid and genetically altered strands of plants.

ASSETS

			FISCAL YEAR	
	2002	2001	2000	1999
Current assets:				
Cash & cash equivalents	203,461	146,992	89,557	72,429
Short-term investments	157,700	90,853	55,650	47,005
Accounts receivable	101,006	72,448	35,543	30,451
Inventories	49,349	30,557	20,512	15,627
Deferred income taxes	32,544	12,953	6,430	350
Other current assets	12,542	9,600	5,398	3,213
Total current assets	556,602	363,403	213,090	169,075
Investments	35,601	51,525	42,508	12,954
Furniture, fixtures, and equipment, net	20,428	10,327	6,972	3,451
Other assets	3,655	2,153	1,078	446
Total assets	616,286	427,408	263,648	185,921

2

In addition to typing into tables, you can import information into tables from external sources. And besides specifying the table's overall properties, you can also use custom ruling and shading to highlight specific information in the table.

In this lesson, you'll learn how to do the following:

• Import text into a table.

• Change the paragraph format of table text.

• Format body cells.

• Indent text within table cells.

• Apply custom ruling and shading to a table.

You'll also use some of the skills you learned in the previous lesson to move information in a table, resize columns, and set up a table's basic design.

Viewing a sample table

During this lesson, you'll import financial data as a table into an annual report and then format the table. Begin by opening and viewing the finished table.

1 Open Finished.fm in the Lesson08 folder.

2 In the status bar, click the Next Page button (⬇) to display page 2 of the annual report. You'll re-create the table that appears at the bottom of the page.

ASSETS				
		FISCAL YEAR		
	2002	2001	2000	1999
Current assets:				
Cash & cash equivalents	203,461	146,992	89,557	72,429
Short-term investments	157,700	90,853	55,650	47,005
Accounts receivable	101,006	72,448	35,543	30,451
Inventories	49,349	30,557	20,512	15,627
Deferred income taxes	32,544	12,953	6,430	350
Other current assets	12,542	9,600	5,398	3,213
Total current assets	556,602	363,403	213,090	169,075
Investments	35,601	51,525	42,508	12,954
Furniture, fixtures, and equipment, net	20,428	10,327	6,972	3,451
Other assets	3,655	2,153	1,078	446
Total assets	616,286	427,408	263,648	185,921

Much of the table's appearance is determined by the table format. For example, the rules around the edge of the table and the rule separating the heading cells from the body of the table are specified in the table format, as are the paragraph formats of the cells. However, the thin rules that extend only partway across two of the rows and the shading for the second column are specified as custom ruling and shading properties for specific parts of the table. Custom ruling and shading are not contained in the table format.

3 Close Finished.fm. If prompted to save changes, click No.

Importing text into a table

First you'll import some financial data into a table.

1 Open Tables.fm in the Lesson08 folder.

2 Choose File > Save As, enter the filename **Tables1.fm**, and click Save.

3 Display page 2 of the annual report.

4 On page 2, click at the end of the text in the right column.

During 2000, we expect to expand our flow of product worldwide, including flora optimized for previously inhospitable regions, through hybrid and genetically altered strands of plants.

5 Choose File > Import > File.

6 Select Assets.txt in the Lesson08 folder.

7 Select Copy into Document and then click Import.

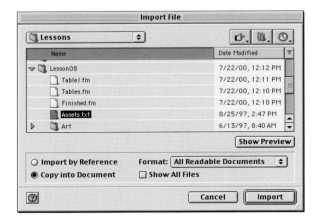

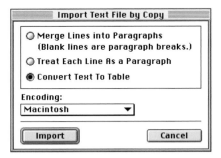 *Online Help provides additional information on file types and filters.*

8 If the Unknown File Type dialog box appears, select Text in the scroll list and click Convert.

9 Select Convert Text to Table. The Encoding pop-up menu selects the appropriate option depending on whether you are running FrameMaker 7.0 on Windows, on a Mac OS, or on a UNIX system.

10 Click Import.

No table format has been set up for financial data, so you'll use one of the default table formats and then modify it later.

11 Select Format A in the Table Format scroll list.

The data is stored as tab-delimited text. That is, each paragraph represents a row of the table, and tabs separate the contents of one cell from another.

12 In the Treat Each Paragraph As area, make sure these options are selected: A Row with Cells Separated By, and Tabs. Then enter **2** in the Heading Rows text box.

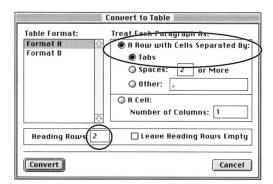

13 Click Convert. The imported information appears in a table.

Table 1:				
Fiscal Year				
	2002	2001	2000	1999
Current assets:				
Cash & cash equiva-lents	203,461	146,992	89,557	72,429
Short-term investments	157,700	90,853	55,650	47,005
Accounts receivable	101,006	72,448	35,543	30,451
Inventories	49,349	30,557	20,512	15,627

The table extends beyond the right side of the text frame and onto page 3 of the annual report. You'll fix these problems later.

Note: In the next several steps, you'll change the paragraph formats of table cells. This part of the lesson extends the type of formatting you did in "Formatting text in table cells" in Lesson 7, "Tables."

Formatting the imported table data

Next you'll change the paragraph format of the table headings.

1 Click in the heading cell that contains the words *Fiscal Year*.

2 Choose Format > Paragraphs > Designer.

3 Choose Default Font from the Properties pop-up menu. (In Windows, you can just click the Default Font tab at the top of the designer.)

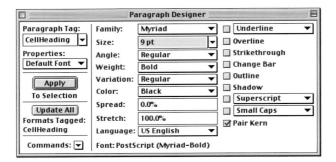

4 Change the Family to Myriad-Roman (Windows) or Myriad (Mac OS and UNIX), the Size to 9, and the Weight to Bold. Then click Update All.

Table 1:				
Fiscal Year				
	2002	**2001**	**2000**	**1999**
Current assets:				
Cash & cash equiva-lents	203,461	146,992	89,557	72,429
Short-term investments	157,700	90,853	55,650	47,005
Accounts receivable	101,006	72,448	35,543	30,451
Inventories	49,349	30,557	20,512	15,627

5 If necessary, click the Zoom In button (Ⓩ) in the status bar until you can read the headings easily.

Now you'll move the heading *Fiscal Year* to the right side of the table.

6 Drag from inside the cell that contains the text *Fiscal Year* through the border of the next cell and then back again to select just the one cell. (You can tell that the cell is selected because the entire cell is highlighted, rather than just the text in it, and because a selection handle appears at the right side of the cell.)

Fiscal Year	
	2002
Current assets:	

$\bigcirc$ *Another way to select the cell is to Control-click the cell (Windows and UNIX) or Option-click it (Mac OS). This method can be easier for selecting single cells.*

7 Choose Edit > Cut, click in the rightmost cell in the row, and choose Edit > Paste. The heading is now in the rightmost cell.

Table 1:				
				Fiscal Year
	2002	2001	2000	1999
Current assets:				

Now you'll make the heading right-aligned and in uppercase letters. To leave the other heading cells centered, you'll create a new paragraph format for this heading.

8 In the Paragraph Designer, choose Uppercase from the pop-up menu.

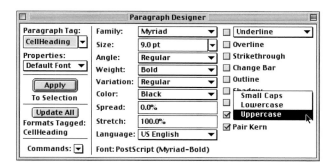

9 Choose New Format from the Commands pop-up menu.

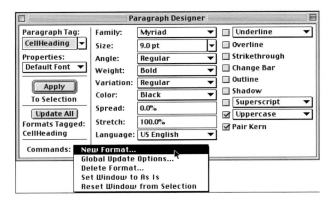

10 Enter **CellHeadingRight** in the Tag text box.

11 Make sure that both options, Store in Catalog and Apply to Selection, are selected, and click Create.

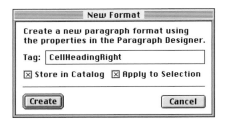

The current paragraph's tag changes to CellHeadingRight, and the CellHeadingRight format is added to the Paragraph Catalog.

Cell contents appear in uppercase.

12 In the Paragraph Designer, choose Basic from the Properties pop-up menu.

13 Choose Right from the Alignment pop-up menu. Then click Update All.

Formatting body cells

Next you'll format the table's body cells.

1 Click in the first body cell (the cell that contains *Current assets*).

2 In the Paragraph Designer, choose Default Font from the Properties pop-up menu.

3 Change the Family to Myriad-Roman (Windows) or Myriad (Mac OS and UNIX), the Size to 8, and click Update All.

	2002	2001
Current assets:		
Cash & cash equivalents	203,461 146,992	
Short-term investments	157,700 90,853	

You'll need two paragraph formats for the body cells. The numbers will be right-aligned, but the row labels will be left-aligned and will contain tab stops. First you'll create the format for the row labels.

4 Drag downward from the cell that contains the text *Current assets* until all the body cells in that column are selected (including the cells on page 3).

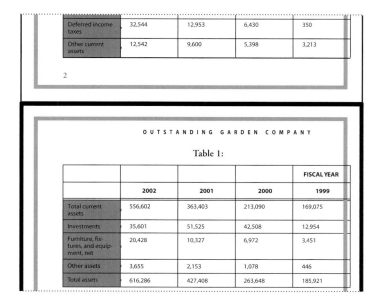

5 In the Paragraph Designer, choose Basic from the Properties pop-up menu.

6 In the Tab Stops area, click Edit.

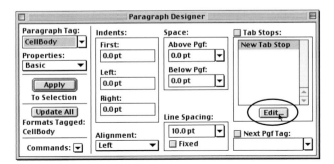

7 Enter **10 pt** in the New Position text box.

8 Make sure that the Alignment is set to Left and that the Leader is set to None. Then click Continue.

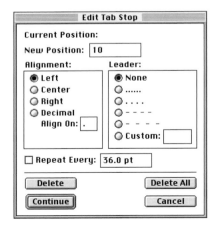

The tab stop appears in the Tab Stops scroll list.

9 With New Tab Stop selected in the Tab Stops scroll list, click Edit again.

10 Enter **20** in the New Position text box, and click Continue.

11 Choose New Format from the Commands pop-up menu.

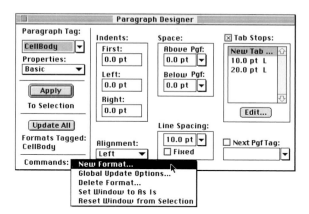

12 Enter **RowLabel** in the Tag text box.

13 Make sure that both options, Store in Catalog and Apply to Selection, are selected.
Then click Create.

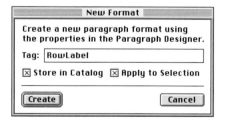

The current paragraph's tag changes to RowLabel, and the RowLabel format is added to
the Paragraph Catalog.

Now you'll change the format for the remaining body cells.

14 Click in one of the body cells that contains a numerical value.

15 In the Paragraph Designer, choose Right from the Alignment pop-up menu and click
Update All.

203,461	146,992	89,557
157,700	90,853	55,650
101,006	72,448	35,543
49,349	30,557	20,512

Body cells are right aligned.

Formatting the table title

You'll change one more paragraph format—the table title. You'll remove the autonumber, left-align the title, and change it to uppercase.

1 Click in the table title and type **Assets**.

Note: You can also insert a system variable, Table Continuation, after the last word in a title. If the table continues to the next page, the title will indicate that it is continued from the previous page. Choose Special > Variable and select Table Continuation.

Table 1: Assets				
				FISCAL YEAR
	2002	2001	2000	1999
Current assets:				
Cash & cash equivalents	203,461	146,992	89,557	72,429

💡 *Inserting the Table Continuation variable will save time if the pagination changes later. (You may have to refresh the screen display in order to see its effect on page 3.)*

2 In the Paragraph Designer, choose Numbering from the Properties pop-up menu.

3 Click the Autonumber Format check box twice to turn it off.

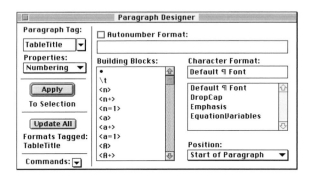

4 Click Update All.

Assets				
				FISCAL YEAR
	2002	2001	2000	1999
Current assets:				
Cash & cash equivalents	203,461	146,992	89,557	72,429

5 Choose Default Font from the Properties pop-up menu.

6 Change the Family to Myriad-Roman (Windows) or Myriad (Mac OS and UNIX) and the Size to 11. Then choose Uppercase from the pop-up menu.

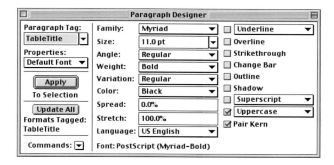

7 Click Update All.

8 Choose Basic from the Properties pop-up menu.

9 Choose Left from the Alignment pop-up menu. Then click Update All.

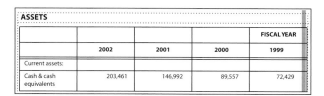

10 Close the Paragraph Designer.

Setting basic table properties

Now you're ready to set overall table properties. First you'll change the space above the table and its cell margins.

1 Make sure that the insertion point is in the table. If the Table Designer is not already open, open it by choosing Table > Table Designer.

2 Choose Basic from the Properties pop-up menu in the Table Designer.

3 Change the Space Above to 20 and the Top cell margin to 4.

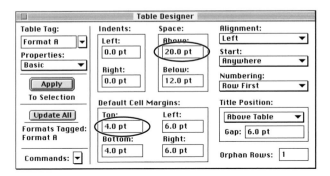

4 Click Update All.

ASSETS				
				FISCAL YEAR
	2002	2001	2000	1999
Current assets:				
Cash & cash equivalents	203,461	146,992	89,557	72,429
Short-term investments	157,700	90,853	55,650	47,005
Accounts receivable	101,006	72,448	35,543	30,451
Inventories	49,349	30,557	20,512	15,627
Deferred income taxes	32,544	12,953	6,430	350
Other current assets	12,542	9,600	5,398	3,213
Total current assets	556,602	363,403	213,090	169,075

Note: To redraw the screen if necessary, press Control+l (lowercase letter L).

Resizing columns

Now you'll resize the table columns. To begin, you'll verify that the table is measured in points. (There are 72 points in an inch.)

1 Choose View > Options.

2 Make sure the Display Units pop-up menu is set to Point and click Set.

3 Drag from the heading cell that contains the text *2002* to the rightmost heading cell. The four cells are selected.

				FISCAL YEAR
	2002	2001	2000	1999

4 Choose Table > Resize Columns.

5 Enter **42** in the To Width text box. Then click Resize.

6 Drag to select several cells in the first column of the table.

Current assets:	
Cash & cash equivalents	203,461
Short-term investments	157,700
Accounts receivable	101,006
Inventories	49,349

7 Drag a selection handle to the right until the table approximately fills the width of the text frame. (You may need to drag several times.)

ASSETS				
				FISCAL YEAR
	2002	2001	2000	1999
Current assets:				
Cash & cash equivalents	203,461	146,992	89,557	72,429
Short-term investments	157,700	90,853	55,650	47,005
Accounts receivable	101,006	72,448	35,543	30,451
Inventories	49,349	30,557	20,512	15,627
Deferred income taxes	32,544	12,953	6,430	350
Other current assets	12,542	9,600	5,398	3,213
Total current assets	556,602	363,403	213,090	169,075
Investments	35,601	51,525	42,508	12,954
Furniture, fixtures, and equipment, net	20,428	10,327	6,972	3,451
Other assets	3,655	2,153	1,078	446

You can make text straddle the cells you select. Here you'll straddle two cells so that the heading fits on one line.

8 Drag to select the cell that contains the text *FISCAL YEAR* and the cell to its left.

	FISCAL YEAR
2000	1999

9 Choose Table > Straddle. The text now spans two cells.

Using tabs in table cells

Earlier in this lesson, you added tab stops to the RowLabel paragraph format that's used for the labels at the left side of each body row. You'll use these tab stops now.

1 Click at the beginning of the second row label (the one that contains the text *Cash & cash equivalents*).

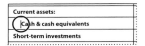

2 Press Esc+Tab to insert a tab.

If you had simply pressed the Tab key as you do in regular body text, the next cell would have been selected.

3 Click at the beginning of a row label and press Esc+Tab to insert a tab in each row label as needed (see below). In the row labels *Total current assets* and *Total assets*, press Esc+Tab twice to increase the indentation.

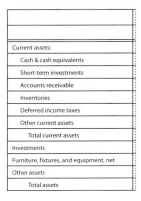

Defining ruling styles

To make the table appear with the ruling called for in the design, create two ruling styles.

1 Choose Table > Custom Ruling & Shading. The available ruling styles appear in the Apply Ruling Style scroll list.

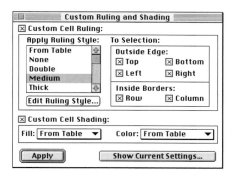

2 Select Medium in the Apply Ruling Style scroll list and click Edit Ruling Style.

3 Type **TableTop** in the Name area. Change the Color to PageRule and the Width to 2.5 points. Click Set.

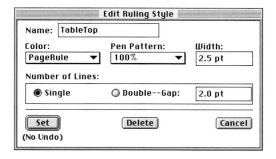

4 In the Apply Ruling Style area, select TableTop. Then click Edit Ruling Style again.

5 Type **TableEdge** in the Name area and change the Width to 1 point. The color is already set to PageRule. Click Set and close the Custom Ruling and Shading dialog box.

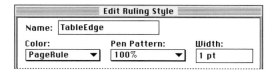

Setting table ruling

Now you're ready to set up the table ruling.

1 Choose View > Borders to hide the borders. Without the borders showing, you'll be able to see the effect of your changes more clearly.

2 Make sure the insertion point is in the table.

3 In the Table Designer, choose Ruling from the Properties pop-up menu.

4 Change the Column Ruling options and Body Row Ruling options to None.

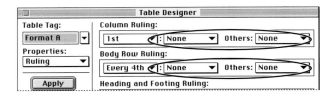

5 Click Update All. The ruling between the body cells is removed.

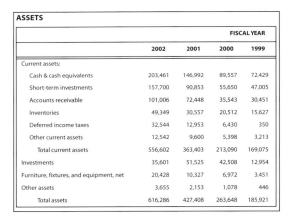

ASSETS				
			FISCAL YEAR	
	2002	2001	2000	1999
Current assets:				
Cash & cash equivalents	203,461	146,992	89,557	72,429
Short-term investments	157,700	90,853	55,650	47,005
Accounts receivable	101,006	72,448	35,543	30,451
Inventories	49,349	30,557	20,512	15,627
Deferred income taxes	32,544	12,953	6,430	350
Other current assets	12,542	9,600	5,398	3,213
Total current assets	556,602	363,403	213,090	169,075
Investments	35,601	51,525	42,508	12,954
Furniture, fixtures, and equipment, net	20,428	10,327	6,972	3,451
Other assets	3,655	2,153	1,078	446
Total assets	616,286	427,408	263,648	185,921

6 In the Heading and Footing Ruling area, change Separators to TableTop and Rows to None.

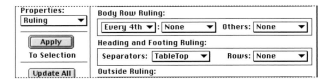

7 Click Update All. The ruling between the row *FISCAL YEAR* and the row containing the years is removed, and the ruling between them and the body cells is replaced with the TableTop ruling you created.

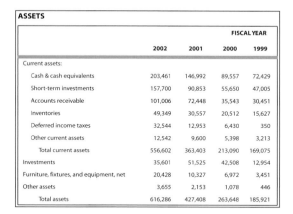

8 In the Outside Ruling area, change the Top to TableTop, the Bottom to TableEdge, Left to TableEdge, and Right to TableEdge. Click Update All.

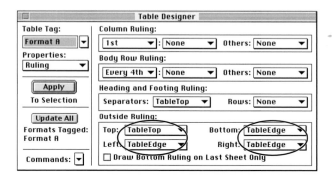

9 Observe the results and then close the Table Designer. Save the document.

ASSETS				
				FISCAL YEAR
	2002	2001	2000	1999
Current assets:				
Cash & cash equivalents	203,461	146,992	89,557	72,429
Short-term investments	157,700	90,853	55,650	47,005
Accounts receivable	101,006	72,448	35,543	30,451
Inventories	49,349	30,557	20,512	15,627
Deferred income taxes	32,544	12,953	6,430	350
Other current assets	12,542	9,600	5,398	3,213
Total current assets	556,602	363,403	213,090	169,075
Investments	35,601	51,525	42,508	12,954
Furniture, fixtures, and equipment, net	20,428	10,327	6,972	3,451
Other assets	3,655	2,153	1,078	446
Total assets	616,286	427,408	263,648	185,921

10 Save the file.

Using custom ruling and shading

The table is almost finished, but you need some additional ruling, and you need to shade the *2002* column to highlight the results. Because the additional ruling and shading you need do not follow a pattern, you can't specify them in the table format. Instead, you'll define some custom ruling and shading for the table.

1 Drag from the heading cell that contains the text *2002* to the rightmost heading cell. The four cells are selected.

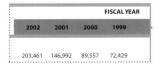

2 Choose Table > Custom Ruling & Shading.

3 Select Very Thin in the Apply Ruling Style scroll list.

💡 *Zooming into a higher percentage makes it easier to see slight differences in line thickness when editing ruling styles.*

4 In the To Selection area, select Top, but turn off the other options.

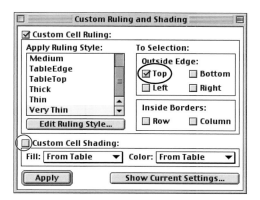

5 At the bottom of the dialog box, make sure the Custom Cell Shading option is off, and click Apply.

6 Click in the body of the table to deselect the cells so you can see the rule above the cells.

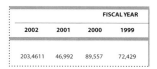

Now you'll add the same rule in two other places. Because the Custom Ruling and Shading dialog box is already set up correctly, you won't need to change the settings.

7 Select the four cells to the right of *Total current assets*.

8 In the Custom Ruling and Shading dialog box, click Apply.

Note: *(Mac OS only) If the dialog box is hidden behind the document window, choose Table > Custom Ruling & Shading.*

9 At the bottom of the table, select the four cells to the right of *Total assets*.

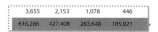

10 In the Custom Ruling and Shading dialog box, click Apply.

11 Click outside of the table to deselect the cells.

ASSETS				
		FISCAL YEAR		
	2002	**2001**	**2000**	**1999**
Current assets:				
Cash & cash equivalents	203,461	146,992	89,557	72,429
Short-term investments	157,700	90,853	55,650	47,005
Accounts receivable	101,006	72,448	35,543	30,451
Inventories	49,349	30,557	20,512	15,627
Deferred income taxes	32,544	12,953	6,430	350
Other current assets	12,542	9,600	5,398	3,213
Total current assets	556,602	363,403	213,090	169,075
Investments	35,601	51,525	42,508	12,954
Furniture, fixtures, and equipment, net	20,428	10,327	6,972	3,451
Other assets	3,655	2,153	1,078	446
Total assets	616,286	427,408	263,648	185,921

Finally, you'll highlight the information in the *2002* column.

12 Select the body cells below the *2002* heading.

ASSETS				
		FISCAL YEAR		
	2002	**2001**	**2000**	**1999**
Current assets:				
Cash & cash equivalents	203,461	146,992	89,557	72,429
Short-term investments	157,700	90,853	55,650	47,005
Accounts receivable	101,006	72,448	35,543	30,451
Inventories	49,349	30,557	20,512	15,627
Deferred income taxes	32,544	12,953	6,430	350
Other current assets	12,542	9,600	5,398	3,213
Total current assets	556,602	363,403	213,090	169,075
Investments	35,601	51,525	42,508	12,954
Furniture, fixtures, and equipment, net	20,428	10,327	6,972	3,451
Other assets	3,655	2,153	1,078	446
Total assets	616,286	427,408	263,648	185,921

13 In the Custom Ruling and Shading dialog box, make sure Custom Cell Ruling is turned off.

14 In the Custom Cell Shading area, make sure Custom Cell Shading is selected. Then change the Fill to 100% and the Color to PageTint.

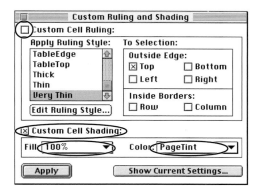

15 Click Apply. Then close the Custom Ruling and Shading dialog box.

16 Click outside of the table to see the results.

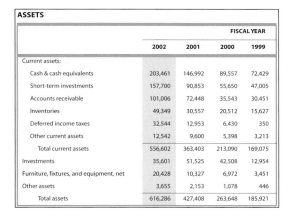

You're finished with the table.

17 Save and close the file.

Moving on

You've completed this lesson. For in-depth information about tables, see Chapter 6, "Tables," in the *Adobe FrameMaker 7.0 User Guide*. For information about file formats, see Chapter 18, "Importing, Linking, and Exporting," in the *Adobe FrameMaker 7.0 User Guide*.

Review questions

1 What is tab-delimited text?

2 How do you remove autonumbering, such as in the heading of a table?

3 What are two ways to resize columns?

4 How do you make the contents of one cell straddle two or more cells?

5 How do you insert tabs in cells?

6 What is the difference between the normal ruling and shading you can apply from the Table Designer and the custom ruling and shading you can apply from the Custom Ruling and Shading dialog box?

7 What is the Table Continuation variable?

Answers

1 In tab-delimited text, each paragraph represents a row of the table, with tabs separating the contents of one cell from another.

2 To remove autonumbering, click in the paragraph you want to change and choose Format > Paragraphs > Designer. Choose Numbering from the Properties pop-up menu. Click the Autonumber Format check box twice to turn it off and then click Apply to Selection or Update All.

3 Select the columns to resize. Then either drag a handle at the right side of the column or choose Table > Resize Columns, enter a value in the To Width text box, and click Resize.

4 Drag from the cell containing the text, through the cells you want the text to straddle. Then choose Table > Straddle.

5 Click in the cell where you want to insert the tab and press Esc+Tab. (If you pressed only Tab, the insertion point would move to the next cell.)

6 Only ruling and shading that extend through the entire table or across one or more rows or columns in a repeating pattern can be created and applied with the Table Designer; they are then part of the table format. Ruling and shading that extend only partway across a table or that span individual cells are created and applied with the Custom Ruling and Shading dialog box. Such ruling and shading are not part of the table format.

7 The Table Continuation variable is a system variable that can be inserted in a title of a table to indicate that the table is continued from the previous page.

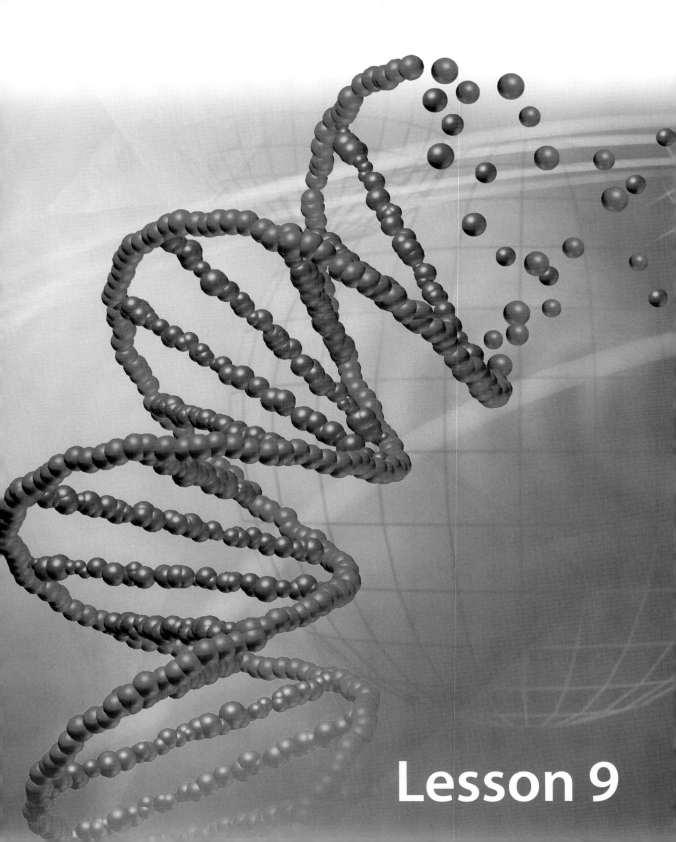

Lesson 9

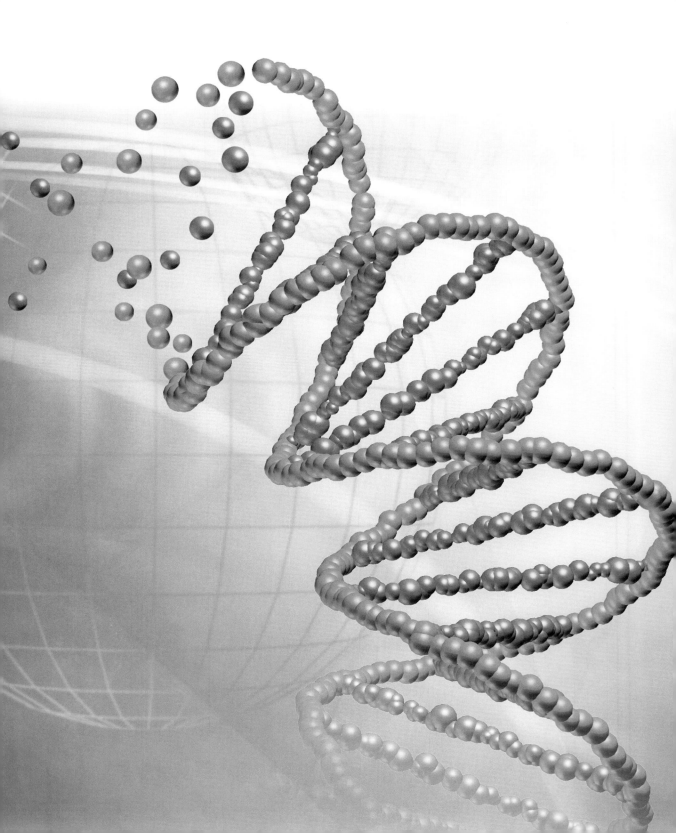

9 | Anchored Frames and Graphics

You can draw illustrations in FrameMaker 7.0 or import them. When you need to keep an illustration with particular document text, you place the illustration in an anchored frame that's positioned in the column of text or in the page margin.

In this lesson, you'll learn how to do the following:

• Import graphics into anchored frames.

• Anchor graphics below a paragraph, at the bottom of a column, in the page margin, in a line of text, and run into a paragraph.

• Copy and reuse anchored frames.

• Create a drop cap.

Editing text containing anchored frames

Throughout this lesson, you'll add graphics to a travel guide on Hawaii. To see the different positions in which you can place graphics and how they move as you edit text, you'll begin by looking at the finished document.

1 If necessary, copy the Lesson09 folder from the *FrameMaker 7.0 Classroom in a Book* CD and start FrameMaker 7.0.

2 If FrameMaker 7.0 is not in standard mode, choose File > Preferences > General, and then select FrameMaker from the Product Interface pop-up menu.

3 Open Finished.fm in the Lesson09 folder.

4 Use the Next Page button (⬇) and Previous Page button (⬆) in the status bar to page through the document.

Each graphic in the document is in an anchored frame; that is, a frame attached to the text. This means that when you edit the text, the frame and the graphic in it move with the text.

The graphics in this document appear in several positions. One graphic is anchored to a spot in the body text, but positioned in the page margin (the "must visit" graphic on pages 1 and 3). Another is run into the paragraph (the flower on pages 2 and 6). Several graphics are anchored between paragraphs or at the bottom of the page (pages 3 through 6). Even text, such as the drop cap on page 1, can be in an anchored frame.

5 Go back to page 1.

6 To see how the graphics move with the text, click at the end of the first body paragraph on page 1 to place the insertion point, and then press Return several times.

The two pieces of art in the margin move down when you press Return. When you press Return enough times, the first piece of art in the margin moves from the left side of the page to the right.

7 Close Finished.fm without saving your changes.

Importing a graphic

Anchors.fm already contains several graphics. You'll add a few more to finish the document. First, you'll add a graphic between two paragraphs in the text column.

1 Open Anchors.fm in the Lesson09 folder.

2 Choose File > Save As, enter the filename **Anchors1.fm**, and click Save.

3 Choose View > Borders and View > Text Symbols to turn on the display of borders and text symbols.

4 Go to page 3 of Anchors1.fm.

5 Click at the end of the first paragraph on the page (at the end of the line *some of these sights*).

ing at the Kailua Pier. This is a particularly good area to take a walk after a meal. Public parking is somewhat limited and is shown on the Kailua-Kona Map. This part of town has lots of shops and restaurants overlooking the water. If you start strolling from the **Kailua Pier** keep an eye out for some of these sights.¶

Kailua Bay is located in the heart of Downtown. Usually pier areas have nasty water, but this one is surprisingly clean due to the daily flushing action of the sea.¶

6 Press Return to create an empty paragraph.

from the **Kailua Pier** keep an eye out for some of these sights. ¶

¶

Kailua Bay is located in the heart of Downtown. Usually pier areas have nasty

7 At the right side of the document window, click the Paragraph Catalog button (¶).

Paragraph Catalog button

8 In the Paragraph Catalog, click Anchor. The properties of the Anchor paragraph format control the spacing around the graphic.

You could create the anchored frame and then import the graphic into it, but you'll usually find it faster to import the graphic at the insertion point. FrameMaker 7.0 will create the anchored frame for you.

9 Choose File > Import > File.

10 Open the Art folder in the Lesson09 folder and select the Tourmap.tif file.

11 Select Import by Reference and click Import.

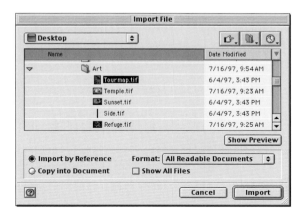

When you import by reference, the graphic file isn't stored in the document. Instead, the document contains a pointer to the graphic file, keeping the file size down. The graphic in the document will be updated automatically whenever the stored file is changed.

12 The Import Graphic Scaling dialog box appears. If it isn't already set to this, select Custom and enter **144** in the Custom dpi text box to specify the size of the graphic. Click Set.

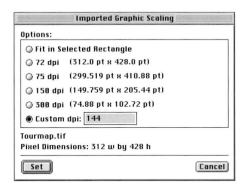

Note: If you had entered 72 dpi, the graphic would have appeared full-sized. You specified twice as many dots per inch (144), so the graphic appears at half of its full size.

FrameMaker 7.0 supports import and export of many types of graphics file formats, including SVG and movies. For more information about file formats, see Chapter 18, "Importing, Linking, and Exporting," in the *Adobe FrameMaker 7.0 User Guide.*

The imported graphic appears in an anchored frame below the empty paragraph. Handles appear around the anchored frame to indicate that the frame is selected. Also, an anchor symbol (⊥) appears at the insertion point, although it's hard to see here at the beginning of the line. The text moves down to accommodate the graphic.

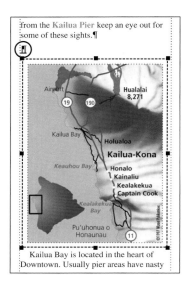

For the graphic to appear in the correct position, you'll need to change the properties of the anchored frame. First you'll eliminate the white space between the anchored frame and the graphic by resizing the anchored frame.

13 Display the Graphics menu to see whether Snap is on or off. If it's on, as indicated by a check mark or check box next to it, turn Snap off by selecting it.

14 Drag the top-left handle of the anchored frame until the edges of the anchored frame line up with the edges of the graphic.

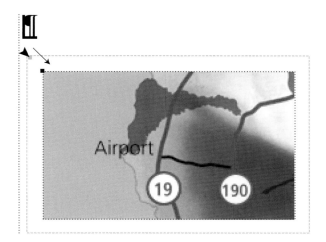

15 Drag the bottom-right handle of the anchored frame until the edges of the anchored frame line up with the edges of the graphic.

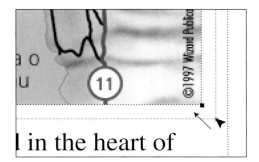

Now you'll change the anchoring position of the frame.

16 With the anchored frame still selected, choose Special > Anchored Frame.

Note: *If the anchored frame is no longer selected, the first button at the bottom of the dialog box is New Frame rather than Edit Frame. If this is the case, click Cancel, click the frame's border, and try again.*

17 Choose At Insertion Point from the Anchoring Position pop-up menu.

18 Change the Distance above Baseline to 0 (zero) and click Edit Frame. The anchor moves to the bottom of the anchored frame.

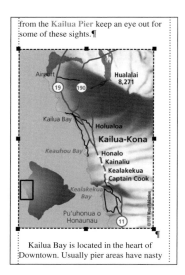

Importing a second graphic

Now you'll import a second graphic on the same page.

1 Click at the end of the first body paragraph in the right column (the paragraph ending with *Kamehamaha insisted*).

2 Press Return.

3 In the Paragraph Catalog, click Anchor. Then close the catalog.

4 Choose File > Import > File.

5 Open the Art folder in the Lesson09 folder and select the Temple.tif file.

6 Make sure Import by Reference is still selected and click Import.

7 Make sure the Custom option is still set to 144 dpi and click Set.

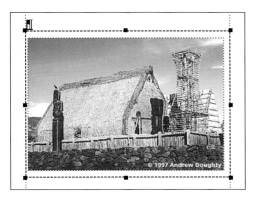

You could change the properties of the anchored frame as you did in the previous section. This time, though, you'll use a shortcut that places the anchored frame into the paragraph and resizes the anchored frame so the graphic just fits inside it. (This is called *shrinkwrapping*.)

8 Make sure the anchored frame is still selected, press Esc m p (the Esc key followed by the letters *m* and *p* in sequence). The graphic now appears with the correct spacing above and below.

Anchoring graphics in the column

Next you'll position a graphic at the bottom of the column. It's a wide graphic, so it will span both columns.

1 Go to page 4.

2 Click at the end of the heading *Elsewhere Along Alii Drive*.

This graphic will appear at the bottom of the column, so you won't need a separate paragraph for it.

3 Choose File > Import > File.

4 Select the Sunset.tif file in the Art folder (within the Lesson09 folder).

5 Click Import and then click Set. The graphic appears in an anchored frame below the heading. An anchor symbol (⊥) appears at the end of the heading.

Anchor symbol

The graphic is wider than the column, and is cropped by the column. You'll turn off the cropping effect so you can display the entire graphic, and then change the anchoring position.

6 With the anchored frame still selected, choose Special > Anchored Frame.

7 Choose At Bottom of Column from the Anchoring Position pop-up menu.

8 Turn off Cropped and click Edit Frame.

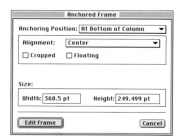

The anchored frame moves to the bottom of the page, and the rest of the graphic appears.

9 Drag the top-left handle of the anchored frame down and to the right until the edges of the anchored frame line up with the edges of the graphic.

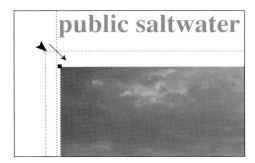

10 Drag the bottom-right handle of the anchored frame up and to the left until the edges of the anchored frame line up with the edges of the graphic.

Using art in the margin

Next you'll add some art in the margin of the page to call attention to several top tourist attractions.

1 Go back to page 1 of Anchors1.fm.

2 In the last paragraph in the left column, click just to the left of *Kiholo Bay*. (It appears in blue.)

> The scenic turnout at the 82-mile marker overlooks Kiholo Bay. Down there you will find a saltwater bay with freshwater calmly oating on top, lots of turtles, and a lava tube with fresh spring water just a few dozen feet from the ocean. Intrigued? I hope so. You can drive there…maybe. Access is a little unusual.¶

3 Choose File > Import > File.

4 Select the Mustvisi.tif file in the Art folder (within the Lesson09 folder) and click Import.

5 In the Import Graphic Scaling dialog box, verify or enter 144 in the custom dpi value box. Then click Set. The graphic appears in an anchored frame below the text.

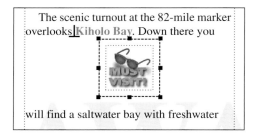

You'll use the same shortcut you used before to shrinkwrap the anchored frame.

6 With the anchored frame still selected, press Esc m p. The anchored frame appears in the line of text, and the insertion point appears to the right of the anchored frame.

The Line Spacing property for the paragraph format is set to Fixed. As a result, the line height of the text doesn't increase to accommodate the height of the frame, and the frame obscures the text. Because you don't want the anchored frame to appear at the insertion point, you'll use the Anchored Frame command to change the anchoring position.

7 Click the border of the anchored frame to select the frame, not the graphic. Handles appear on the frame. (If no handles appear, you probably selected the graphic, not the frame.)

8 Choose Special > Anchored Frame.

9 Choose Outside Column from the Anchoring Position pop-up menu.

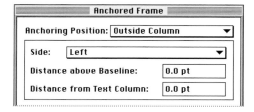

You want to be able to add text above the frame, and if the frame moves to the right column, you want the graphic to appear on the right side of the column. To do this, you'll change the Side setting.

10 Choose Side Closer to Page Edge from the Side pop-up menu, and then click Edit Frame. The graphic moves to the left edge of the column.

Next, you'll move the anchored frame down to align the graphic's text with the line of text that contains the anchor symbol.

11 With the anchored frame still selected, point on the bottom of the frame between two handles (not on a handle) and Shift-drag the frame downward until the baseline of the word *MUST* is approximately aligned with the baseline of the line of text that contains the anchor symbol. (If you accidentally select and move the graphic inside the frame instead of moving the frame, choose Edit > Undo and try again.)

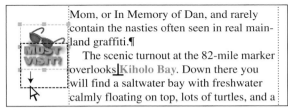

Shift-drag the anchored frame.

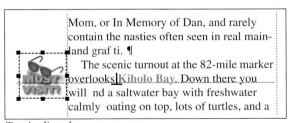

Text is aligned.

💡 *Press Control + l (lower case L) for a quick way to redraw or refresh the display after a format edit.*

Copying anchored frames

You'll use this same graphic in two other locations in the document. You could import and position the graphic each time, but you can save time by copying and pasting the anchored frame and graphic.

1 With the anchored frame still selected, choose Edit > Copy.

2 In the right column on page 1, click just to the left of *Makalawena Beach,* which appears in blue.

> If you're looking for a stunning secluded beach and don't mind walking for 15–20 minutes, Makalawena Beach (described in Beaches) is west of the 89-mile marker.¶

3 Choose Edit > Paste. Because you specified that the graphic should appear on the side closer to the page's edge, the graphic appears at the right side of the column. The frame's Anchoring Position setting, and its vertical position with respect to the anchor symbol, are already set appropriately, so you don't need to adjust the frame's position.

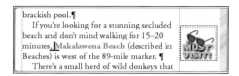

4 Go to page 3 of Anchors1.fm.

5 Under the heading *Downtown Kailua-Kona,* click just to the left of *Ahuʻena Heiau.*

> **Downtown Kailua-Kona ¶**
> To the right (north) of the pier is the Ahuʻena Heiau. Now wonderfully maintained and very picturesque, this was King

6 Choose Edit > Paste. The graphic appears at the left side of the column.

Using inline graphics

Now you'll add a few small graphics in lines of text.

1 Go to the last page of Anchors1.fm.

The coffee information at the bottom of the page appears in a frame that's anchored at the bottom of the column. The text appears in a text frame that's drawn inside the anchored frame, and the picture of coffee beans is in an anchored frame that's run into the paragraph.

2 Click just to the left of *Kona Coffee* in the first sentence of coffee information.

3 Choose File > Import > File.

4 Select the Mug.tif file in the Art folder (within the Lesson09 folder) and click Import.

5 In the Import Graphic Scaling dialog box, verify that 144 dpi is selected and click Set.

The graphic appears in an anchored frame under Kona Coffee.

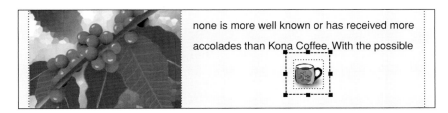

6 With the anchored frame still selected, press Esc m p. The anchored frame appears in the line of text, and the insertion point appears to the right of the anchored frame.

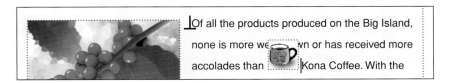

7 Press the spacebar to add a space between the frame and *Kona*.

The graphic is sized correctly, but appears too high in the line.

8 Click the frame's border to select the frame.

You could drag the frame downward or use the arrow keys to reposition the frame, but you'll use the Anchored Frame command this time.

9 Choose Special > Anchored Frame.

10 Enter **-11** (type a hyphen, then the number eleven) in the Distance above Baseline text box to move the frame down 11 points. Then click Edit Frame.

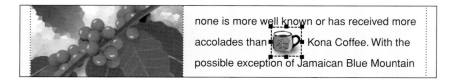

Reusing anchored frames

Now you'll import two more small pieces of art. Because the anchored frame is already positioned the way you want it, you'll reuse it by copying and pasting the frame elsewhere in your document.

1 With the anchored frame still selected, choose Edit > Copy.

2 Click in the second sentence of the same paragraph, just to the left of the word *world*.

3 Choose Edit > Paste. A copy of the anchored frame, with the graphic of the coffee mug, appears at the insertion point.

4 Press the spacebar to add a space between the frame and the following word.

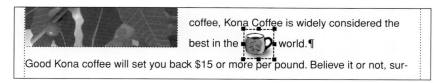

5 Click just to the left of the words *from many* in the fourth sentence of the final paragraph.

6 Choose Edit > Paste and press the spacebar.

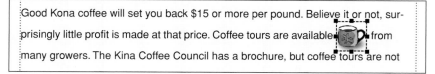

Now you'll replace the coffee mugs in the two pasted frames with the correct art.

7 Click on the second coffee mug to select it. (Click inside the frame, not on the frame's border.) Notice that the handles on the graphic appear inside the border of the anchored frame.

8 Choose File > Import > File. If you selected the graphic correctly, you'll see the Replace button instead of the Import button in the dialog box.

9 Select the Globe.tif file in the Art folder (within the Lesson09 folder), click Replace, then click Set in the Import Graphic Scaling dialog box.

The graphic appears in the frame.

10 Click on the last coffee mug to select it.

> Good Kona coffee will set you back $15 or more per pound. Believe it or not, sur-prisingly little pro t is made at that price. Coffee tours are available ![mug]from many growers. The Kina Coffee Council has a brochure, but coffee tours are not

11 Choose File > Import > File.

12 Select the Coffeebe.tif file in the Art folder (within the Lesson09 folder) and click Replace.

13 Click Set in the Import Graphic Scaling dialog box.

💡 *Alternatively, you can double-click on the .tif file name to select and replace the file in a single step.*

The appropriate graphic now appears in the frame.

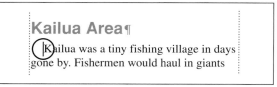

Using run-in art

Next you'll add a graphic that's run into the beginning of a paragraph.

1 Go to page 2 of Anchors1.fm.

2 Click at the beginning of the first paragraph under the heading *Kailua Area*.

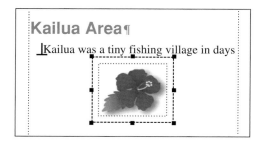

3 Choose File > Import > File.

4 Select the Flower.tif file in the Art folder (within the Lesson09 folder), click Import, then click Set in the Import Graphic Scaling dialog box.

The graphic appears in the frame.

Unlike the graphics in the previous section, the graphic you imported here is too large, so you'll scale it down.

5 Click the graphic to select it.

6 Choose Graphics > Scale, enter **69** in the Factor text box to scale it to 69 percent of its current size, and click Scale.

Note: FrameMaker 7.0 allows you to scale or resize an imported graphic relative to the original size of the original graphics file.

7 Press Esc m p to resize the frame to fit the graphic.

8 Select the frame border and choose Special > Anchored Frame.

9 Choose Run into Paragraph from the Anchoring Position pop-up menu.

10 Enter **2** in the Gap text box and click Edit Frame. The frame now runs into the beginning of the paragraph. FrameMaker 7.0 uses a 2-point gap between the frame and the surrounding text.

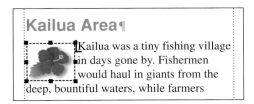

11 Save the document.

12 FrameMaker 7.0 also supports drag and drop functions for importing graphics that are specific to the Windows, Mac OS, and UNIX platforms. See chapter 9, "Graphics," in the *Adobe FrameMaker 7.0 User Guide* for platform-specific information.

Creating a drop cap

A *drop cap* is a large capital letter that drops down into the text. The last art you'll add is a drop cap at the beginning of this document. This time, you'll create the anchored frame first. Then you'll add the drop cap afterward.

1 Go to page 1 of Anchors1.fm.

2 Delete the letter *B* at the beginning of the first paragraph of body text (beginning with *Back on Highway 19*).

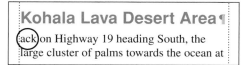

3 With the insertion point still at the beginning of the paragraph, choose Special > Anchored Frame.

4 Make sure that Anchoring Position is still set to Run into Paragraph and that the Gap is set to 2 points.

5 Click New Frame. An empty anchored frame appears at the insertion point.

6 At the right side of the document window, click the Tools button.

Tools button

7 In the Tools palette, click the text line tool (**A**). This tool lets you create a single line of text that FrameMaker 7.0 treats independently from other text. You can apply character formats to this kind of text, but not paragraph formats.

8 Click inside the anchored frame and type the letter **B**.

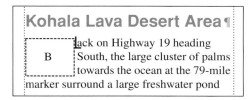

9 Close the Tools palette.

10 Do one of the following to select the text line:

- (Windows and UNIX) Control-click the letter *B*.

- (Mac OS) Option-click the letter *B*.

Now you'll apply a preset group of font properties to the letter.

11 At the right side of the document window, click the Character Catalog button.

Character Catalog button

12 In the Character Catalog, click DropCap. Then close the Character Catalog.

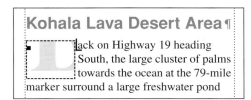

The letter *B* should still be selected.

13 Drag the letter until it's positioned at the top-left corner of the anchored frame.

14 Select the anchored frame and drag its bottom-right handle until the edges of the anchored frame line up with the edges of the letter.

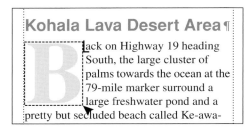

The drop cap is done and you've finished adding graphics to the document.

15 To see how the document will look when printed, choose View > Borders and View > Text Symbols, and page through the document. When done, save and close Anchors1.fm.

Importing movies into documents

Adding motion pictures to your documents can enhance them. In the last lessons of this *Classroom in a Book*, you'll learn to develop publications for the *Adobe Acrobat*, HTML, and other formats. Multimedia is an exciting component of designing for these uses.

Windows media in FrameMaker 7.0 files

You can add movies, animation, and other multimedia segments into your documents by embedding .avi, .mov (if you have QuickTime installed), or other types of files.

Here you'll add a movie file to a document.

1 Start a new default portrait document by choosing File > New Document.

2 In the New Document window, select Portrait, and a new document appears.

3 Choose > File > Import Object.

The Import Object dialog box appears.

4 Choose Create from File.

5 Browse to the Lesson09 Art folder, select Cyclers.avi, click Open to insert the file name into the dialog box. Click OK.

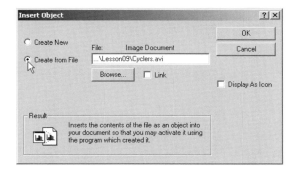

6 The movie is imported like any other graphic. The difference is that you have now embedded an active object into the document. To watch the movie, double-click the imported graphics frame.

Sample Windows movie playing in a FrameMaker 7.0 document window.

Note: *Don't rotate the movie. You won't be able to play it until you return it to its original orientation.*

For more information, see "Using OLE (Windows)" in Chapter 18 of the Adobe FrameMaker 7.0 User Guide.

When you print a document containing an object, only the object's title appears.

Note: *Don't move or delete the original .avi movie file. The entire movie is not copied into your document. Instead, it is played in your document through linking to the movie as a reference.*

Mac OS media files in FrameMaker 7.0 files

You import a QuickTime® movie in the same way that you import other graphics. On the Mac OS, Flash and other types of media files must be converted to one of the QuickTime output formats in order for Adobe FrameMaker 7.0 to recognize them for import into a document.

Here you'll add a QuickTime movie (.mov) file to a document.

1 Start a new default portrait document. Choose > File > Import File. Locate the Lesson09 Art folder, where you will find Cyclers.mov to import. If you have a movie you would like to try out and QuickTime is installed in your system, import that.

 To help you quickly navigate through your disk system, try changing the import format you are seeking to QuickTime Movie. Only importable movies will display in your lists.

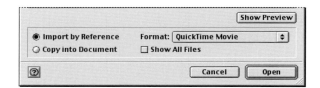

2 To play the movie in the document, double-click the film icon. The graphic frame will convert to a movie player. (Make your frame a little bit taller if it does not reveal the whole set of player controls.) Click on the Play button.

Note: *Don't rotate the movie—you won't be able to play it until you return it to its original orientation.*

View of an imported movie.

3 Choose Graphics > Object Properties. Change the Height to **204** pt and click Set. This will allow the movie's player controls to be completely visible when you play it.

4 To watch the movie, double-click the film icon.

Sample movie playing in a
FrameMaker 7.0 document window.

When you print a document containing a QuickTime movie, only the movie's title appears.

Note: Don't move or delete the original QuickTime movie file, even if you used the Copy into Document option when you imported it. Even with this option, the entire QuickTime movie is not copied into your document. Instead it is played in your document through linking to the movie as a reference.

For details, see "Using the Import command to import graphics" in Chapter 18 of the *Adobe FrameMaker 7.0 User Guide*.

Using graphic insets (UNIX)

A graphic inset is a graphic created in a special UNIX application—a graphic inset editor—and then inserted in a document. You use the inset editor to create or modify the graphic inset, or you can start the editor from within FrameMaker.

Moving on

You've completed this lesson. For in-depth information on anchored frames, see Chapter 10, "Anchored Frames," in the *Adobe FrameMaker 7.0 User Guide*. For in-depth information on importing graphics, see Chapter 18, "Importing, Linking, and Exporting," in the *Adobe FrameMaker 7.0 User Guide*.

Review questions

1 What is an anchored frame? How is an anchored graphics frame useful?

2 Name three kinds of places a graphic can be positioned in a document.

3 If a graphic has a resolution of 72 dpi, and you import it at 144 dpi, what happens to the size of the imported graphic?

4 Why might you want to reuse—that is, copy and paste—an anchored frame?

5 What is a drop cap?

6 What does the text line tool do?

7 What is the shortcut for resizing a frame to fit a graphic?

8 How do you import a QuickTime® movie into a document?

Answers

1 An anchored frame is a frame that can contain a graphic or text and is anchored to the text. The frame and its contents move with the anchor, so you don't have to reposition the graphic or text when you edit the document.

2 Graphics can appear in several positions, such as between words; between paragraphs; anchored to a spot in the text, but positioned in the page margin; or relative to a spot on the page (such as at the top).

3 Doubling the dpi makes the imported graphic half the size of the original.

4 It might contain the graphic that you want to use. It might also have properties that you want to apply to another graphic, such as size and position.

5 A drop cap is a large capital letter set into a piece of body text. It usually occurs at the beginning of a section of text.

6 The text line tool lets you create a single line of text that FrameMaker 7.0 treats independently from other text.

7 Press Esc m p to resize the frame to fit the graphic.

8 Start a new default portrait document. Choose > File > Import File and locate the movie file to import.

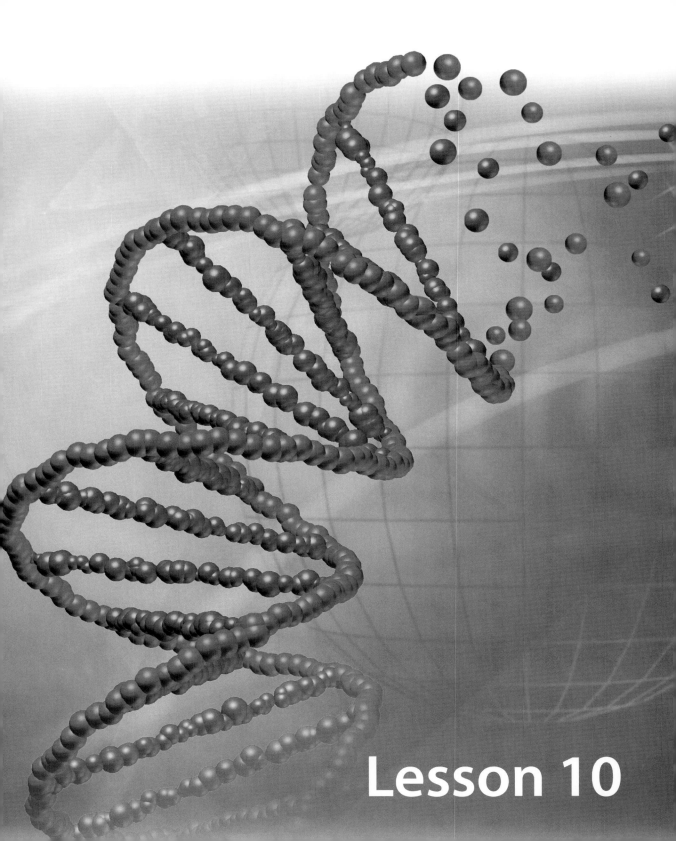

Lesson 10

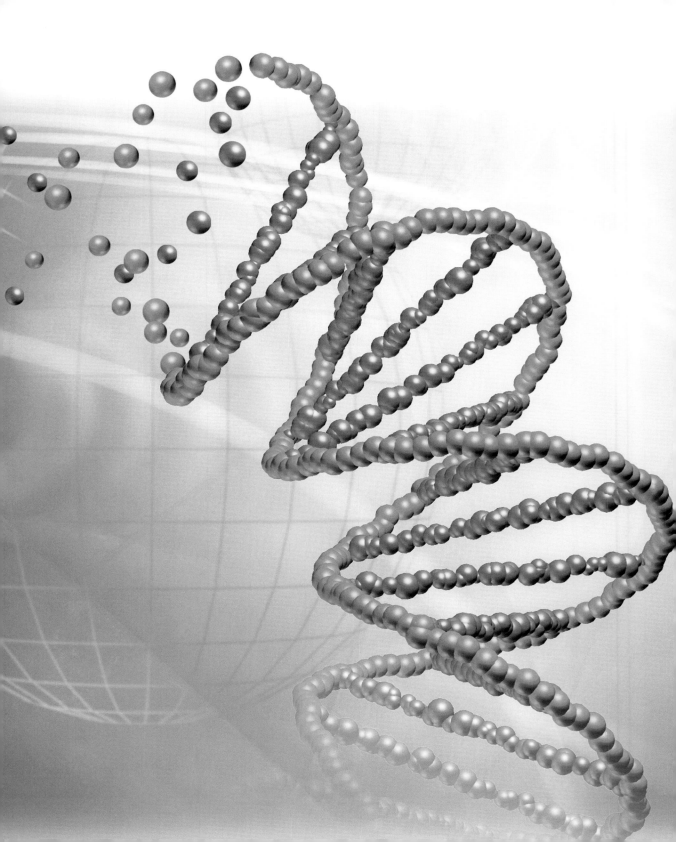

10 | Cross-References and Footnotes

When you need a cross-reference, you specify its source and the wording to use (for example, See "Installing" on page 7). Later, if page numbers or headings change when you edit the source documents, FrameMaker 7.0 can automatically update the cross-references. FrameMaker 7.0 also rearranges and renumbers footnotes as you edit your document.

This lesson uses a travel guide on Hawaii as its sample. You will add some cross-references and footnotes to it. If you want to see completed versions of the sample files, open the Finished folder in the Lesson10 folder.

In this lesson, you'll learn how to do the following:

• Insert cross-references to headings and to specific words or phrases in a paragraph.

• Create and edit cross-reference formats.

• Insert cross-references to other documents.

• Fix unresolved cross-references.

• Insert footnotes.

• Change footnote properties.

Inserting a paragraph cross-reference

In this exercise, you'll create an internal cross-reference to a heading. An internal cross-reference is one with links to the same document in which it originates.

1 Open Ref1.fm in the Lesson10 folder. You will be making changes directly to the sample files in this lesson. If you want to start over, you can get fresh copies of the files from the CD-ROM.

An alert message tells you that the document contains unresolved cross-references.

This means that FrameMaker 7.0 can't update at least one cross-reference in the document because it can't find the source of the cross-reference. You'll fix this problem later.

2 Click OK.

3 Go to page 4 of Ref1.fm.

4 In the left column, click at the end of the first paragraph, as shown.

Finally, dismount and run a 26.2 mile marathon. All this done under the tropical Sun. This is the best opportunity you'll ever have to look into the faces of mass excellence.

You'll now start to insert a cross-reference to a heading. This is called a *paragraph cross-reference* because the reference is to an entire paragraph.

Note: *A paragraph is any amount of text that ends with a paragraph symbol (¶). This means that even a one-line heading is a paragraph.*

5 Press the spacebar and type **For more information, see** and then press the spacebar again.

After these words, you'll insert a cross-reference to another section of the travel guide.

6 Choose Special > Cross-Reference.

The Cross-Reference dialog box appears, which lets you specify the paragraph you want to refer to (the *source* for the cross-reference) and the wording you want to use (the *cross-reference format*).

You'll refer to a heading.

7 Select Heading1 located in the Paragraph Tags scroll list. The text of all the Heading1 paragraphs appears in the Paragraph scroll list.

8 Select South of Kailua-Kona located in the Paragraphs scroll list.

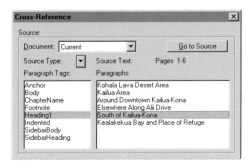

Next, you specify the format for the cross-reference, which you choose from the Format pop-up menu. The name of the format appears in the pop-up menu, and the definition appears below the pop-up menu.

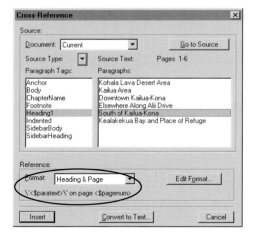

9 Be sure to choose Heading & Page in the pop-up menu. This format is defined to include the text of the heading and the page number on which it occurs.

10 Click Insert. The cross-reference appears at the insertion point.

> Finally, dismount and run a 26.2 mile marathon. All this done under the tropical Sun. This is the best opportunity you ll ever have to look into the faces of mass excellence. For more information, see South of Kailua-Kona on page 5

11 Type a period to end the sentence. Save the document.

12 Click once on the cross-reference (the text that FrameMaker 7.0 just inserted). Notice that the entire cross-reference is selected, indicating that the cross-reference is considered a single object by FrameMaker 7.0, not a series of words.

You can't edit the text of the cross-reference directly. The text will change automatically as the source changes. However, you can change it by choosing a different cross-reference format, by referring to a different heading, or by editing the definition of the format.

Insert headings, figure titles, and table titles in the form of cross-references rather than typing them directly. Adobe FrameMaker 7.0 will automatically track and update them.

Displaying the source of a cross-reference

You can use the cross-reference to go to the source paragraph quickly.

1 Double-click the cross-reference you just inserted. The Cross-Reference dialog box appears.

2 At the top-right of the dialog box, click Go to Source. FrameMaker 7.0 displays page 5, which contains the source heading.

3 Choose View > Text Symbols to display the marker symbol (T) that appears at the beginning of the heading. The marker defines the location of the source of the cross-reference.

> **South of Kailua-Kona¶**
>
> If you head south out of Kona, you'll come to a series of small towns, all above 1,000 feet. It's usually cool up here, some-

The marker symbol is difficult to see because it's at the beginning of the paragraph. You can confirm that it's there by zooming to 400%.

Inserting an external cross-reference

The cross-reference you inserted was to a heading in the same document. Now you'll insert an external cross-reference, that is, a cross-reference to a heading in a different document.

1 Add Ref2.fm to your work space by opening it from the Lesson10 folder.

Note: To create an external cross-reference, both the source and destination files must be open.

2 Arrange the two documents, Ref1.fm and Ref2.fm, so that you can see at least part of both of them. (In Windows, you can choose Window > Tile.)

3 On page 6 of Ref1.fm, click at the end of the second sentence of the paragraph that begins with *Napoʻopoʻo Beach*, as shown.

> strangers were mere mortals, not the gods
> some felt them to be.¶
>   Napoʻopoʻo Beach used to be a fabu-
> lous beach fronting the heiau. Most "cur-
> rent" guidebooks still rave about (it.) Too
> bad it doesn't exist anymore. It had been

4 Press the spacebar, type **See**, and press the spacebar again.

5 Choose Special > Cross-Reference.

6 Choose Ref2.fm from the Document pop-up menu at the top of the dialog box.

Verify that Heading1 is still selected in the Paragraph Tags scroll list.

7 Select *Napoʻopoʻo Beach* located last in the Paragraphs scroll list.

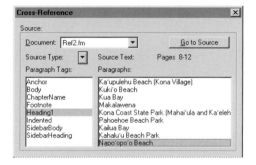

8 Click Insert. The cross-reference appears at the insertion point.

Napoʻopoʻo Beach used to be a fabu-
lous beach fronting the heiau. Most "current" guidebooks still rave about it. See
"Napoʻopoʻo Beach" on page 12 Too bad it
doesn't exist anymore. It had been eroding

9 Type a period and press the spacebar.

10 In Ref1.fm, the cross-reference to the Heading1 in Ref2.fm has been made. In the next exercise, you'll create another one that inserts the file name of the external source.

11 Save both documents. Now that the cross-reference is inserted and saved, FrameMaker 7.0 will update its text and page number automatically whenever you print or open the file.

Creating a cross-reference format

The document already contains cross-reference formats for headings and tables, but it doesn't have an appropriate format for a cross-reference to a chapter title. Here, you'll create such a format so that you'll be able to cross-reference a chapter title later.

1 With the insertion point still in Ref1.fm, choose Special > Cross-Reference.

2 Make sure that the Heading & Page format is chosen in the Format pop-up menu. Then click Edit Format. The definition for the Heading & Page format appears in the Definition text box.

You'll use the Edit Cross-Reference dialog box to create the *format* for the cross-reference. The format definition comes from three sources:

• Building blocks specify information about the source of the cross-reference. For example, the <$paratext> building block specifies the paragraph text, and the <$pagenum> building block specifies the page number.

• Text you type yourself in the Definition text box will appear in the format just as you typed it. For example, typing the words *on page* adds those words to the format.

• Character formatting comes from special building blocks so that, for example, portions of the cross-reference appear in bold or italics.

3 Delete the contents of the Name text box and enter **Chapter** in its place.

4 In the Definition text box, place the insertion point at the very beginning or left of the <$paratext> building block.

Note: In Windows and on UNIX systems, the backslash sequences in the Definition text box indicate curved quotation marks. On the Mac OS, you literally see curved quotation marks: "and " instead of: \` and \'.

5 Type **the chapter** and press the spacebar. Carefully proofread the words, because Spelling Checker does not check text that is inserted into dialog boxes.

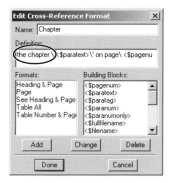

6 Click to set the cursor at the left of the building block <$paratext>.

7 Click once on the <Emphasis> building block at the bottom of the Building Blocks list.

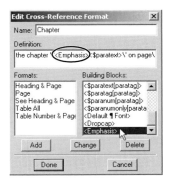

8 Select the remainder of the definition (*on page\ <$pagenum>*), then press Backspace (Windows) or Delete (Mac OS).

Be sure that you delete everything to the right, including any blank spaces.

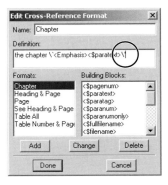

9 Click Add. The new cross-reference format (Chapter) appears in the Formats scroll list.

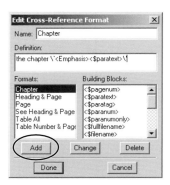

10 Click Done in the Edit Cross-Reference dialog box, then click Done in the Cross-Reference dialog box itself.

11 Save the document.

Using the new cross-reference format

Now you'll use the cross-reference format you just created.

1 Go to page 5 of Ref1.fm.

2 In the second column, in the paragraph that begins with, "Next to the church", click at the end of the first sentence, as shown.

> Next to the church is **Kahalu'u Beach Park** where you'll find some of the easiest access to good snorkeling on the island. Kahalu'u had a large population in the old

3 Press the spacebar, type **See**, and press the spacebar again.

4 Choose Special > Cross-Reference.

5 Choose Ref2.fm from the Document pop-up menu at the top of the dialog box.

6 In the Paragraph Tags scroll list, select ChapterName, then select Beaches near Kona in the Paragraphs scroll list.

The Format is still set to Chapter.

7   Click Insert. The cross-reference appears at the insertion point.

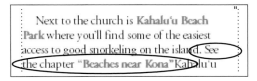

8   Type a period and press the spacebar.

9   Save the document.

Inserting a spot cross-reference

Spot cross-references refer to an individual word or phrase in a paragraph, rather than to an entire paragraph. In this exercise, you'll use a spot cross-reference to refer to a beach that's described in the middle of a paragraph of text.

Paragraph and spot cross-references use markers at the source location. When you insert a *paragraph* cross-reference, a cross-reference marker is automatically inserted at the beginning of the paragraph. However, before you insert a *spot* cross-reference, you must manually insert a marker to mark the spot.

1   In the left column on page 5 of Ref1.fm, put the insertion point just to the left of *White Sands Beach*. (It appears in color about a third of the way down the page.)

Near the 3-mile marker is Pahoehoe Beach Park. No sand here, but recently renovated. It's a nice place to have a picnic, or to just sit on a bench and watch the surf. White Sands Beach (it has several other names) is a little farther down with good

2   Choose Special > Marker.

3   Choose Cross-Ref from the Marker Type pop-up menu.

4 Enter **White Sands Beach** in the Marker Text box, or drag to select the actual text to make it appear in the Marker Text area, then click New Marker.

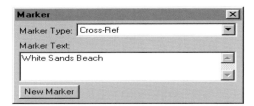

5 The marker symbol ($\top$) now appears at the insertion point. (If the marker symbol isn't visible, choose View > Text Symbols.)

6 Close the Marker dialog box.

Now that the marker is in place, you're ready to insert the cross-reference in Ref2.fm.

7 Go to page 10 (the third page) of Ref2.fm.

8 Place the insertion point at the end of the last paragraph on the page.

> it too exciting. Lots of fish here as well.
> Located north of the 4-mile mark on Alii
> Drive in Kailua (just north of White Sands
> Beach).

9 Press the spacebar, type **See**, and press the spacebar again.

10 Choose Special > Cross-Reference.

11 Choose Ref1.fm from the Document pop-up menu.

12 Choose Cross-Reference Markers from the Source Type pop-up menu.

The text of all the cross-reference markers in Ref1.fm appears in the Cross-Reference Markers scroll list.

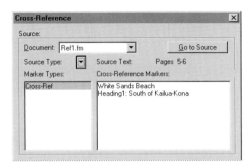

Notice that the Cross-Reference Markers scroll list contains the text of two markers—the one that you just inserted and another one that FrameMaker 7.0 inserted for you when you inserted the paragraph cross-reference earlier in this lesson.

13 Select White Sands Beach, located in the Cross-Reference Markers scroll list.

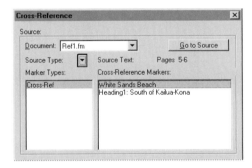

14 Choose Page from the Format pop-up menu, then click Insert.

15 Type a period to end the sentence.

16 Save the document.

Resolving cross-references

Cross-references become *unresolved* when the source of the cross-reference (the Cross-Ref marker at the source) is deleted, when the source has been moved to another document, or if the source document cannot be found or opened for some reason (it may be locked by another user).

When you opened Ref1.fm at the beginning of this lesson, an alert message warned you that this document contained unresolved cross-references. You'll fix this problem next.

1 In Ref1.fm (not Ref2.fm), choose Edit > Update References.

2 Select All Cross-References and click Update.

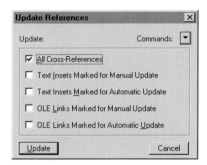

The Update Unresolved Cross-References dialog box appears.

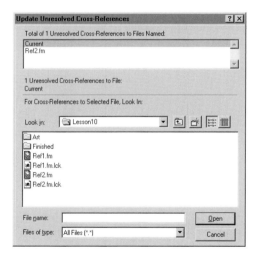

The text above the top scroll list tells you the total number of unresolved cross-references. The scroll list contains all the documents to which the current document's cross-references refer.

3 In the Total of Unresolved Cross-References scroll list, click Ref2.fm. The text below the scroll list tells you that there are no unresolved cross-references to Ref2.fm.

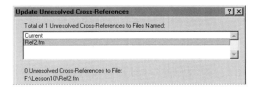

4 In the Total of Unresolved Cross-References scroll list, click Current. The text below the scroll list tells you that one of the internal cross-references is unresolved.

If the cross-reference were unresolved because the source was *deleted,* you'd have to fix the problem by closing this dialog box and re-creating the source or by deleting the cross-reference. Before doing that, it's a good idea to see if the cross-reference is unresolved because its source has been *moved* (in this case, moved from Ref1.fm to Ref2.fm). When this is the cause of the problem, you can fix the problem right in this dialog box.

5 Do one of the following:

• (Windows and UNIX) In the Look In list, select Ref2.fm as the document to search for the missing cross-reference source, then click Open.

• (Mac OS) Click Change to File, select Ref2.fm, and click Select.

The Update Unresolved Cross-References dialog box reappears, but this time it shows that no unresolved cross-references remain.

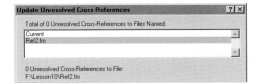

6 Do one of the following:

• (Windows) Click Cancel.

• (Mac OS and Unix) Click Done.

7 Save Ref2.fm and close the file.

8 Save Ref1.fm, but do not close the file.

Inserting footnotes

Next you'll add two brief footnotes to the text.

1 Go to page 2 of Ref1.fm.

2 Choose View > Text Symbols to turn on text symbols, if necessary.

3 In the right column, click at the end of the second sentence under the *Kailua Area* heading, as shown.

Kailua Area

Kailua was a tiny shing village in days gone by. Fishermen would haul in giants from the bountiful waters, while farmers tended their fields up the slopes of Hualalai. Kona weather and Kona waters were known

4 Choose Special > Footnote. A footnote reference number now appears where you clicked.

bountiful waters, while farmers tended their fields up the slopes of Hualalai. Kona weather and Kona waters were known

Also, an empty footnote appears at the bottom of the page with a separator line between it and the body text.

island. The winds we do get are usually from wraparound sea breezes. The rains from them have already been wrung out.¶

_____

1.) §

The insertion point now appears in the footnote.

5 Type **Many of the great chiefs of old chose this part of the island as their home.**

6 Click at the end of the long paragraph in the left column, as shown.

> housing Maine lobsters. When the lobsters
> arrive from the mainland they have a nasty
> case of jet lag.¶
>   An excellent tide-pool is nearby at
> **Wawaloli Beach.**¶

7 Choose Special > Footnote. A new footnote is inserted at the bottom of the left column. Notice that the footnote in the right column is automatically renumbered from 1 to 2.

8 Type **The lab gives free hour-long tours every Thursday.**

9 Choose Special > Footnote again to move the insertion point back into the body text.

10 Save the document.

Online Help and the Adobe FrameMaker 7.0 User Guide (Chapter 7) provide information on creating one footnote with multiple references or multiple references to one footnote. For example, create a table footnote with references in several cells.

Also explore the usage of endnotes, which are numbered notes at the end of a document, and can be used instead of footnotes at the bottom of pages.

Changing how footnotes look

Footnote properties come from two sources. First, because footnotes are paragraphs of text, a normal paragraph format controls a footnote's indents, font, and so on. Second, to handle a footnote's unique aspects (such as its numbering style), there is a special Footnote Properties dialog box. In this section, you'll make changes to properties from both sources.

Changing numbering style

The footnotes in Ref1.fm are numbered sequentially throughout the document. You'll change the footnote properties so the footnotes are marked with special characters whose sequence begins anew on each page.

First you'll change the footnote numbering.

1 Choose Format > Document > Numbering.

2 Choose Footnote from the top pop-up menu.

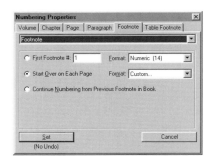

3 Click Start Over on Each Page, then choose Custom from the Format pop-up menu.

In Windows and on UNIX systems, the Custom Numbering dialog box contains \d and \D. These are backslash sequences for a dagger (†) and a double-dagger (‡).

4 Click Set, then click Set again.

The first footnote now appears with an asterisk, and the second one now appears with a dagger.

After the 96-mile marker is a lava road leading to the sea. It goes to **Kaloko-Honokohau National Historical Park.**	times **Kailua Town.** Kailua-Kona is nestled in the lee of Hualalai Volcano, meaning that it is sheltered from the trade
*)The lab gives free hour-long tours every Thursday.§	†)Many of the great chiefs of old chose this part of the island as their home.§

Removing the separator line

Now you'll remove the line that separates the body of the text from the footnotes. The separator is specified on a special *reference* page, so you'll change it there. (A reference page is a nonprinting page containing unanchored graphic frames. The contents of the graphic frames can be used by paragraph formats and footnotes.)

1 If necessary, choose View > Borders to turn on borders.

2 Choose View > Reference Pages.

The reference page contains several reference frames. The first one contains the footnote separator line. When you insert the first footnote in a column, FrameMaker 7.0 uses this reference frame to determine how much space to leave between the body text and the footnote. If the reference frame contains a line, FrameMaker 7.0 displays that line within the space.

3 Display the Graphics menu to see whether Snap is turned on. If it is, turn it off.

4 Click the line inside the Footnote frame to select the line (not the frame). You may want to zoom in to 200% so that clicking the line inside the frame is easier.

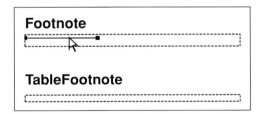

5 Press Delete to remove the line, leaving just the empty frame. The empty frame will define the space between the body text and the first footnote in the column.

6 Choose View > Body Pages to redisplay page 2. The separator line is now gone but the space is still there.

After the 96-mile marker is a lava road leading to the sea. It goes to **Kaloko-Honokohau National Historical Park.**	times **Kailua Town.** Kailua-Kona is nestled in the lee of Hualalai Volcano, meaning that it is sheltered from the trade
*)The lab gives free hour-long tours every Thursday.§	†)Many of the great chiefs of old chose this part of the island as their home.§

Making footnotes span columns

In the sample you've been working with, each footnote appears at the bottom of the column that contains the footnote reference. By changing the paragraph format for the footnote, you'll make the footnotes span the columns.

1 Click in a footnote at the bottom of a page. Note that the status line's tag area displays Footnote. This is the tag of the format you'll change.

2 Choose Format > Paragraphs > Designer.

3 Choose Pagination from the Properties pop-up menu.

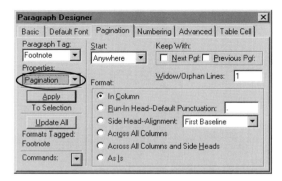

4 In the Format area, select Across All Columns. This will allow the footnotes to span the columns in the text frame.

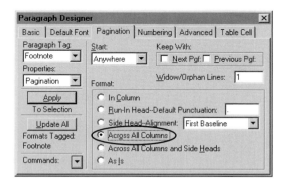

5 On the left side of the Paragraph Designer, click Update All. The footnotes now span the columns.

After the 96-mile marker is a lava road leading to the sea. It goes to Kaloko-Honokohau National Historical Park.	times Kailua Town. Kailua-Kona is nestled in the lee of Hualalai Volcano, meaning that it is sheltered from the trade

*)The lab gives free hour-long tours every Thursday.§
†)Many of the great chiefs of old chose this part of the island as their home.§

6 Close the Paragraph Designer.

7 Save and close Ref1.fm.

You're finished with inserting cross-references and footnotes.

Moving on

You've completed this lesson. For in-depth information on cross-references and footnotes, see Chapter 7, "Cross-References and Footnotes," in the *Adobe FrameMaker 7.0 User Guide*.

Review questions

1 What are some of the differences between a paragraph cross-reference and a spot cross-reference?

2 How can you quickly display the source of a cross-reference?

3 What controls the wording and appearance of a cross-reference?

4 What are the two main ways a cross-reference could become unresolved?

5 After you've typed the text of a footnote, how can you return to the spot you left off in the body text?

6 What controls the look of a footnote?

7 How do you resolve an external cross-reference?

8 When should you choose Edit > Update References?

9 What are endnotes?

Answers

1 A paragraph cross-reference refers to the text of an entire paragraph; a spot cross-reference refers to a location within a paragraph. Inserting a paragraph cross-reference places a marker at the source automatically; you must insert a marker manually at the source before you insert a spot cross-reference.

2 To quickly display the source of a cross-reference, double-click the cross-reference and then click Go to Source.

3 The cross-reference format, which is chosen in the Cross-Reference dialog box, determines the wording and appearance of a cross-reference. The cross-reference format is created and edited by clicking Edit Format in that dialog box.

4 A cross-reference could become unresolved if the source of the cross-reference has been deleted or moved to a different document. Also, the source document could be locked by another user and therefore could not be opened.

5 Choosing Special > Footnote again returns the insertion point to the body text.

6 The look of a footnote is determined by the settings in the Footnote Properties dialog box and by the paragraph format specified for footnotes.

7 You resolve an external cross-reference in the same way that you resolve an internal cross-reference but with both the source and reference documents open.

8 You should choose Edit > Update References, whenever you have added or edited cross-references or footnotes.

9 Endnotes are numbered notes at the end of a document; they are used instead of footnotes at the bottom of pages.

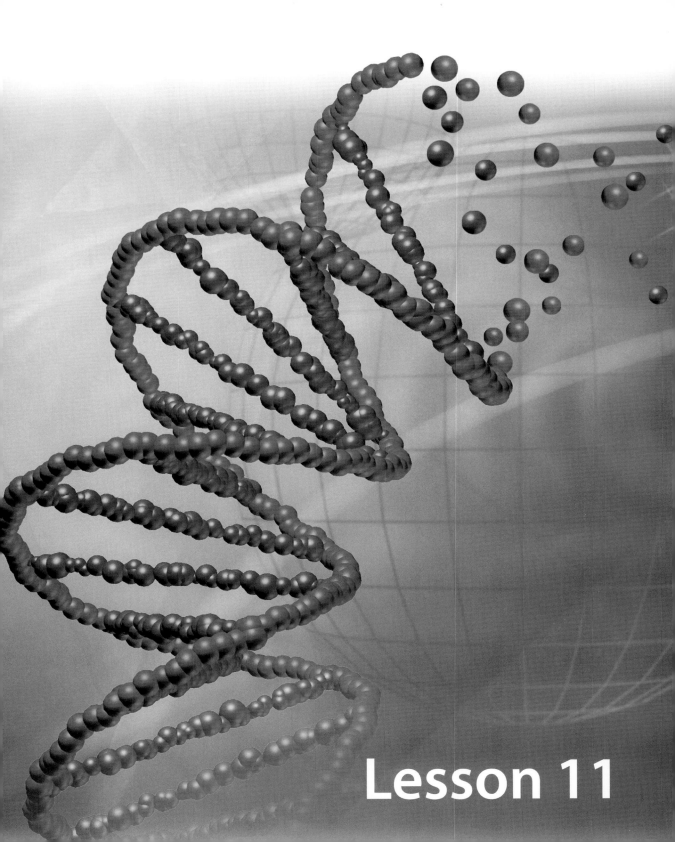

Lesson 11

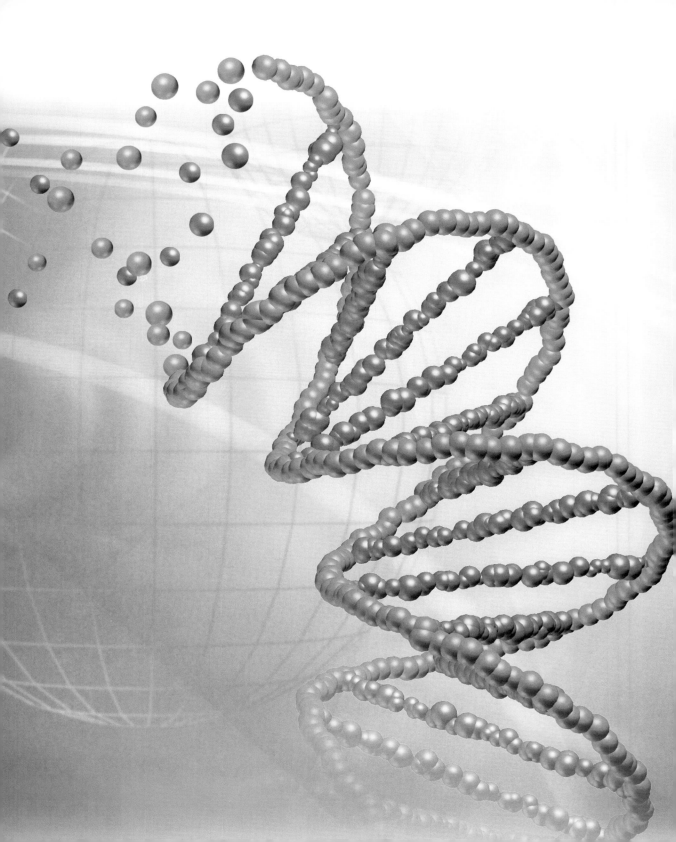

11 | Books

You can group separate FrameMaker 7.0 documents into one book. This grouping lets you generate a single table of contents or index for the documents, and it greatly simplifies printing, numbering, cross-referencing, and formatting.

This lesson uses four sample files: three chapter files and a preface file. You'll collect these files into a book and then generate a table of contents from all the files in the book. If you want to see completed versions of the sample files, open the Finished folder in the Lesson11 folder.

In this lesson, you'll learn how to do the following:

• Create a book file from one of the documents in the book.

• Add documents to a book and paginate them.

• Add a table of contents to a book.

• Format a table of contents.

Viewing the finished book file

You'll create a *book file*—a file that lets you group and work with several documents together—for a small, three-chapter guide to commercial printing. Working from a book file, rather than with individual files lets, you easily paginate across files, update all cross-references, and generate special documents such as an index or table of contents for the book.

You'll begin by familiarizing yourself with the finished version of the Press.book file.

1 Choose File > Open > Lesson11 > Finished > Press.book.

The default mode is to display the chapters as Adobe FrameMaker 7.0 formatted file names.

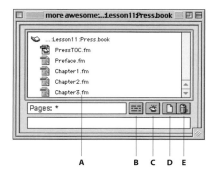

*A. File names in .fm mode **B.** Display Heading Text button **C.** Update Book button **D.** Add File to Book button **E.** Delete Selected File from Book button*

2 Click on the Display Heading Text button (⚏).

The files are listed to display contents from the chapters.

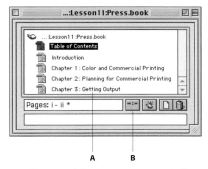

A. *Files named from contents* **B.** *Display File Names button*

3 Close the finished version of Press.book, but do not save it. You'll create one of your own in this lesson.

Creating a book file

First you'll create a new book file. Then you'll explore working in a book window and compare it to working in a document window.

1 Open Chapter1.fm. Be sure to open it from the main Lesson11 folder. You won't be making copies of the sample files in this lesson. If you want to start over, you can get fresh copies of the files from the CD-ROM.

2 Choose File > New > Book.

3 Click Yes when FrameMaker 7.0 displays an alert message asking if you want to add Chapter1.fm to the new book.

A book window appears showing the book's contents, so far only Chapter1.fm (the file from which the book was created).

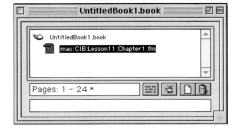

When you're working in a book window, the menu bar contains only commands appropriate for books. For example, the File menus for a book and for a document contain somewhat different commands.

File   Edit   Add   Format   View   Window   Scripts   Help

Main file menu when a book is the active file.

Note: On UNIX systems, the book menu bar appears as part of the book window. In Windows and on the Mac OS, the menu bar remains at the top of the application window.

4 Compare the File menu for the book window with the File menu for the document window by doing one of the following:

• (Windows and Mac OS) Click in the book window and observe the File menu. Then click in Chapter1.fm and observe the difference in the File menu.

• (UNIX) Display the File menu in the book window. Then display the File menu in the document window for Chapter1.fm.

For the rest of this lesson, you'll work with the book rather than with individual files in the book.

5 Close Chapter1.fm, but leave open the book window you just created.

The book was assigned a default name (UntitledBook1.book), but you'll save the book using a more appropriate filename.

6 Choose File > Save Book As, enter the filename **Press.book**, be sure that the destination folder is Lesson11, and click Save.

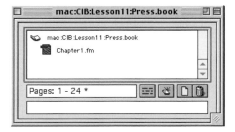

Note: The Save Book As command saves the book file only. The component files of the book are saved individually. If you save the book to a new location, open and save each individual component file to that location as well.

Adding documents to the book

Your book will eventually contain a table of contents, a preface, and three chapters. You'll add another chapter now.

1 Choose Add > Files.

2 Navigate to the folder containing the chapter files; if necessary, select Chapter2.fm and click Add.

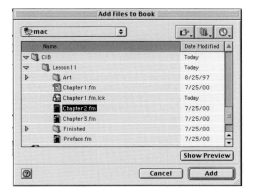

To add a file to a book, you can also click the Book Add button ( ) at the bottom of the book window.

Now, you'll add the third chapter and the preface.

3 Choose Add > Files and do one of the following:

• (Windows) Hold down Control while you select Chapter3.fm and Preface.fm, then click Add.

• (Mac OS) Hold down Shift while you select Chapter3.fm and Preface.fm, then click Add.

• (UNIX) Select Chapter3.fm and click Add, select Preface.fm and click Add, then click Done.

The book window now shows that the book contains three chapters and a preface.

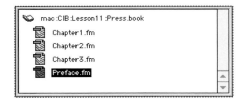

Notice that the preface appears at the bottom of the list in the book window instead of at the beginning where it should be. You can fix that easily.

4 Select Preface.fm in the book window and drag it above Chapter1.fm.

5 You can rearrange one or more files in a book window by selecting them and dragging them where you want them to appear in the book. The files are now in the correct order.

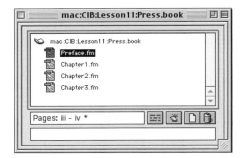

6 Choose File > Save Book to save the book file.

Opening files from the book window

Before adding a table of contents to the book, you'll take a quick look at the individual chapters in the book.

1 Double-click Chapter1.fm in the book window.

Double-clicking a filename is a quick way to open an individual file. However, you can open many files at once by using a shortcut.

2 Close Chapter1.fm.

3 In the book file, hold down Shift and choose File > Open All Files in Book. All the documents in the book are opened.

Note: In Windows and on UNIX systems, the documents are minimized, so you'll need to open the minimized windows to see their contents.

Notice that each chapter is numbered *Chapter 1* and begins on page 1. When you update the book later in the lesson, the chapter and page numbers will be renumbered correctly.

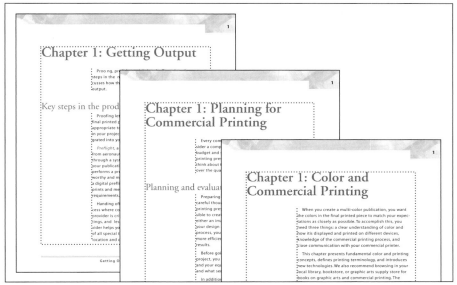

Initially, all three chapter numbers are 1.

4 Hold down Shift and choose File > Close All Files in Book to close the preface and all three chapters. Leave the book window open.

Adding a table of contents

The book is now complete except for the table of contents. The table of contents will be a *generated file*—a file whose entries are generated from the other files in the book.

Adding a table of contents is a twofold process. First, you add a description of the table of contents to the book file. Then you generate (create) the table of contents from the other files in the book.

1 In the book window, select Preface.fm because you want the book's table of contents to appear before the preface.

2 Choose Add > Table of Contents.

In the dialog box that appears, you'll choose chapter titles and one level of headings to be included in the table of contents.

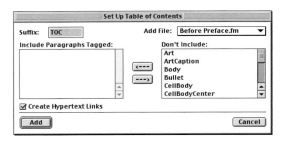

Initially, the tags of all the paragraph formats in the files of the book appear in the Don't Include scroll list on the right. When you set up a table of contents, you decide which tags to include in it. FrameMaker 7.0 will look in the files of the book for any text that's formatted with these tags. When it finds a paragraph formatted with one of the tags, FrameMaker 7.0 copies the text into the table of contents.

You'll include the paragraph tagged ChapterTitle in the table of contents by moving it from the right scroll list (the Don't Include scroll list) to the left scroll list (the Include Paragraphs Tagged scroll list).

3 Select ChapterTitle in the right scroll list (you may need to scroll down) and move it to the left scroll list by clicking the left arrow (**‹---**).

Moving ChapterTitle to the Include Paragraphs Tagged scroll list means that the text of any paragraph tagged ChapterTitle will be included in the book's table of contents. Each chapter contains a single paragraph tagged ChapterTitle.

4 Now double-click Heading1 in the Don't Include scroll list to move it to the Include Paragraphs Tagged scroll list. (Double-clicking an item in a scroll list moves it to the opposite list.)

The text of any paragraph tagged Heading1 will also be included in the table of contents. Each chapter contains several paragraphs tagged Heading1.

5 Scroll in the Don't Include list (if necessary) until you see PrefaceTitle.

6 Double-click PrefaceTitle to move it to the Include Paragraphs Tagged scroll list.

The text of any paragraph tagged PrefaceTitle will also be included in the table of contents.

7 Turn off Create Hypertext Links. Click Add.

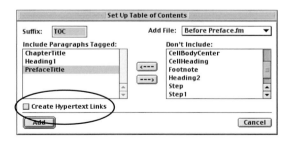

Generating the table of contents

In the Update Book dialog box that appears, the *filename* of the table of contents, PressTOC.fm, appears in the Generate list on the left. The filename is based on the book's name (*TOC* indicates that the file is a table of contents.)

The PressTOC.fm *file* doesn't actually exist until FrameMaker 7.0 *generates* it (meaning that FrameMaker 7.0 gathers the paragraphs tagged with the formats you want included (ChapterTitle, Heading1, and PrefaceTitle) and puts them into a new file called PressTOC.fm).

1 In the Update Book dialog box, deselect Apply Master Pages.

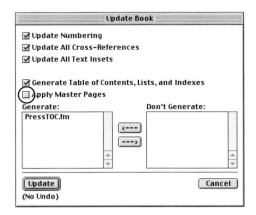

2 Click Update to generate the table of contents for your book.

Note: If the program fails to update the book and generate the table of contents, hold down the Shift key and choose File > Open All Files in Book. Then proceed to Update the book.

At the same time, FrameMaker 7.0 updates the chapter numbering, page numbering, and cross-references in the book.

Messages appear in the status bar at the bottom of the book window as FrameMaker 7.0 examines each file in the book. After a few moments, the table of contents appears. Initially, the table of contents uses the page layout of the first document in the book (the preface).

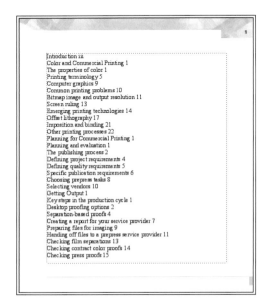

Note: In Windows and on UNIX systems, the table of contents is minimized, so you'll need to open the minimized window to see its contents.

3 Click in the first paragraph of the table of contents (the single-line paragraph whose text is *Introduction*) and notice the tag that appears in the status bar: PrefaceTitleTOC.

4 Press the Down Arrow key several times to move the insertion point down the page, noticing that the other paragraphs also have tags that end in *TOC* (ChapterTitleTOC and Heading1TOC).

FrameMaker 7.0 created and assigned these TOC paragraph formats when the table of contents was generated. Because these three formats are initially identical, the entries in the table of contents all look the same. Later, you'll redefine the formats and apply them to the entries in the table of contents.

💡 *If you had placed a document in the book folder that was already named PressTOC.fm and that already contained definitions for the TOC formats, FrameMaker 7.0 would have used that document for the table of contents instead of creating a new one. In this way, you can use a* template *to speed up formatting a generated file.*

5 Minimize the table of contents again (Windows and UNIX) or move it out of the way and click in the book file (Mac OS).

Setting up chapter numbering

After adding the table of contents to your book, you'll need to be sure that the chapters are numbered correctly.

1 Double-click Chapter2.fm in the book window to open the document. Notice that the chapter is still numbered *Chapter 1*. (FrameMaker 7.0 does not continue paragraph numbering across all the files of the book unless you tell it to by using the Format > Document > Numbering command.)

2 Return to the book window and select both Chapter2.fm and Chapter3.fm.

3 Choose Format > Document > Numbering.

4 Choose Chapter from the pop-up menu, select Continue Numbering from Previous FIle in Book, and click Set.

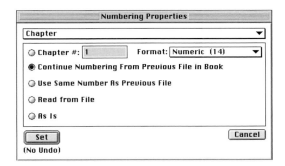

5 Choose Edit > Update Book, then click Update.

6 Display both Chapter2.fm and Chapter3.fm to confirm that FrameMaker 7.0 has correctly renumbered them.

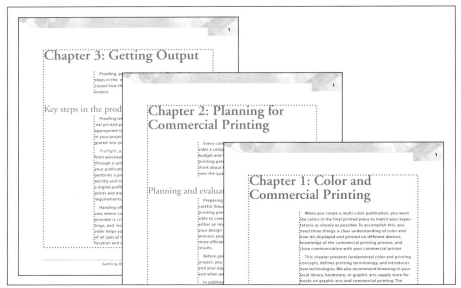

All three chapters are now numbered correctly.

Fixing the pagination

The table of contents shows you how FrameMaker 7.0 has paginated the book. Notice that the chapter titles for Chapter 2 (*Planning for Commercial Printing*) and Chapter 3 (*Getting Output*) incorrectly begin on page 1. FrameMaker 7.0 does not number the pages consecutively in a book unless you tell it to.

1 Make sure the book file is open and visible.

Next you'll choose a command that will let you adjust how the second and third chapters paginate. You could choose the Document > Numbering command from the Format menu. Instead, you'll use a *context menu*, which is a convenient shortcut when working in a book window. (A context menu contains commonly used commands applicable to the item under the pointer.)

2 Select Chapter2.fm and Chapter3.fm in the book window, then do one of the following:

• (Windows and UNIX) Right-click in the book window.

• (Mac OS) Hold down Control and click in the book window.

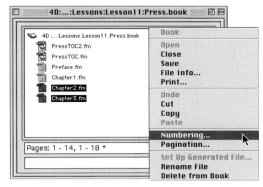

Context menu for a book

3 Choose Numbering from the pop-up menu.

4 Choose Page from the pop-up menu in the Numbering Properties dialog box.

5 Click Continue Numbering from Previous Page in Book.

6 Click Set.

Any time you make a change to a file in a book—either to its contents or to its setup—you should update the book to see the change reflected in the book's generated files.

7 Choose Edit > Update Book, then click Update.

8 Reopen the table of contents to see the new numbering. Notice that the book's pages are now numbered sequentially.

You'll make one more change to the book's contents.

9 Click in Chapter3.fm, and change the title of this chapter from *Getting Output* to *Good-Looking Output*.

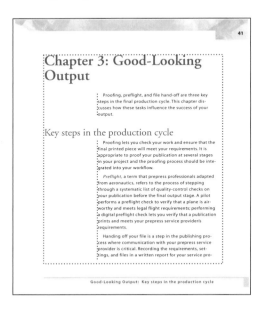

10 Save and close Chapter3.fm.

11 From the book file, generate the table of contents again by choosing Edit > Update Book, then clicking Update.

💡 *To update a book, you can also click (⛷) at the bottom of the book window.*

12 Inspect the updated table of contents and note that the entry for this chapter now correctly reads *Good-Looking Output*.

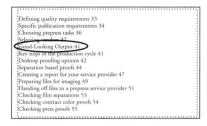

13 Save the table of contents and the book and keep them open.

Changing the layout

The preface and chapters in the book use a side-head area at the left side of each page. To make the TOC consistent with the rest of the book, you'll apply the same layout.

First convert the TOC's own page number to roman, like in the Preface.fm file.

1 Choose Format > Document > Numbering.

2 In the first pop-up area, select Page.

3 Click on First Page # and type **1** if it isn't already there.

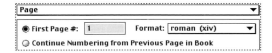

4 In the Format pop-up area, select *roman (xiv)* and click Set. Observe the number at the top right corner of the Table of Contents document. It is in roman numerals.

Next you'll format the page layout of the text contents of the TOC itself.

5 Click anywhere in the table of contents, and then choose Format > Customize Layout > Customize Text Frame.

6 Select Room for Side Heads. Change the Width to 92. Verify that the Gap is 14 and the Side is set to Left.

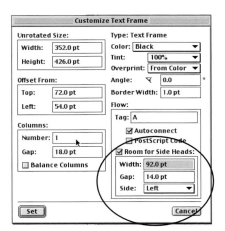

7 Click Set. The entries move into the body-text area at the right side of the text frame.

Adding a title

Before you format the entries in the table of contents, you'll add a title.

1 Click outside the frame to deselect it and then click at the beginning of the first paragraph of the table of contents (*Introduction*).

2 Press Return and then press the Up Arrow key to place the insertion point in the new empty paragraph above *Introduction*.

3 Type **Table of Contents**.

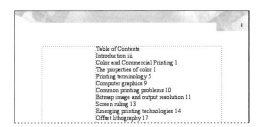

4 Choose Format > Paragraphs > Designer.

5 Choose New Format from the Commands pop-up menu.

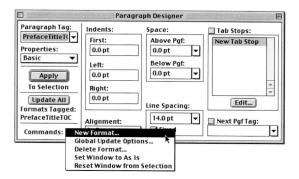

6 Enter **ContentsTitle** in the Tag text box. Make sure that both options, Store in Catalog and Apply to Selection, are selected.

7 Click Create.

The tag of the title you just typed is changed to ContentsTitle (as shown in the status bar), and the format is stored in the Paragraph Catalog.

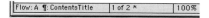

When you generate the table of contents again, FrameMaker 7.0 will update only the paragraphs whose tags end in *TOC*. The title will remain because the tag you typed (ContentsTitle) doesn't end in *TOC* and because the paragraph appears at the start of the text flow.

8 In the Paragraph Designer, choose Default Font from the Properties pop-up menu. (In Windows, you can just click the Default Font tab at the top of the designer.)

9 Change the Size to 30, the Color to HeadingColor, and the Family to:

• (Windows) AGaramond-Semibold, Weight Regular.

• (Mac OS and UNIX) Adobe Garamond, Weight Semibold.

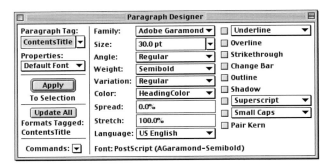

10 Click Update All to apply the changes to the title and to update the format in the catalog.

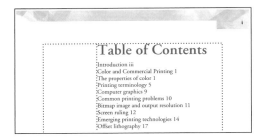

11 Choose Basic from the Properties pop-up menu.

12 Change the Space Below Pgf to 72 and click Update All.

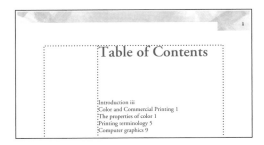

The title will look better if it spans both the side-head area and the body-text area, so you'll make that change next.

13 Choose Pagination from the Properties pop-up menu.

14 Click Across All Columns and Side Heads, then click Update All.

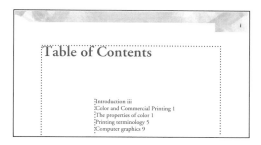

Now you're ready to format the entries in the table of contents.

Formatting the entries

Formatting a table of contents is a twofold process:

- In this section, you'll format the entries as you would any paragraphs.

- In the next section, you'll make changes that affect the contents of the entries, instead of their formats.

Formatting a generated file takes some time, but you need to do it only once for the book because FrameMaker 7.0 reuses your formatting each time you generate the file. You can also use the formatted table of contents from one book as a template for others, so the investment you make in formatting a table of contents pays off quickly.

Changing paragraph formats

First, you'll change the paragraph formats of the entries.

1 Click in the first entry (the preface title, *Introduction*).

2 In the Paragraph Designer, display the Default Font properties.

3 Change the Family to:

- (Windows) AGaramond-Semibold, Weight Regular.

- (Mac OS and UNIX) Adobe Garamond, Weight Semibold.

4 Click Update All.

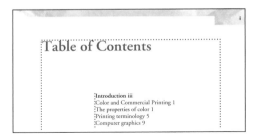

5 Click in the second entry (the title of Chapter 1, *Color and Commercial Printing*).

6 In the Paragraph Designer, Change the Family to:

• (Windows) AGaramond-Semibold, Weight Regular.

• (Mac OS and UNIX) Adobe Garamond, Weight Semibold.

7 Click Update All. All three chapter titles change.

8 Display the Basic properties in the Paragraph Designer.

9 Change the Space Above Pgf to 14 and click Update All.

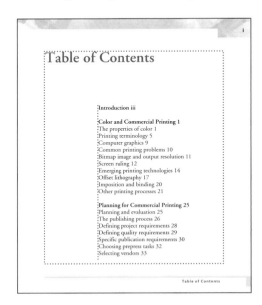

10 Now click in the first entry for Chapter 1, *The properties of color.*

11 Display the Default Font properties in the Paragraph Designer.

12 Change the Family to Myriad-Roman (Windows) or Myriad (Mac OS or UNIX), the Size to 10, and click Update All.

13 Display the Basic properties again, change Line Spacing to 14, and click Update All.

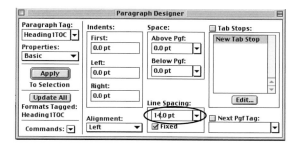

14 Save the document.

Adding tab leader dots

A table of contents often places page numbers at the right side of the page with dots between the text and the page numbers.

To do this for all Heading1 entries, you need to make a few more changes to the format of the entries.

1 Choose View > Rulers to display the document rulers.

2 If the formatting bar isn't visible, choose View > Formatting Bar (Windows), or click the formatting bar toggle at the left side of the top ruler (Mac OS and UNIX).

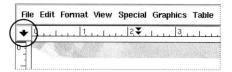

The formatting bar contains several formatting pop-up menus and tab wells that you can use to set some paragraph properties. You'll use the tab wells.

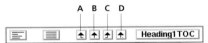

A. *Left-aligned tab well* **B.** *Centered tab well* **C.** *Right-aligned tab well* **D.** *Decimal-aligned tab well*

3 Click anywhere in the first entry for Chapter 1, *The properties of color*. Then drag a right-aligned tab stop from the tab well to just under the right indent on the ruler.

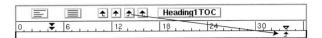

You won't see any result from having added the tab stop yet, because the Heading1 paragraphs don't contain tab characters. (Tab characters will be inserted automatically in the table of contents when it's generated.)

4 Double-click the tab stop (the little arrow) under the ruler.

5 Select the first dotted leader in the Leader area of the Edit Tab Stop dialog box.

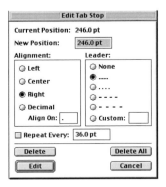

6 Click Edit.

7 In the Paragraph Designer, click Update All. The entries in the table of contents don't change, because they don't contain a tab character yet. You'll fix that in the next section.

8 Close the Paragraph Designer.

9 Choose View > Rulers to hide the rulers and save the document.

Changing the contents of entries

The table of contents now has the general appearance you want, but the entries still may not be quite right for the intended design. For example, suppose you'd like the preface and chapter titles to appear without page numbers. Also, all the Heading1 entries now need to contain tab characters to correspond to the tab stop you defined in the Heading1TOC format in the previous section.

Changes such as these affect the contents of entries rather than their formats. For this reason, you won't be using the Paragraph Designer to make the changes. Instead, FrameMaker 7.0 provides a special place to edit the contents of TOC entries: a *reference page*.

1 Choose View > Reference Pages.

The reference page that first appears contains graphics that are used to highlight notes to the reader in the chapter. You'll work on a different page.

2 Click the Next Page button in the status bar until you reach the *TOC* Reference page (on page 7). The name of the reference page appears in the status bar.

The page contains a special text flow that controls the contents of the entries in the table of contents. The first paragraph—which is just one line long and whose text is <$paratext> <$pagenum>—is tagged PrefaceTitleTOC.

This paragraph contains two *building blocks*, <$paratext> and <$pagenum>. Building blocks are special pieces of text that control the content of an entry. In this case, <$paratext> and <$pagenum> indicate that the text of the preface title and its page number should appear in the table of contents. The space between the two building blocks tells FrameMaker 7.0 to insert a space between the text and the page number.

3 Place the insertion point at the end of the first paragraph (tagged PrefaceTitleTOC) and press Backspace to delete the <$pagenum> building block and the space before it. This instructs FrameMaker 7.0 to place only the text of the preface title in the table of contents.

4 Press the Down Arrow key until the insertion point is in the last paragraph (tagged ChapterTitleTOC). The paragraph tag appears in the status bar.

5 Place the insertion point at the end of the paragraph and press Backspace to delete the <$pagenum> building block and the space before it. This instructs FrameMaker 7.0 to place only the text of each chapter title in the table of contents.

6 Press the Up Arrow key to place the insertion point in the second paragraph (tagged Heading1TOC).

7 Select the space between the two building blocks and press Tab to replace the space with a tab character.

The special text flow on the TOC reference page now looks like this.

8 Choose View > Body Pages.

Your recent changes are not reflected in the table of contents until you generate the table of contents again.

9 Save the table of contents and keep it open.

10 Return to the book window and choose Edit > Update Book.

11 Click Update.

12 Review the updated table of contents and notice that page numbers no longer appear next to the preface or chapter titles, and that all the Heading1 page numbers are now right-aligned with leader dots.

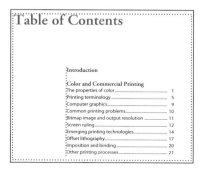

13 Save and close the table of contents, any open chapters, and the book file.

Finishing the Preface.fm file

In order to learn the formatting of the Table of Contents, you left the Preface.fm file in a basic unformatted state. The Table of Contents bases its format on the file that is active at the time of its generation.

Self-guided exercise

As a self-guided exercise, upgrade the formatting of Preface.fm.

1 Open and review the finished version supplied with the lesson files.

2 Open the unformatted version used in Press.book.

3 Apply formats through the Paragraph Designer and through File > Import > Formats.

4 Compare your results with the finished version.

Moving on

You've completed this lesson. For in-depth information about books, tables of contents, and other generated lists such as lists of figures and lists of tables, see Chapter 14, "Tables of Contents and Indexes," and Chapter 15, "Books," in the *Adobe FrameMaker 7.0 User Guide*.

Review questions

1 What are some of the advantages of using a book file?

2 Where do you find the commands you need for working with a book file?

3 How do you list book files so that the contents of the chapters are displayed?

4 How do you access a context menu for a book window?

5 When you set up a table of contents for a book, why do you have to move some tags to the Include Paragraphs Tagged scroll list?

6 How do you control the pagination of a file in a book?

7 When you add a title to a table of contents, why doesn't FrameMaker 7.0 overwrite it when it updates the file?

8 What are the two basic steps you need to perform to format entries in a table of contents?

Answers

1 A book file creates and keeps current a bookwide table of contents or index. It also simplifies chapter and page numbering and helps to maintain accurate cross-references.

2 Commands that apply to a book file appear in the File, Edit, and Add menus when a book window is active (Windows and Mac OS) or at the top of a book window (UNIX). Also, you can access a book window's context menu for a subset of the commands.

3 Click on the Display Heading Text button (▤).

4 To display a context menu, right-click (Windows and UNIX) or Control-click (Mac OS) in the book window.

5 Moving tags in the Set Up Table of Contents dialog box tells FrameMaker 7.0 which paragraphs to include when it creates and updates the table of contents.

6 Select one or more files in the book window and choose Format > Document > Numbering. Then choose Page from the pop-up menu in the Numbering Properties dialog box.

7 FrameMaker 7.0 leaves alone any paragraph that appears at the start of a generated file whose tag does not end with *TOC*.

8 To format entries in a table of contents you need to modify the paragraph formats for the entries in the table of contents. Then, you need to modify the special text flow on the reference page.

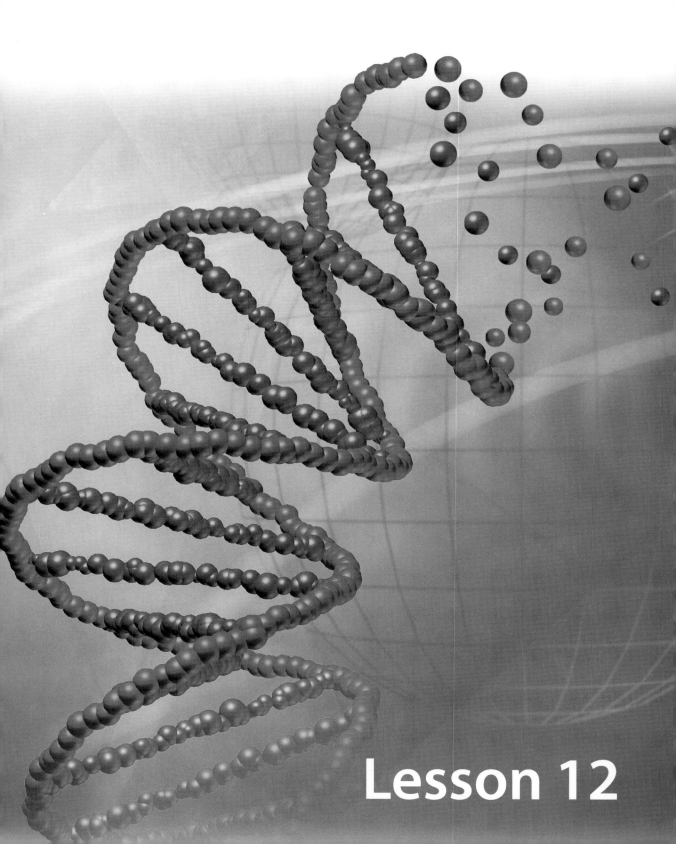

Lesson 12

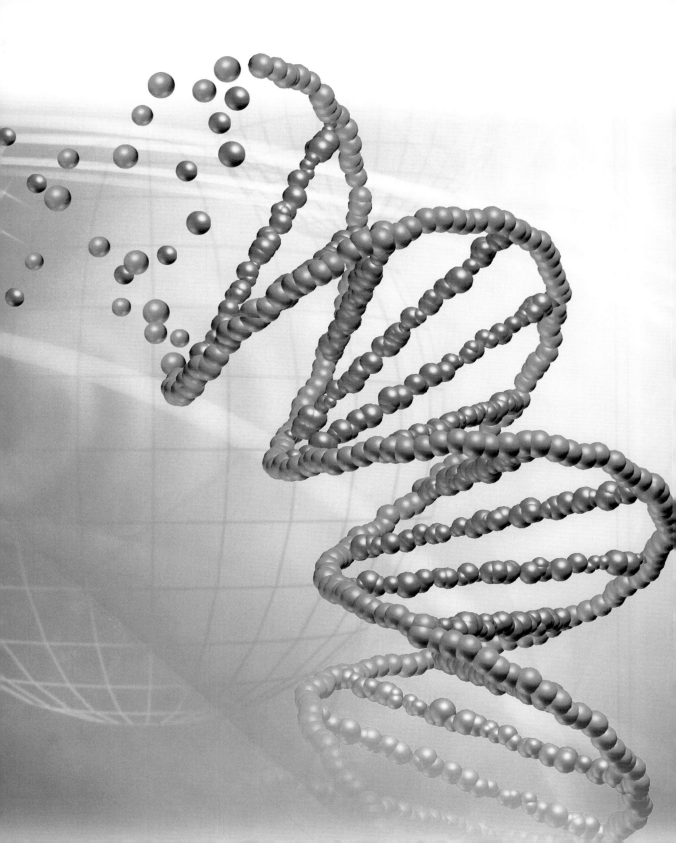

12 | Indexes

You prepare an index by using special markers. After the markers are inserted, you can generate the index for a document or for an entire book. When you move or edit a marker, you generate the index file again so that it's up-to-date.

This lesson uses a version of the book file you created in the previous lesson. If you want to see completed versions of the sample files, open the Finished folder in the Lesson12 folder.

In this lesson, you'll learn how to do the following:

- Add an index to a book.

- Generate and update an index.

- Lay out and format an index.

- Insert and edit index entries.

Adding an index to the book

Adding an index to a book is a twofold process. First you add a description of the index to the book file. Then you generate the index from index markers that are already inserted in the book's chapters. (Later in this lesson, you'll insert and edit some index entries on your own.)

1 Open Press.book from the Lesson12 folder. (You won't be saving copies of the sample files in this lesson. If you want to start over, you can get fresh copies of the files from the CD-ROM.)

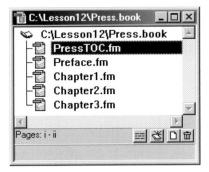

The book contains a table of contents (PressTOC.fm), a preface (Preface.fm), and three chapters (Chapter1.fm, Chapter2.fm, and Chapter3.fm).

2 Select Chapter3.fm in the book file because you want the index to follow the last chapter in the book.

3 Choose Add > Standard Index.

The dialog box that appears is already set up for a standard index.

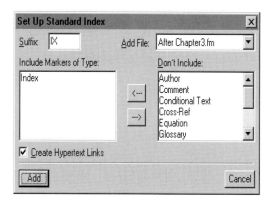

4 Make sure that Create Hypertext Links is selected so that FrameMaker 7.0 will include a hypertext link with each index entry. You'll use this feature later to display the source of an index entry by clicking the entry's page number. Click Add.

The index *filename* (PressIX.fm) appears in the Update Book dialog box. The filename is based on the book's name (*IX* indicates that the file is an index.) The PressIX.fm *file* doesn't actually exist until *FrameMaker 7.0* generates it (meaning that *FrameMaker 7.0* gathers and sorts the markers of type Index into the index file). Click Update.

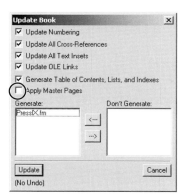

Note: If the program fails to update the book and generate the index, hold down the Shift key and choose File > Open All Files in Book. Then proceed to Update the book.

5 Messages appear in the status bar at the bottom of the book window as FrameMaker 7.0 scans each file in the book. After a few moments, the index appears.

Note: In Windows and UNIX systems, the index is minimized. Open the minimized window to see its contents.

A
Additive color model 7
B
Binding 24
Bitmap image
  defined 13
  resolution of 15
  tonal range in 15
Bleed, checking 50
Blueline 46
C
Chroma 6
CMS. *See* Color management system
CMY color model 8
Color
  characteristics of 6
  checking definitions 50
  displaying on monitors 6
  high-fidelity 19
  in imported illustrations 50
  matching 10
  perception of 6
  proofing 41, 42–47
  screening 10
  systems for managing 19
  tints of 10
Color bars 55
Color gamut 8
Color management system 19
Color model 7

The index has content because the chapters already contain index markers. If you hadn't yet inserted any index markers, the index would be empty. (You'll add more index markers yourself later.)

Changing the layout

Initially, the index uses the page layout of the first document in the book (the preface). If you had a template for the index, you could have generated a formatted index, and you'd be finished now. However, there is no template for this index, so you'll need to format it yourself.

Formatting an index is a multistep process, but you need to do it only once. When you generate the index again, it will retain your formatting changes. You can use the formatted index as a template for other indexes.

The first changes you'll make to the appearance of the index are to its layout and to its page numbering. You'll change the index to a three-column layout.

1 In the index file, choose View > Master Pages to display the Right master page.

2 Click in the main text frame and choose Format > Customize Layout > Customize Text Frame.

3 In the Columns area, change the number of columns to 3, change the gap to 10, and select Balance Columns.

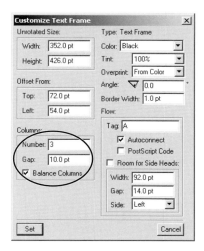

When columns are balanced, text on the last page of the index is evenly distributed across the columns.

4 Turn off Room for Side Heads and click Set.

5 In the status bar, click the Previous Page button (⬆) to display the Left master page.

6 Click in the main text frame and choose Format > Customize Layout > Customize Text Frame.

7 Make the same changes you made in step 3 and step 4, and click Set.

8 Choose View > Body Pages to display the first page of the index.

The layout changes throughout the index.

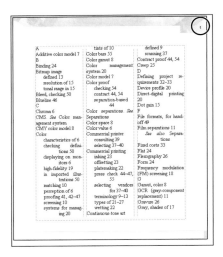

The page numbering is incorrect. (You may need to scroll up to see that the first page is numbered 1 instead of 59, the next page in the book). You'll fix that next.

9 Return to the book file, select PressIX.fm, and choose Format > Document > Numbering.

10 Click Continue Numbering from Previous Page in Book, and click Set. The next time you generate the index, the pages will number correctly.

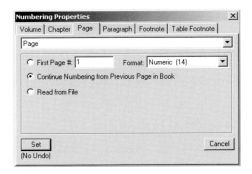

11 Return to the index file and save it.

Adding a title

Before you format the index entries, you'll add a title.

1 Click at the beginning of the first paragraph of the index (on the left side of the group title *A*) and press Return.

2 Click in the new empty paragraph and type **Index**.

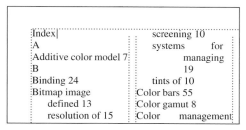

3 Choose Format > Paragraphs > Designer.

4 Choose New Format from the Commands pop-up menu.

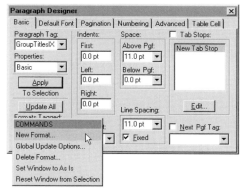

5 Enter **IndexTitle** in the Tag text box.

6 Make sure that both options, Store in Catalog and Apply to Selection, are selected.

7 Click Create.

The tag of the current paragraph changes to IndexTitle, and the IndexTitle format is added to the Paragraph Catalog.

Because FrameMaker 7.0 will replace only the paragraphs whose tags end in *IX*, the title will remain when you generate the index again as long as it is at the start of the text flow.

8 In the Paragraph Designer, choose Default Font from the Properties pop-up menu. (In Windows, you can click the tab at the top of the designer to display a group of properties.)

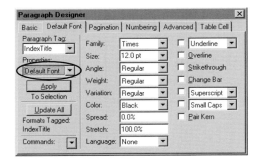

9 Change the Size to 30, the Color to HeadingColor, and the Family to:

• (Windows) AGaramond-Semibold, Weight Regular.

• (Mac OS and Unix) Adobe Garamond, Weight Semibold.

10 Click Update All to apply the changes to the title and to update the format in the catalog.

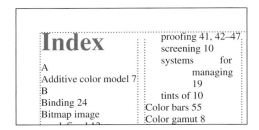

11 Choose Basic from the Properties pop-up menu.

12 Change the Space Below Pgf to 18, then click Update All.

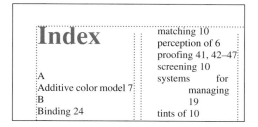

The title area would look nice if it spanned all three columns, so you'll make that change next.

13 Choose Pagination from the Properties pop-up menu.

14 In the Format area, click Across All Columns, then click Update All.

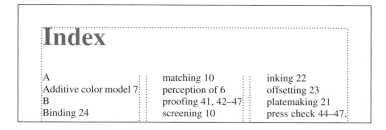

15 Save the index file.

Updating the page footer

The running page footer for a chapter in this book contains the chapter title; in the table of contents, the word *Contents* appears in the page footer. For consistency, the index title (the word *Index*) should appear in the footer of the index.

1 Choose View > Master Pages to display the Right master page.

2 Click the running header/footer variable once in the footer text frame to select the variable. (You may need to scroll down to see the footer text frame.)

If the footer appears as a gray bar rather than as text, click the Zoom In button (⊡) in the status bar until the header appears as text.

3 Choose Special > Variable, then click Edit Definition.

The variable definition uses the <$paratext> building block along with the paragraph tags for the titles of the chapter, preface, and table of contents. This definition makes the variable display the text of the chapter, preface, or table of contents title, depending on which of these appears on the page. To make the index title appear in the footer, you add the paragraph tag for the index title to the variable definition.

4 Click just inside the right bracket near the end of the variable definition.

5 Enter a comma, a space, and **IndexTitle**. (The tag you type must match exactly the paragraph format name you created in the previous section, "Adding a title.")

6 Click Edit, then click Done.

7 Choose View > Body Pages to redisplay the first page of the index. The word *Index* now appears in the page footer.

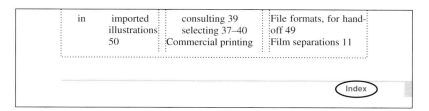

At this point, you're ready to format the entries.

Formatting the entries

When you first generated the index, FrameMaker 7.0 created and assigned paragraph tags to the entries.

1 Click in the first index entry (whose text is *Additive color model*) and notice the tag that appears in the status bar: Level1IX.

2 Press the Down Arrow key several times to move the insertion point down the page, noticing (in the status bar) that the other paragraphs also have a tag that ends in *IX* (GroupTitlesIX, Level1IX, and Level2IX).

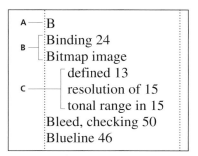

A. GroupTitlesIX B. Level1IX C. Level2IX

Formatting main entries

First you'll format the main entries (the ones tagged Level1IX).

1 Click in the first index entry (*Additive color model*).

2 In the Paragraph Designer, display the Default Font properties.

3 Change the Family to Myriad-Roman (Windows) or Myriad (Mac OS and UNIX), the Size to 8, the Spread to 5, and click Update All.

All the main entries are reformatted. Page numbers differ on different systems.

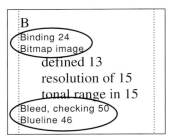

Main entries

4 Display the Basic properties in the Paragraph Designer.

5 Change the Alignment to Left and the Left Indent to 12, then click Update All.

The left indent makes multiline entries easier to read.

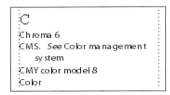

6 Display the Pagination properties.

7 Change the Widow/Orphan Lines setting to 3. This setting controls the minimum number of lines that can appear alone at the top or bottom of a column. Changing this setting to 3 will prevent multiline entries from splitting across columns or pages.

8 Click Update All.

9 Display the Advanced properties.

10 Click Hyphenate twice to turn it off, then click Update All.

The main (Level1IX) entries are formatted.

Formatting subentries

Now you'll format the subentries (the ones tagged Level2IX).

1 Click in the first subentry under *Bitmap image* (the text of the subentry is *defined*).

2 With the Advanced properties displayed in the Paragraph Designer, click Hyphenate twice to turn it off.

3 Click Update All.

4 Display the Pagination properties, change the Widow/Orphan Lines setting to 3, and click Update All.

5 Display the Default Font properties.

6 Change the Family to Myriad-Roman (Windows) or Myriad (Mac OS and UNIX), the Size to 8, and the Spread to 5.

7 Click Update All.

8 Display the Basic properties.

9 Change the Alignment to Left, the First Indent to 6, the Left Indent to 12, and click Update All.

The subentries (Level2IX entries) are formatted.

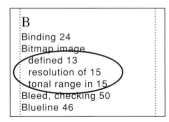

Subentries

Formatting group titles

Finally, you'll format the group titles (the paragraphs containing the letters *A, B, C,* and so on). Group titles are tagged GroupTitlesIX.

1 Click in the first group title (the letter *A* in the first line under the title).

2 With the Basic properties displayed in the Paragraph Designer, change the Space Above Pgf to 14 and click Update All.

3 Display the Default Font properties, and change the Family to Myriad-Roman (Windows) or Myriad (Mac OS and UNIX), the Size to 9, the Weight to Bold, and the Color to HeadingColor.

4 Click Update All.

The group titles are formatted.

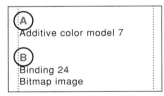

Group titles

5 Save the index.

All that remains to be formatted are the page numbers for index entries. You'll format them next.

Formatting page numbers

The format for index entry page numbers is controlled from a special page called a *reference page*.

1 Choose View > Reference Pages. Click the Page Down icon (⬇) until the one named *Reference* appears.

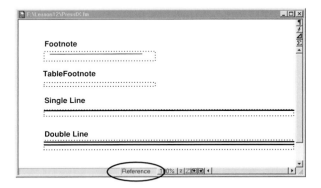

The name of the reference page called *Reference* appears in the status bar.

2 In the status bar, click the Next Page button ( ) until the IX reference page is displayed.

The reference page contains a text flow tagged IX, which contains paragraphs that specify several aspects of the index's appearance, including the format of the page numbers.

3 Click in the IndexIX paragraph (the single-line paragraph whose text is <$pagenum>).

The <$pagenum> building block specifies that the index include page numbers (rather than paragraph numbers). The paragraph's Default Font properties specify the font properties of the page numbers in the index.

You'll change the Default Font properties so that the page numbers will look the way you want when you update the index.

4 With the Default Font properties displayed in the Paragraph Designer, change the Family to Myriad-Roman (Windows) or Myriad (Mac OS and UNIX), the Size to 8, and the Spread to 5.

5 Click Update All.

You'll see the result of making this change when you generate the index again later.

Fixing bad line breaks

The entries have the general appearance you want, but the line breaks of some entries need improvement.

Changing index separators

In some entries, the page number appears alone on a line.

1 Choose View > Body Pages.

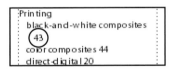

You can fix this problem by changing the character that separates the entry text from the first page number. An index entry such as *Proofing 41, 42–47* uses three types of *separators:*

- The separator between the entry text and the first page number (in this sample, a space).

- The separator between page numbers (a comma and a space).

- The separator between numbers in a page range (an en dash, –).

You can change any of these separators in an index. In this section, you'll change the space after the entry text to a comma followed by a nonbreaking space. This change will prevent bad line breaks after the entry text.

The separators that FrameMaker 7.0 uses are stored on the IX reference page.

2 Choose View > Reference Pages.

3 Choose View > Text Symbols to display text symbols.

4 Select the space at the beginning of the SeparatorsIX paragraph.

5 Type a comma and then enter a nonbreaking space by doing one of the following:

- (Windows and UNIX) Press Control+space.

- (Mac OS) Press Option+space.

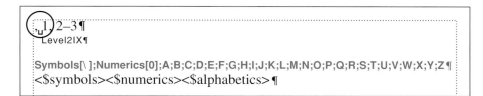

6 In the Paragraph Designer, change the Family to Myriad-Roman (Windows) or Myriad (Mac OS and UNIX), the Size to 8, and the Spread to 5.

7 Click Update All, then close the Paragraph Designer.

8 Choose View > Text Symbols to turn off text symbols.

9 Choose View > Body Pages to display the first page of the index.

Changes you make to the reference page are not reflected on the body pages until you generate the index, so the separators haven't changed yet.

10 Do one of the following:

- (Windows and Mac OS) Click in the book window, and choose Edit > Update Book.

- (UNIX) Choose Edit > Update Book in the book window.

11 Click Update.

12 Return to the index and notice that a comma now appears after the text of every entry, and that line breaks no longer occur between the entry and the page number.

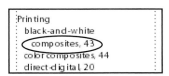

Preventing line breaks in page ranges

The index still contains some bad line breaks. In a few entries, the line breaks between page numbers in a range.

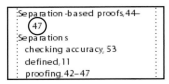

Bad line break in a page range

The line breaks after the en dash (–) between numbers in a page range because the document allows line breaks at en dashes. You'll change that next.

1 Click in the index and choose Format > Document > Text Options.

2 In the Allow Line Breaks After text box, do one of the following to prevent line breaks after en dashes:

• (Windows) Delete the forward slash (/) at the beginning of the line, the equal sign (=), and the space following it. (This backslash sequence represents an en dash in Windows dialog boxes.)

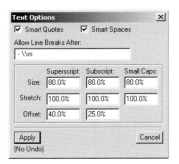

Windows

- (Mac OS) Delete the second dash and the space following it.

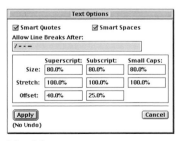

Mac OS

- (UNIX) Delete the second dash and the space following it.

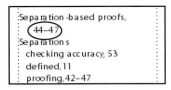

UNIX

3 Click Apply. The line no longer breaks at an en dash.

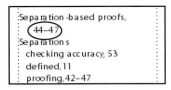

4 Save the index.

Adding index entries

You'll add a main entry and a subentry to the index. An index entry is contained in a *marker* that you insert in the source text.

1 In the book window, double-click Chapter1.fm to open the first chapter.

2 Choose View > Text Symbols to display text symbols.

3 In the chapter's status bar, click the Next Page button (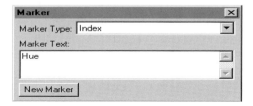) to display the second page of the chapter.

4 Click just to the left of the word *Hue* in the middle of the second line of text (at the beginning of the second sentence).

> ¶We describe color in terms of three characteristics—
> hue, value, and saturation. |Hue is the wavelength of
> light reflected from or transmitted through an object.
> More commonly, hue is identifed by the name of the
> color, such as orange, pink, or green.

5 Choose Special > Marker.

6 Move the Marker dialog box so it doesn't obscure your view of the insertion point in the chapter.

7 In the Marker dialog box, make sure Index is chosen in the Marker Type pop-up menu.

8 Click in the Marker Text box and enter **Hue**.

Marker	✕
Marker Type:	Index ▼
Marker Text:	
Hue	
New Marker	

9 Click New Marker to insert the index marker. A marker symbol (⊤) appears at the insertion point. The next time you generate the index, an entry will appear for *Hue*.

> ¶We describe color in terms of three characteristics—
> hue, value, and saturation.⊤Hue is the wavelength of
> light reflected from or transmitted through an object.
> More commonly, hue is identifed by the name of the
> color, such as orange, pink, or green.

10 In the chapter's status bar, click the Previous Page button (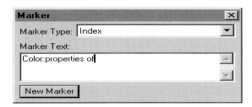) to redisplay the first page of the chapter.

11 Click at the beginning of the heading *The properties of color.*

12 In the Marker dialog box, enter **Color:properties of** in the Marker Text box. This is the text of an index entry for "Color" with a subentry of "properties of." The colon indicates a subentry; two colons would create nested subentries.

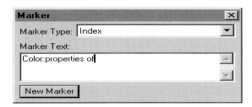

Note: If the document window obscures the Marker dialog box, you can redisplay the dialog box (choose Special >Marker) or click its title bar to bring it forward.

13 Click New Marker and close the Marker dialog box.

14 Save and close Chapter1.fm.

15 From the book window, choose Edit > Update Book.

(⬛)*Online Help provides a list of building blocks and their meanings for adding index markers with subentries, multiple entries, and page ranges.*

16 Click Update in the Update Book dialog box to generate the index. After a few moments, the index is updated.

17 Display the first page of the index. The new entry for *Hue* now appears on the first page in the third column. Also, the new subentry for *Color* appears in the first column.

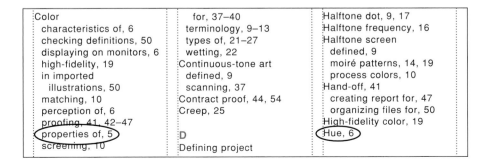

Editing index entries

After you generate an index, you may find errors in the index. For example:

• An inconsistency may cause an incorrect entry.

```
P
Page creep.  See
Perfect binding, 25
Pixel, 13
Pixels, 15
Platemaking, 21
```

Two entries should appear on one line.

• A typographical error may cause a problem in a page range.

```
O
Object-level overprinting, 12
Object-oriented graphic, 13
Offset lithography, 21–??
Offset litography, ??–24
Offsetting, 23
```

Spelling error

• A *cross-reference* entry (a *see* entry that refers the reader to another index entry) may include a page number.

```
L
Laminate proof, 46
Lightness, 6
Linescreen.  See Screen
    ruling 5
Linked graphics, 50
```

Page number appears where it shouldn't.

When you set up the index, you selected Create Hypertext Links. This lets you trace entries back to their corresponding markers in the chapters. You'll use these hypertext links to locate the index markers whose text you need to change.

Correcting an inconsistency

First you'll correct the spelling inconsistency.

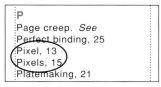

Two entries should appear as a single entry.

You'll remove the *s* from the second entry so that the index will contain one entry for *Pixel*, with two page numbers.

1 Display the second page of the index.

2 Place the text cursor (I) over the *Pixels* entry.

3 Do one of the following to display the source of the entry:

• (Windows) Press Control-Alt over the page number and the cursor changes to a pointing finger. Then click the entry.

• (Mac OS) Control-Option-click the entry.

• (UNIX) Control-right-click the entry.

The first chapter appears, with the index marker selected.

> both the clarity of detail and the tonal range that can be reproduced from bitmap images.¶
>
> A pixel is the smallest distinct unit of a bitmap image. A high-resolution bitmap image contains enough data— a description of each pixel's location and what color is

4 Choose Special > Marker.

5 Delete the *s* at the end of *Pixels* in the Marker Text box and click Edit Marker.

6 Save Chapter1.fm.

The next time you generate the index (you'll do this later), a single index entry, *Pixel*, appears with both page numbers on one line.

Correcting a spelling error

Next you'll edit a marker to fix a problem in a page range that results from a spelling error.

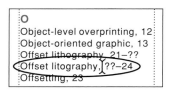

Spelling error

You indicate a page range for an index entry by inserting two markers in the text. The first marker indicates the start of the page range; the second indicates the end of the range. In this case, the second marker contains a spelling error.

1 On the second page of the index, place the pointer on the second entry with a broken page range (the entry with the spelling error *Offset litography*).

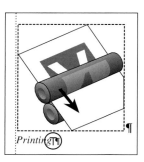

2 Do one of the following to display the end of the page range:

• (Windows) Control-Alt-click over the page number. The cursor changes to a pointing finger. Then click the entry.

• (Mac OS) Control-Option-click the entry.

• (UNIX) Control-right-click the entry.

3 If the Marker dialog box is obscured, redisplay it.

4 Click between the *t* and *o* of *litography* in the Marker Text box.

5 Enter an **h** and click Edit Marker.

6 Save Chapter1.fm.

When you generate the index again (you'll do this later), the page range will appear correctly.

Removing a page reference

Now you'll remove the page number from a cross-reference (*See*) entry.

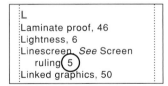

Page number appears where it shouldn't.

1 On the second page of the index, place the pointer on the page number of the *Linescreen* entry in the first column.

2 Do one of the following to display the beginning of the page range:

• (Windows) Control-Alt-click over the page number. The cursor changes to a pointing finger. Then click the entry.

• (Mac OS) Control-Option-click the entry.

• (UNIX) Control-right-click the entry.

3 If the Marker dialog box is obscured, redisplay it.

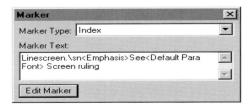

In the Marker Text box, the text enclosed in angle brackets indicates formatting instructions. <Emphasis> tells FrameMaker 7.0 to format the text that follows with the Emphasis character format (usually italics) stored in the Character Catalog of the index. <Default Para Font> tells FrameMaker 7.0 to change back to the paragraph's default font.

You'll add a building block that suppresses the page number.

4 Click at the beginning of the text in the Marker Text box.

5 Enter **<$nopage>**.

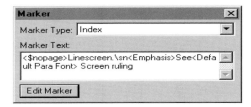

6 Click Edit Marker and close the Marker Dialog box.

7 Save and close Chapter1.fm.

8 Do one of the following:

• (Windows and Mac OS) Click in the book window, then choose Edit > Update Book.

• (UNIX) Choose Edit > Update Book in the book window.

9 Click Update in the Update Book dialog box to generate the index. After a few moments, the index is updated and the three errors you fixed no longer appear.

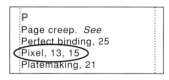

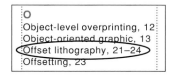

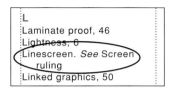

10 After inspecting the finished index, save and close both the index and the book file.

Moving on

You've completed this lesson. For in-depth information about indexes, see Chapter 14, "Tables of Contents and Indexes," in the *Adobe FrameMaker 7.0 User Guide*.

Review questions

1 When you first add an index to a book file, does FrameMaker 7.0 automatically create that file on disk?

2 When you add a title to the index, how does FrameMaker 7.0 know not to update it as it does for all the other paragraphs?

3 How do you change the text that is used to separate two pages in a page range in an index?

4 When you find an error in an index, do you fix it in the index or in the source document?

5 How are the paragraph formats Level1IX and Level2IX created and used?

6 What does a colon (:) do when entered in an index marker?

Answers

1 Adding an index to a book file only sets up some of the properties for the index file, such as its pagination and what markers will be used to compile it. You must use the Update Book dialog box to actually generate (create) the index file for the first time.

2 As long as the title is at the start of the text flow and its paragraph format does not end in *IX*, FrameMaker 7.0 will not replace the title text you type.

3 You edit the SeparatorsIX paragraph on the IX reference page to change the text that is used to separate two pages in a page range in an index.

4 You should fix index errors in the source document. Then when you generate and update the index again, the correction appears in the index.

5 FrameMaker 7.0 automatically creates and assigns these formats to the main index entries (Level1IX) and to subentries (Level2IX). By modifying the properties of these formats, you can quickly format the text of the index entries.

6 A colon separates the main entry from a subentry, or separates a subentry from a subsubentry.

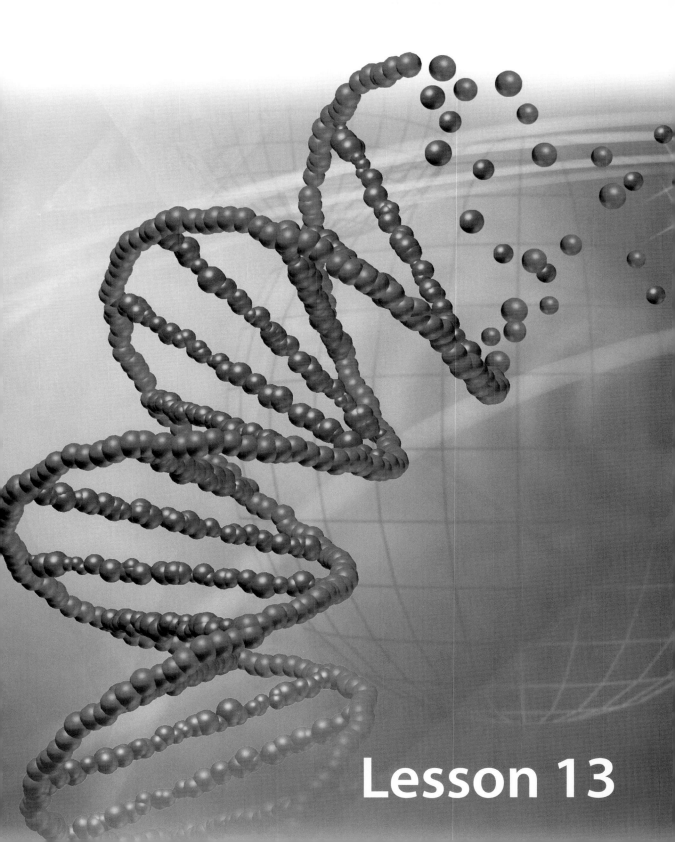

Lesson 13

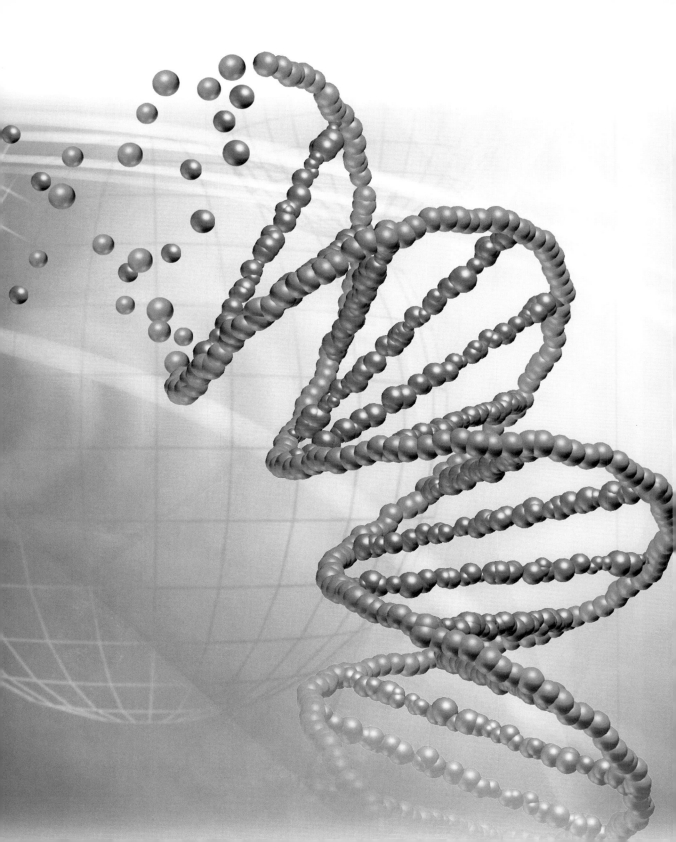

13 | Conditional Text

ModuLine CEO
High-Back Of ce Seat
Model 225K

Completely adjustable
Ergonomically designed

The CEO is our deluxe office chair with full lumbar support and
adjustable seat angle, height, and backrest positions. Comes
standard with armrests.

Colors		Coverings	
⬛	Black	⬛	Leather
⬜	Gray	⬜	Natural Wool
⬛	Tan		All fabric is pretreated with stain and moisture guard.
⬛	Sienna		

If you're preparing several versions of a document, each with minor differences, you can use a single FrameMaker 7.0 document for all the versions. When you later revise the contents, you'll be revising all the versions at the same time. The one document can contain both conditional text and conditional graphics.

This lesson's sample is a card that's designed to be attached to office furniture. The card already contains information about the ModuLine CEO office chair. You'll use conditional text to add information about a second model, the ModuLine Professional. When you're finished, the two versions of the card will be contained in one document.

In this lesson, you'll learn how to do the following:

• Create condition tags and assign condition indicators.

• Apply condition tags to text, graphics, and table rows.

• View different versions of a conditional document.

• Save versions of conditional documents.

Viewing conditional text

Before you add information about the ModuLine Professional, you'll take a look at the finished document.

1 In the Lesson13 folder, open Finished.fm.

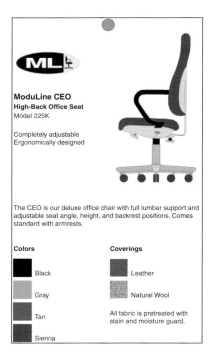

Finished.fm already contains information about both models of office chairs. The information on the CEO office chair is visible, and the information on the Professional office chair is hidden.

2 Choose Special > Conditional Text.

3 Click Show/Hide.

You'll now swap the two conditions—showing the one that's hidden, and hiding the one that's shown.

4 In the Show/Hide Conditional Text dialog box, double-click CEO to move it from the Show scroll list to the Hide scroll list.

5 Double-click Professional to move it from the Hide scroll list to the Show scroll list.

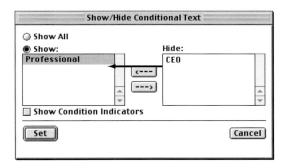

6 Click Set.

Now the information on the Professional office chair is visible, and the information on the CEO office chair is hidden. Notice that some of the text is different, that the picture of the chair is different, and that the available coverings are different.

 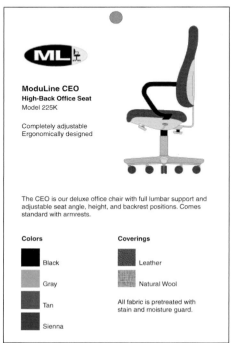

The same document showing the Professional condition (left) and the CEO condition (right)

7 Click Show/Hide.

8 Select Show Condition Indicators, then click Set.

The text that is specific to the Professional chair appears underlined and in blue.

Note: Condition indicators (in this example, the blue underlining) are present so that you can easily identify what text is in which condition. When the document is ready for final printing, you would turn these indicators off.

9 Close Finished.fm without saving your changes. Leave the Conditional Text dialog box open because you'll use it often during this lesson.

Setting up your document

The document you'll be working with contains only the information on the CEO office chair. You will add the conditional information on the Professional model.

1 Open Condit.fm in the Lesson13 folder.

2 Choose File > Save As, enter the filename **Condit1.fm**, and click Save.

When working with conditional text, it is often helpful to have borders and text symbols showing.

3 Choose View > Borders and then choose View > Text Symbols.

4 Before you begin working with conditional text, take a few moments to explore the document. Notice the following:

• The gray circle at the top (indicating the location of a hole to be drilled in the card) is drawn on the master page, so you can't select it or modify it here.

• The ModuLine corporate logo is also not selectable because it is included as part of the format of the paragraph just below it (*ModuLine CEO*). The logo is selectable only on a special *reference page,* from which FrameMaker 7.0 copies it to this body page. Placing often-used graphics on a reference page and making them part of a format reduces file size because the graphic only needs to be copied into the document once.

• The card is laid out in two columns; the descriptive paragraph in the middle of the page spans both body columns.

• The illustration of the chair is in an anchored frame that's anchored to the preceding paragraph, *Ergonomically designed*.

• The colors and coverings at the bottom of the card are arranged in tables. Each color swatch in the table is in an anchored frame.

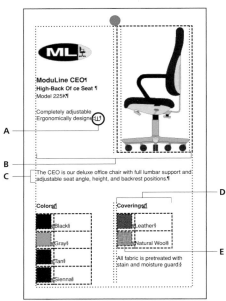

A. Anchor symbol B. Two-columns C. Paragraph spans columns D. Table E. Anchored frame

Now that you're more familiar with the document, you're ready to begin working with conditional text.

Creating condition tags

First you'll create the condition tags that will indicate the new version of this document.

1 If the Conditional Text dialog box isn't open, choose Special > Conditional Text.

2 Click Edit Condition Tag.

3 Replace the contents of the Tag text box with **Professional**.

4 Choose Underline from the Style pop-up menu and Blue from the Color pop-up menu.

5 Click Set. The new condition tag appears in the Conditional Text dialog box.

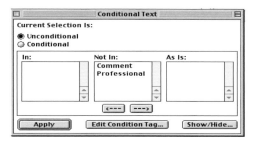

6 Click Edit Condition Tag again.

7 This time, replace the contents of the Tag text box with **CEO**. Then choose Strikethrough from the Style pop-up menu and Burgundy from the Color pop-up menu.

8 Click Set. The new condition tag appears in the Conditional Text dialog box.

The document contains a third condition tag (Comment). You won't need this tag, so you'll delete it.

9 Select Comment in the Not In scroll list and then click Edit Condition Tag.

10 Click Delete. Now only two tags appear in the Conditional Text dialog box.

11 Save the document.

Adding conditional text

Now you're ready to add some conditional text. You'll be selecting text as you work, so click the Zoom In button (☑) in the status bar whenever you want to magnify the document window contents.

Adding the model name

First you'll add conditional text for the model name.

1 Place the insertion point at the end of the *ModuLine CEO* paragraph, under the logo.

2 Press the spacebar and then type **Professional**.

3 Select *CEO* and the space before it.

4 In the Conditional Text dialog box, double-click CEO to move it to the In scroll list.

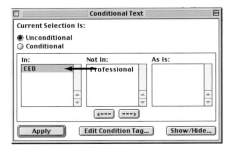

5 Click Apply. The selected text appears in the strikethrough style and the color burgundy. (To see the text more clearly, click anywhere in the document to deselect the text.)

6 Now select *Professional* and the space before it. (Drag from the right of *Professional* back to the end of the word *CEO*.)

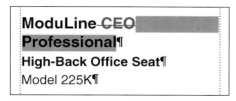

Note: Be careful not to select the paragraph symbol (¶). If you accidentally make the paragraph symbol conditional, the next paragraph will run into the current one when you show only the CEO version of the card.

7 In the Conditional Text dialog box, double-click Professional to move it to the In scroll list.

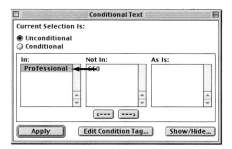

8 Click Apply.

9 Click anywhere to deselect the conditional text, which is now underlined and blue (which indicates the Professional condition).

Now you'll change the conditional text settings to see the results of your work.

10 In the Conditional Text dialog box, click Show/Hide.

11 Double-click Professional to move it to the Hide scroll list, and then click Set.

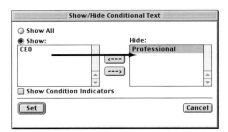

The text that's specific to the Professional version is now collapsed into a special marker (⊤). When you edit a document that contains hidden conditional text, be careful not to delete these markers. If you do, you'll delete hidden text.

12 In the Conditional Text dialog box, click Show/Hide.

13 Double-click Professional to move it to the Show scroll list.

14 Double-click CEO to move it to the Hide scroll list. Then click Set.

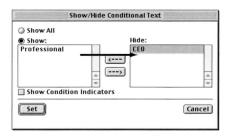

The text that's specific to the CEO version is now hidden.

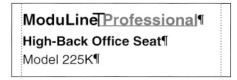

You'll now show both conditions before adding more conditional text.

15 Click Show/Hide. Then click Show All and click Set.

> **ModuLine** ~~CEO~~
> Professional¶
> **High-Back Office Seat¶**
> Model 225K¶

Adding a brief description

Now you'll add an entire paragraph of conditional text.

Place the insertion point at the end of the second paragraph, *High-Back Office Seat*.

1 Press Return and type **Low-Back Office Seat**.

> **ModuLine** ~~CEO~~
> Professional¶
> **High-Back Office Seat¶**
> **Low-Back Office Seat¶**
> Model 225K¶

2 Triple-click *High-Back Office Seat* to select the entire paragraph (including the paragraph symbol).

> **ModuLine** ~~CEO~~
> Professional¶
> **High-Back Office Seat¶**
> **Low-Back Office Seat¶**
> Model 225K¶

3 In the Conditional Text dialog box, double-click CEO to move it to the In scroll list. Then click Apply.

4 Triple-click *Low-Back Office Seat* to select the entire paragraph (including the paragraph symbol).

5 In the Conditional Text dialog box, double-click Professional to move it to the In scroll list. Then click Apply.

ModuLine CEO
Professional¶
High-Back Office Seat¶
Low-Back Office Seat¶
Model 225K¶

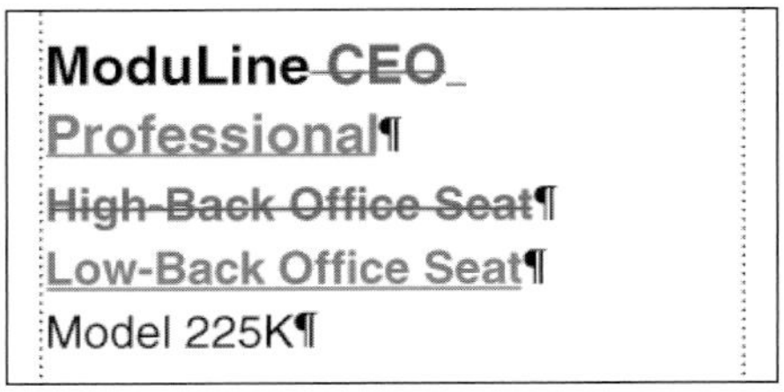

Adding a model number

Next you'll add the model number of the Professional chair.

1 Click at the end of the paragraph containing the model number, *Model 225K*.

2 Press the spacebar and then type **186P**.

3 Select *225K* and the space before it.

ModuLine CEO
Professional¶
High-Back Office Seat¶
Low-Back Office Seat¶
Model 225K 186P¶

4 In the Conditional Text dialog box, double-click CEO to move it to the In scroll list. Then click Apply.

5 Now select *186P* and the space before it. (Drag from the right of *186P* back to the end of the *225K*. Dragging back from the end of the line prevents you from selecting the paragraph symbol.)

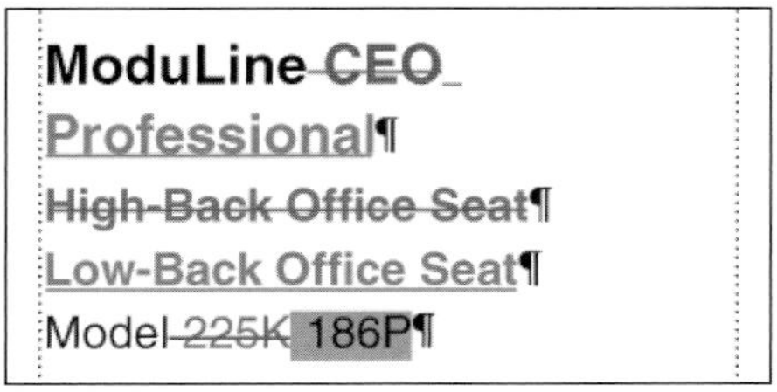

ModuLine CEO
Professional¶
High-Back Office Seat¶
Low-Back Office Seat¶
Model 225K 186P¶

6 In the Conditional Text dialog box, double-click Professional to move it to the In scroll list. Then click Apply.

7 Experiment with showing different conditions to make sure that the conditional text works the way you want. You can also turn off borders and text symbols. When you're finished, show all conditional text again, and make sure that borders and text symbols are visible.

ModuLine CEO	**ModuLine Professional**
High-Back Office Seat	**Low-Back Office Seat**
Model 225K	Model 186P

CEO version (left) and the Professional version (right)

Adding more conditional text

Finally, you'll add some conditional text to the body paragraph below the graphic. (Make sure that borders, text symbols, and all conditions are visible.)

1 Click to the right of the word *CEO* in the body paragraph that spans both columns.

> The CEO is our deluxe office chair with full lumbar support and adjustable seat angle, height, and backrest positions.¶

2 Press the spacebar, type **Professional**, and press the spacebar again.

3 Click to the right of the word *deluxe* in the same paragraph.

4 Press the spacebar, type **standard**, and press the spacebar again.

5 Use the Conditional Text dialog box to apply the CEO tag to the words *CEO* and *deluxe*, and to apply the Professional tag to the words *Professional* and *standard*.

Note: *Be sure to apply the tag to the space before each word as well as to the word itself. If you don't, some versions of the document may have too many spaces and others may have too few.*

> The CEO Professional is our deluxe standard office chair with full lumbar support and adjustable seat angle, height, and backrest positions.¶

Tagging text as you type

If you need to work extensively with conditional text, you may find it easier to use keyboard shortcuts to apply and remove condition tags. Next, you'll use keyboard shortcuts to add conditional text to the body paragraph.

1 Click to place the insertion point at the end of the body paragraph that spans both columns.

The ~~CEO~~ Professional is our ~~deluxe~~ standard office chair with full lumbar support and adjustable seat angle, height, and backrest positions.¶

First you'll type a sentence using the CEO condition tag.

2 Press Control+4. The status bar changes to prompt you for a condition tag.

3 Type the letter **C**. Because the CEO condition tag is the only one that begins with the letter *C*, the prompt changes to indicate that tag.

Note: In Windows and on UNIX systems, you don't need to type the letter C, because the first condition tag in alphabetical order appears in the Tag area of the status bar when you press Control+4.

4 Press Return. The condition tag is applied to the text at the insertion point.

5 Press the spacebar and type **Comes standard with armrests**. Then type a period to end the sentence.

Notice that the status bar shows the CEO condition tag in parentheses. If you type more text at the insertion point, the text will continue to use the CEO condition. Next you'll type a sentence that uses the Professional condition, so you'll need to remove the CEO condition. You'll use a keyboard shortcut that removes all conditions.

6 Press Control+6. The status bar now shows no condition tags, which means text you type at this point would be unconditional.

7 Press Control+4, then type the letter **P**. The status bar prompt changes to the Professional tag.

8 Press Return. Now the Professional condition tag is applied at the insertion point.

9 Press the spacebar and type **Available with or without armrests**. Then type a period to end the sentence.

10 Save the document.

Adding a conditional graphic

The card currently contains a graphic of the CEO office chair. The graphic is in an anchored frame whose anchor symbol appears at the end of the paragraph *Ergonomically designed*.

For this document to work as the single source for the cards for both the CEO chair and the Professional chair, the graphic as well as the text needs to be conditional. You'll do this next by importing a graphic for the Professional chair, and then making the graphic's anchored frame conditional.

1 Click the bottom border of the anchored frame to select the frame. Handles appear around the anchored frame.

Note: Be sure you click at the edge of the anchored frame to select the frame and not the graphic. If you can't see all eight handles around the selected frame, you probably accidentally clicked the graphic instead of the frame.

2 Choose Edit > Copy.

3 Click to the right of the paragraph *Ergonomically designed* to place the insertion point to the right of the anchor symbol.

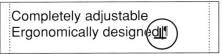

4 Choose Edit > Paste. Now the document contains two anchored frames. Don't worry about their placement. When you display only one condition tag, the document will be formatted correctly.

5 Click the graphic that appears in the new anchored frame (the one on the left) to select it. (Don't select the anchored frame.)

6 Choose File > Import > File.

7 Select Pro.tif in the scroll list and click Replace.

8 In the Imported Graphic Scaling dialog box, click 72 dpi to indicate the dots per inch for the graphic, and then click Set.

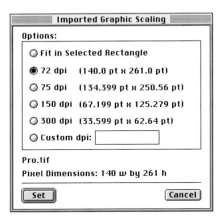

The graphic of the Professional office chair now appears in the left-hand anchored frame, replacing the original.

The bottom of the graphic is slightly cropped by the anchored frame. You'll reposition it to fix this.

9 Display the Graphics menu to make sure that Snap is turned off. If it's not turned off, choose Graphics > Snap.

10 Drag the graphic a bit up and to the left until it's no longer cropped.

Now you'll make the graphics conditional by selecting the anchored frames and then applying the appropriate condition tag.

11 Click the bottom edge of the anchored frame that contains the graphic of the CEO chair (the one with armrests). This selects the anchored frame. Don't select the graphic itself.

12 Press Control+4, type the letter **C**, and press Return.

13 Select the anchored frame that contains the graphic of the Professional chair (the one without armrests).

14 Press Control+4, type the letter **P**, and press Return.

15 Experiment with showing different conditions to see how the conditional text and graphics work together. You can also turn off borders, text symbols, and condition indicators.

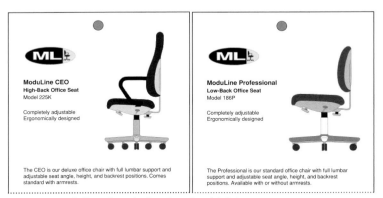

CEO version (left) and Professional version (right)

16 Show all conditional text again, and make sure that borders, text symbols, and condition indicators are visible.

17 Save the document.

Adding conditional table rows

Just one more change is needed before the document is fully conditionalized. The CEO model is available in several types of chair coverings, but the Professional model is available in only one. For this reason, you'll need to make one of the rows in the Coverings table conditional.

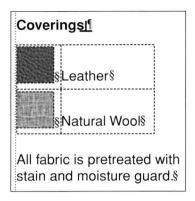

When you make a table row conditional, the entire row disappears when you hide its condition. (If you were to apply a condition to the *contents* of a table cell instead of the row itself, the text would disappear when you hide the condition, but the empty table cell would remain.)

1 Click the Next Page button (⊡) in the status bar to display page 2.

2 Drag from the table cell containing the word *Leather* into the cell to its left, containing the leather swatch. Both cells are selected.

3 Press Control+4, type the letter **C**, and press Return.

4 Click anywhere on the page to deselect the row. The row appears with a cross-hatched border whose color indicates the condition (in this case, the CEO condition).

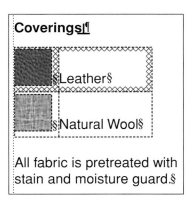

5 Click the Previous Page button (⊡) in the status bar to display page 1.

6 Experiment with showing different conditions to see how the conditional table row works. When you're finished, show all conditional text again.

7 Save the document.

Saving versions of a conditional document

When a conditional document is complete, you may want to create a separate document for each of the versions. For example, you may need to hand off the files to a commercial printer or to someone who might be confused by the presence of the conditional markers in the text. Always retain the original conditional document, so you can edit the versions easily if the need arises.

Saving the CEO version

First you'll save a CEO version of the document. You'll do this by deleting the conditional text and graphic for the Professional version.

1 Use the File > Save As command to save the document as CEO.fm.

2 In the Conditional Text dialog box, select Professional in a scroll list and click Edit Condition Tag.

3 In the Edit Condition Tag dialog box, click Delete.

4 In the Delete Condition Tag dialog box, click Delete the Text.

5 Click OK. The document now contains just the CEO version.

6 If condition indicators are visible, click Show/Hide in the Conditional Text dialog box, turn off Show Condition Indicators, and click Set.

7 Choose View > Borders and View > Text Symbols to see how the document will look when printed.

8 Save and close CEO.fm.

Saving the Professional version

Now you'll save a Professional version by deleting the conditional text and graphic for the CEO version.

1 Open Condit1.fm again.

2 Use the File > Save As command to save the document as Pro.fm.

3 In the Conditional Text dialog box, select CEO in a scroll list and click Edit Condition Tag.

4 In the Edit Condition Tag dialog box, click Delete.

5 In the Delete Condition Tag dialog box, click Delete the Text and then click OK. The document now contains just the Professional version.

6 If condition indicators are visible, click Show/Hide in the Conditional Text dialog box, turn off Show Condition Indicators, and click Set.

7 Choose View > Borders and then View > Text Symbols.

8 Save and close Pro.fm.

9 Close the Conditional Text dialog box.

Moving on

You've completed this lesson. For in-depth information about conditional text, see Chapter 16, "Conditional Text," in the *Adobe FrameMaker 7.0 User Guide*.

Review questions

1 What are the advantages of a conditional document?

2 Why is it useful to work with condition indicators showing?

3 Why is it important to apply conditions to spaces and paragraph symbols carefully?

4 How can you tell if text is conditional?

5 How can you apply a condition to text?

6 How can you make text unconditional?

7 How do you make a graphic conditional?

8 What is the main difference between conditionalizing the contents of a table cell and conditionalizing the entire row?

Answers

1 A conditional document lets you work in a single source but different versions of the same document. This reduces redundancy and improves efficiency.

2 Condition indicators make it easy to see what text is in which condition. This reduces the chances of errors when editing.

3 If the spaces surrounding conditional text are not also conditional, there may be too many or too few spaces in the versions. Making a paragraph symbol conditional means that the paragraph return will be hidden when that condition is hidden—resulting in the paragraph running into the next.

4 If text is conditional, then the status line displays the condition tag for the selected text or the insertion point.

5 You can apply a condition to text by pressing Control+4, typing the letters of the condition tag until it appears in the status line, and then pressing Return. You can also use the Special > Conditional Text command, moving the condition tag to the In scroll list, and then clicking Apply.

6 You can make text unconditional by pressing Control+6.

7 You make a graphic conditional by placing it in an anchored frame, selecting the frame, and then applying a condition to the frame just as you would with text.

8 When you hide a condition that has been applied to the contents of a table cell, the contents disappear but the cell remains. When you hide a condition that has been applied to the entire row of a table, the whole row disappears.

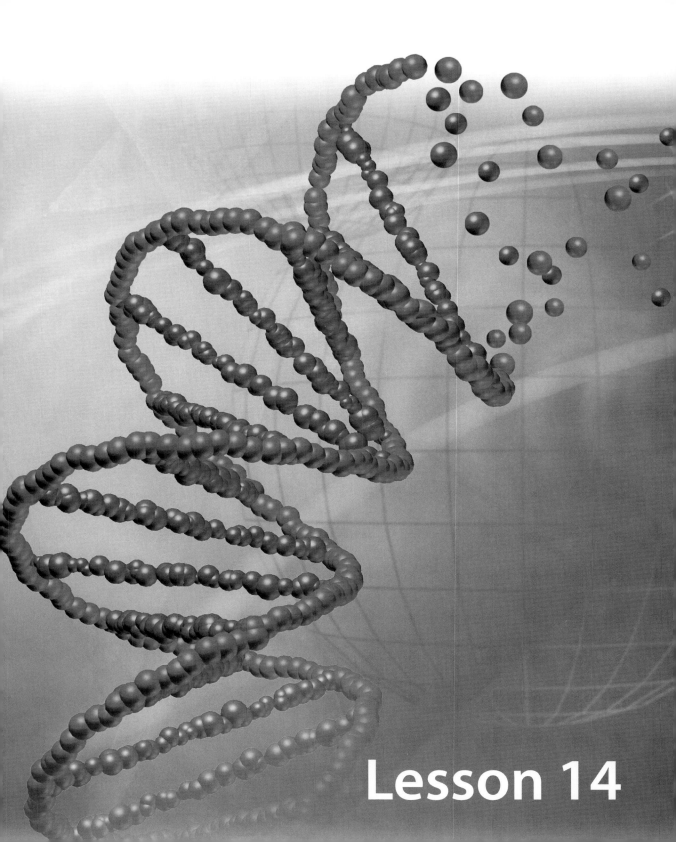

Lesson 14

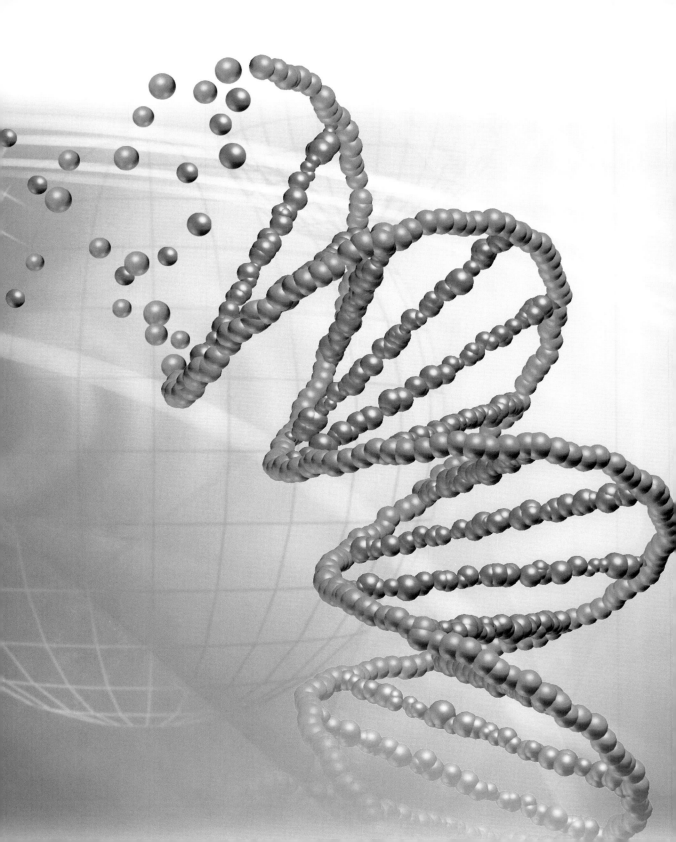

14 | Hypertext and PDF

Hypertext documents make it easy to access information in a nonlinear way. Hypertext commands let readers easily move around in a view-only document. FrameMaker 7.0 includes a robust set of hypertext commands that can turn a document into an online application. You can also save a document as a Portable Document Format (PDF) file, which preserves the design of the original and includes many hypertext features. The PDF file can be viewed with Acrobat or Acrobat Reader or directly in a Web browser.

This lesson uses a book file that contains two chapters of a textbook on electricity. You'll generate a table of contents and index that are linked to the chapters by means of hypertext commands. You'll then see how cross-references can become hypertext links in view-only files. You'll enhance the documents for online use by adding hypertext navigation buttons. Finally, you'll convert the files to Portable Document Format (PDF) to compare this type of online distribution with FrameMaker 7.0's built-in ability to create view-only hypertext documents.

If you want to see completed versions of the sample files, open the Finished folder in the Lesson14 folder.

You'll learn how to do the following:

• Create a table of contents and an index that contain hypertext links.

• Modify a cross-reference format to make it clearer that cross-references work as hypertext links.

• Test hypertext commands in the documents of a book.

• Add a graphical navigation bar that uses hypertext commands.

• Save a book file in PDF and test the hypertext links in the converted files.

Creating a hypertext TOC and index

One of the easiest ways to create hypertext commands is to generate a table of contents (a TOC) or an index so that entries in these files automatically contain hypertext links to the locations they refer to.

Setting up a book file

Hyper.book already has a table of contents and an index set up for you. You only have to make a small adjustment to the setup of these files to create hypertext links automatically.

1 In the Lesson14 folder, open Hyper.book. (You won't be saving copies of the sample files in this lesson. If you want to start over, you can get fresh copies of the files from the CD-ROM.)

This book file contains a table of contents, two chapter files, and an index.

2 Select Hyper1.fm in the book window by clicking it once.

3 Choose Add > Table of Contents. A dialog box appears to Set up TOC.

4 Move Heading1, Heading 2, and Heading3 from Don't Include to Include Elements/Paragraphs by double-clicking each or by using the move arrow (<---).

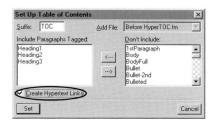

5 Make sure that Create Hypertext Links is checked.

6 Click Add.

7 You won't generate the table of contents yet, so click Cancel to close the Update Book dialog box that appears.

Now you'll set up the index to contain hypertext links.

8 Select Hyper2.fm by clicking on it once.

9 Choose Add > Standard Index. The Setup Standard Index dialog box appears.

10 Be sure that Create Hypertext Links is checked. Then click Add.

Now you'll generate the table of contents and the index from the Update Book dialog box.

11 Be sure the two files (HyperTOC.fm and HyperIX.fm) are in the Generate list on the left.

12 Deselect Apply Master Pages. Click Update.

Note: If the program fails to update the book, hold down the Shift key and choose File > Open All Files in Book. Then proceed to Update the book.

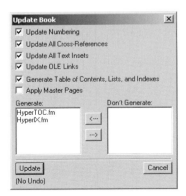

Using a hypertext TOC and index

You can now see how each TOC index entry is linked to its source.

1 Double-click HyperTOC.fm in the book window to open the new table of contents.

The table of contents is nicely formatted because a template for it already existed in the folder.

2 Locate the section on the first page called "The Achievements of Nicola Tesla" and do one of the following to activate the hypertext link embedded in the TOC entry:

- (Windows) Control-Alt-click the entry.

- (Mac OS) Control-Option-click the entry.

- (UNIX) Control-right-click the entry.

FrameMaker 7.0 opens Hyper1.fm and displays and selects the section heading that contains the hypertext marker (*The Achievements of Nicola Tesla*).

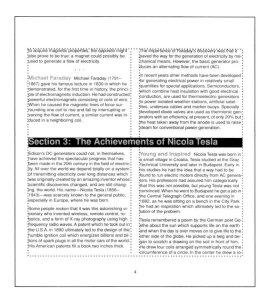

3 If you want, go back to the TOC and repeat the previous step on another entry.

4 Double-click the index file in the book window and test the hypertext links there by following the procedure in step 2, putting the cursor on the page number. (To activate a hypertext link in an index, you usually click a page number instead of the text of the index entry.)

5 When you're finished, close all the documents, but keep the book window open.

6 Save the book file.

Using cross-references as hypertext links

Now you're ready to explore another way that FrameMaker 7.0 automatically creates hypertext links. Every cross-reference you insert in a document can be used as a hypertext link to its source.

Testing a cross-reference link

First you'll see how a cross-reference can be a hypertext link.

1 Double-click Hyper1.fm in the book window to open the first chapter file.

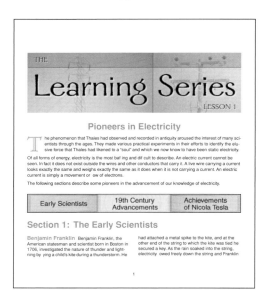

2 Go to page 3.

3 Locate the last paragraph in the subsection on Thomas Alva Edison. The last sentence in this paragraph has a cross-reference to a section named "The Achievements of Nicola Tesla."

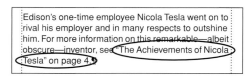

4 Do one of the following to activate the hypertext link embedded in the cross-reference:

• (Windows) Control-Alt-click the cross-reference.

• (Mac OS) Control-Option-click the cross-reference.

• (UNIX) Control-right-click the cross-reference.

FrameMaker 7.0 jumps to the source of this cross-reference entry—in this case, to the start of the section on Nicola Tesla on page 4.

Formatting a hypertext cross-reference

When you are creating a hypertext application for online use, it's helpful to draw attention to objects that are links. This is especially true with cross-references, which usually look like regular paragraph text.

1 Go back to page 3 to the last paragraph in the subsection on Thomas Alva Edison and double-click the cross-reference "The Achievements of Nicola Tesla." This opens the Cross-Reference dialog box.

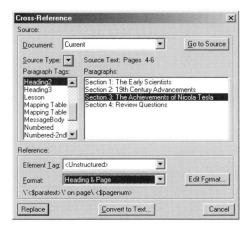

You'll change the format for this cross-reference so that it will stand out as a hypertext link.

2 Click Edit Format.

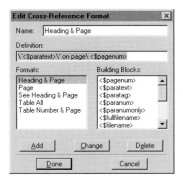

The format for this cross-reference is called Heading & Page, whose definition is \'<$paratext>\' on page\ <$pagenum>.

On the Mac OS, the format's definition is this: "<$paratext>" on page\ <$pagenum>.

This format uses a backslash-sequence for some special characters:

• (Windows and UNIX) \'results in an open double quotation mark (") and \' results in a closing double quotation mark (").

• \ (space) results in a nonbreaking space.

You'll now modify this format to use a character format that will make the text purple and underlined, so that it's clear that a cross-reference is a hypertext link.

3 Click at the start of the definition to place the insertion point.

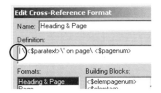

4 Scroll to the end of the Building Blocks list to find the character format building block named <Link>, then click it. The definition now includes < Link> and looks like this: <Link>\'<$paratext>\' on page\ <$pagenum>.

On the Mac OS, the definition is this: <Link>"<$paratext>" on page\ <$pagenum>.

Hyper1.fm already has a Link character format stored in the character catalog. This format will make text purple and underlined so that hypertext jumps are easy to spot in the document.

5 Click Change, then click Done. The Update Cross-References dialog box appears.

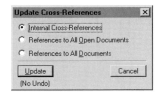

6 Make sure Internal Cross-References is selected, then click Update.

7 Click Done to close the Cross-Reference dialog box.

All the cross-references in the document that use the Heading & Page format change to purple and underlined. (There are two of them, both on page 3.)

> away to the critical gap which extinguished the light.
> As a researcher and lecturer at the Royal Institution
> Davy worked closely with Michael Faraday (see
> "Michael Faraday" on page 4) who rst joined the in-
> stitution as his manservant and later became his
> secretary.¶

> Edison's one-time employee Nicola Tesla went on to
> rival his employer and in many respects to outshine
> him. For more information on this remarkable—albeit
> obscure—inventor, see "The Achievements of Nicola
> Tesla" on page 4.¶

8 Save and close the document.

Testing hypertext links

As you saw in the previous sections, you can always test a hypertext link by using a special keystroke. This sort of testing is handy for checking the source of a link (that is, for seeing where the hypertext jumps to).

However, for a better idea of what the overall document will look like and how it will work as part of an online application, you can *lock* the document to put it in view-only format. A document in view-only format has all its hypertext commands active.

In this section, you'll see how to make a document view-only to test hypertext links.

1 From the book file, hold down Shift and choose File > Open All Files in Book. If the documents open minimized, restore them to their normal size.

2 From one of the documents (it doesn't matter which one), choose Special > Hypertext.

3 Click Make View-Only in the Hypertext dialog box and leave the dialog box open.

Note: *On the Mac OS, clicking a document brings it to the front, which might obscure the Hypertext dialog box. You may have to move or resize the document window so that both it and the Hypertext dialog box are visible.*

FrameMaker 7.0 locks the document, making it view-only, and activates hypertext links.

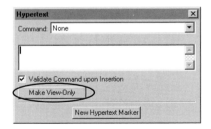

4 Lock each remaining document by clicking in a document, then clicking Make View-Only in the Hypertext dialog box. Leave the dialog box open.

5 From the book file, hold down Shift and choose File > Save All Files in Book.

Now that the files are locked and saved, you can test them more fully.

6 Display the HyperTOC.fm file to view the table of contents.

7 Click the page number of a TOC entry to display that page.

8 Right-click or Control-click (Mac OS) on the document to display the context menu.

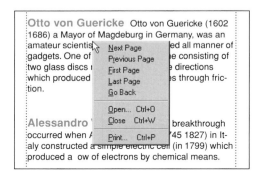

This context menu contains several handy commands for getting around in view-only documents.

9 Choose Last Page from the context menu.

10 Display the HyperIX.fm file to view the index.

11 Click a page number for an index entry to display that page.

12 Display the Hyper1.fm file again and find one of the purple, underlined cross-references on page 3.

13 Click one of the cross-references to jump to its source.

14 If you want, continue navigating around the files by clicking more hypertext TOC and index links and using the commands on the context menu. Leave the Hypertext dialog box open; you'll use it in the next group of steps.

Adding navigation buttons

A reader moves through a FrameMaker 7.0 hypertext system by scrolling, by using commands on the Navigation menu, by using commands on the context menu that appears after a right-click (a Control-click on the Mac OS), or by clicking specially prepared *active areas*.

You've already seen that FrameMaker 7.0 creates several types of active areas automatically—cross-references and entries in generated TOCs and indexes automatically become active when they are in a view-only document. However, there are other types of hypertext commands you can create yourself that can help users navigate in a hypertext system.

In this section, you'll enter hypertext commands to create a navigation bar. The finished document will look like this (the navigation bar is in the upper right corner):

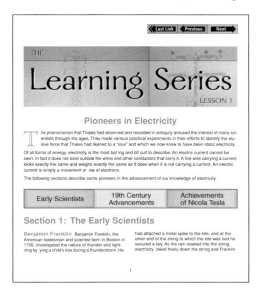

Preparing an active area

To add a navigation bar, you'll need to add graphics for the bar buttons to the master pages of the document. Adding a graphic to the master pages instead of to body pages is an easy way to make it appear on all the pages of the documents.

First, you'll copy the graphic and paste it on a master page of one of the chapter files.

1 Open all the files in the book, if necessary, and unlock each of them by clicking the Make Editable button in the Hypertext dialog box.

💡 SHORTCUT FOR UNLOCKING DOCUMENTS: *If you closed the Hypertext dialog box at the end of the last section, you can unlock the documents by using a keyboard shortcut instead.*

- Press Esc.
- Then press Shift+f.
- Then type l (lowercase L) k.

2 Open Buttons.fm from the Lesson14 folder. This document has been included because it contains a simple graphic that you'll use for the navigation bar.

Each of the three arrow graphics will represent a different hypertext command.

3 Click the graphic to select it and choose Edit > Copy.

4 Close Buttons.fm and display Hyper1.fm.

5 Choose View > Master Pages.

6 Choose Edit > Paste. The graphic is pasted in the center of the master page.

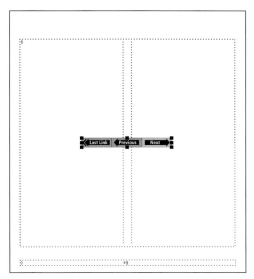

7 Drag the graphic to the upper right corner, outside the text frame.

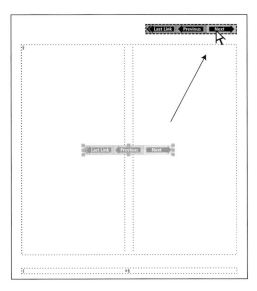

8 Display the Tools palette by clicking the Tools palette button (▲).

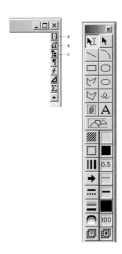

To make each arrow graphic work as a separate hypertext command, each will have to have its own text frame around it (and each text frame will contain a hypertext command).

9 Click the Text Frame tool (▦) and drag a text frame over the leftmost button graphic. (If you have trouble making the text frame the size you want, turn off the snap grid by choosing Graphics > Snap.)

10 When you release the mouse button, FrameMaker 7.0 asks what kind of frame you want to draw here. Click Background Text and then click Add.

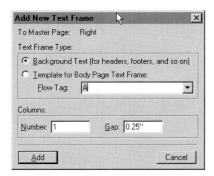

11 With the text frame selected, choose None from the Fill pop-up menu (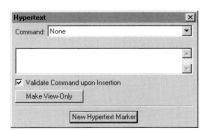) in the Tools palette.

12 Repeat step 9 through step 11 for the other two button graphics. Use the selection handles to adjust the size of the frames if you need to.

13 If the text boxes appear to have a white background, go to Window > Refresh or press control + l (lowercase L) to redraw the screen.

All three graphics now have their own text frames over them, and you're ready to add hypertext commands.

Adding hypertext commands

The best way to insert a hypertext command into a document is to use the Hypertext dialog box.

1 With the Smart Select tool (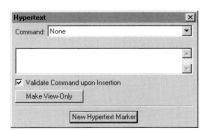), click in the leftmost text frame to place the insertion point there.

2 If the Hypertext dialog box isn't open, choose Special > Hypertext.

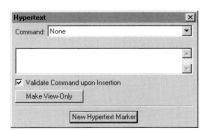

3 From the Command pop-up menu, choose Jump Back, and then click New Hypertext Marker. You've inserted a previouslink hypertext command. All hypertext commands entered through this dialog box are contained in markers (T).

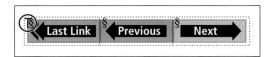

In a view-only document, the previouslink command moves you back to the last pages you jumped to, in turn, even if the pages are in different documents.

4 Click in the middle text frame.

5 In the Hypertext dialog box, choose Jump to Previous Page from the Command pop-up menu, then click New Hypertext Marker. You've inserted a previouspage hypertext command. The previouspage command moves you to the previous page of the view-only document.

6 Click in the rightmost text frame.

7 In the Hypertext dialog box, choose Jump to Next Page from the Command pop-up menu, then click New Hypertext Marker. You've inserted a nextpage hypertext command. The nextpage command moves you to the next page of the view-only document.

8 Drag a selection box around the entire graphic and the three text frames to select them all.

9 Choose Graphics > Group to group them as a single object. (Refresh the screen if necessary.)

10 Choose Edit > Copy, scroll to the other master page, and choose Edit > Paste. The grouped graphic is now placed in the same spot on all the master pages of the document, which means it will appear on every page.

11 Choose View > Body Pages.

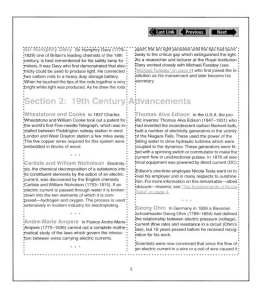

12 In the Hypertext dialog box, click Make View-Only to lock the document so you can test the hypertext commands you just inserted.

13 Choose Fit Page in Window from the Zoom pop-up menu so that the whole page is visible.

14 Click the graphic buttons to see how they work as navigation tools.

15 If you want, you can paste the graphic onto the master pages of the other documents of the book as well.

16 When you're finished, make sure all the documents are unlocked (including the index and table of contents), then close the Hypertext dialog box.

17 Close all the documents, but leave the book window open. If prompted to save the documents, click Yes.

Saving as Hypertext, HTML

To convert a FrameMaker document to HTML, save it as an HTML file. Saving as HTML sets up definitions for how each FrameMaker format converts, or maps, to an HTML element. You can save a whole book as HTML.

FrameMaker automatically creates the mappings of formats to HTML elements upon initial conversion to HTML, but you can fine-tune them.

It is a good idea to choose a separate directory for the files created by a conversion to HTML because you could create a number of them. Keeping the files in a separate directory also makes it possible to move them without changing their relative relationships.

To save a document in HTML format:

1 Open any document in the book.

2 Choose File / Save As and from the pop-up menu, select HTML.

3 Give the filename an extension of .html, specify the file location, and click Save.

The converted file is saved where you specified.

4 Open the HTML file in a Web browser to review the converted file.

Saving as PDF

FrameMaker 7.0 lets you save a document or a book directly as a Portable Document Format (PDF) file. Readers use Acrobat Reader or Acrobat Exchange to view PDF files. PDF files can also be viewed in most Web browser windows.

Saving as PDF preserves the design and format of the original and creates a compact, online system with many automatic hypertext features enabled. For example, cross-references in FrameMaker 7.0 become links in the PDF file.

Note: To save a document as PDF in FrameMaker 7.0, you must have installed Acrobat Distiller 5.05, which comes on your program CD. Ordinarily, you should have installed Acrobat Distiller when you installed FrameMaker 7.0. If you didn't, or if you removed it, you won't be able to perform the following steps until you install it.

1 If it isn't already open, open the book file Hyper.book.

2 Choose File > Save Book As, and navigate to the folder where you want to save the PDF file.

3 Choose PDF from the pop-up menu, and enter **Hyper.pdf** as the filename. Click Save.

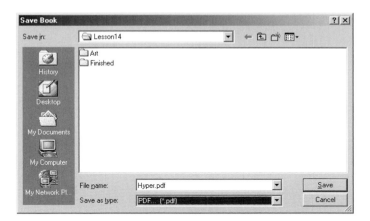

The PDF Setup dialog box now appears.

4 Choose Bookmarks from the pop-up menu. Here, you'll use the next few steps to specify what paragraphs you want to appear as Acrobat "bookmarks" in the final PDF file—ChapterTitleTOC, Heading1, Heading2, Heading3, and TitleTOC/Index.

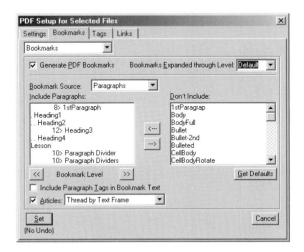

5 Hold down Shift and click the move Right Arrow button (--->) to move all the paragraphs to the Don't Include scroll list.

6 Scroll in the Don't Include list until you see ChapterTitleTOC, then double-click it to move it back to the Include Paragraphs list.

7 Repeat step 6 to move the following paragraphs back to the Include Paragraphs list: Heading1, Heading2, Heading3, and TitleTOC/Index.

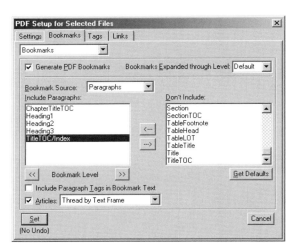

Now indent the headings to show how the Acrobat bookmarks will be nested in the PDF file.

8 Select Heading2, then click the right Bookmark Level arrow button once. Heading2 is now indented below Heading1.

9 Select Heading3, then click the right Bookmark Level arrow button twice. Heading3 is now indented below Heading2.

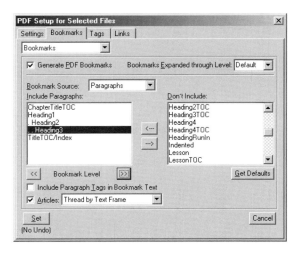

10 Click Set. After a few moments, the Hyper.pdf file appears in the folder you specified.

If you have Acrobat Reader or Exchange installed, you can now look at the PDF file.

11 Open Acrobat Reader or Exchange and open the Hyper.pdf file.

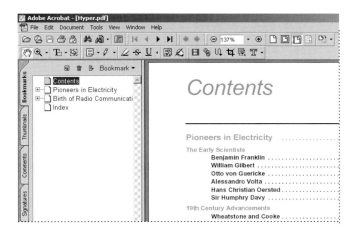

Because you generated the table of contents and the index with hypertext links, those links are active in the PDF file as well.

12 Click an entry in the TOC to move to the section indicated.

13 Click Index to display the index and find the entry for Thales. Click the page number there to move to the corresponding place in the text.

14 When you're finished exploring, quit Acrobat or Acrobat Reader, and close all open files in FrameMaker 7.0.

Moving on

You've completed this lesson. For in-depth information about hypertext, see Chapter 19, "Hypertext and View-Only Documents," in the *Adobe FrameMaker 7.0 User Guide*. For in-depth information about PDF, see Chapter 20, "HTML and PDF Conversion."

Review questions

1 How can you automatically create hypertext links for an index?

2 What other type of hypertext link does FrameMaker 7.0 automatically create?

3 How can you try out a hypertext link when the document is still editable?

4 What are the advantages of placing a graphic on master pages instead of body pages?

5 How does the previouslink hypertext command differ from the previouspage command?

6 If you closed the Hypertext dialog box, how can you unlock the documents?

7 How do you specify Acrobat bookmarks when you save as PDF?

Answers

1 Select the Create Hypertext Links option when the Set Up Standard Index dialog box appears.

2 Any cross-reference you insert into a document automatically becomes a hypertext link in a view-only document.

3 You can use a special keystroke to activate any hypertext command in an editable document. The keystroke is (Windows) Control-Alt-click, (Macintosh) Control-Option-click, or (UNIX) Control-right-click.

4 A graphic on a master page is copied in the document only once but appears many times. To achieve the same effect without using master pages, you'd have to copy the graphic on each body page, increasing the document size dramatically. If you need to change the graphic, you can update it in a single place (the master page), and your changes will be automatically reflected on whatever body pages use that master page.

5 The previouspage command displays whatever page precedes the current one. The previouslink command retraces the places you've gone before, regardless of what the page number is.

6 Press Escape. Then press Shift + F. Then type **l** (lowercase L) **k**.

7 Whatever paragraph formats you include in the Bookmarks' left scroll box in the Acrobat Setup dialog box become Acrobat bookmarks. The indentations of the paragraph formats in the scroll box determine how the bookmarks are nested in Acrobat.

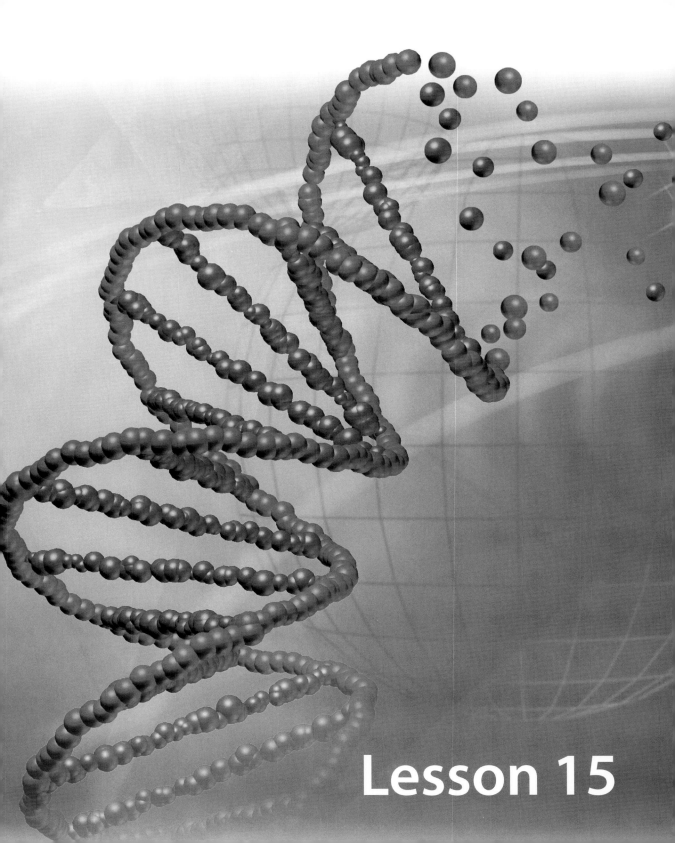

Lesson 15

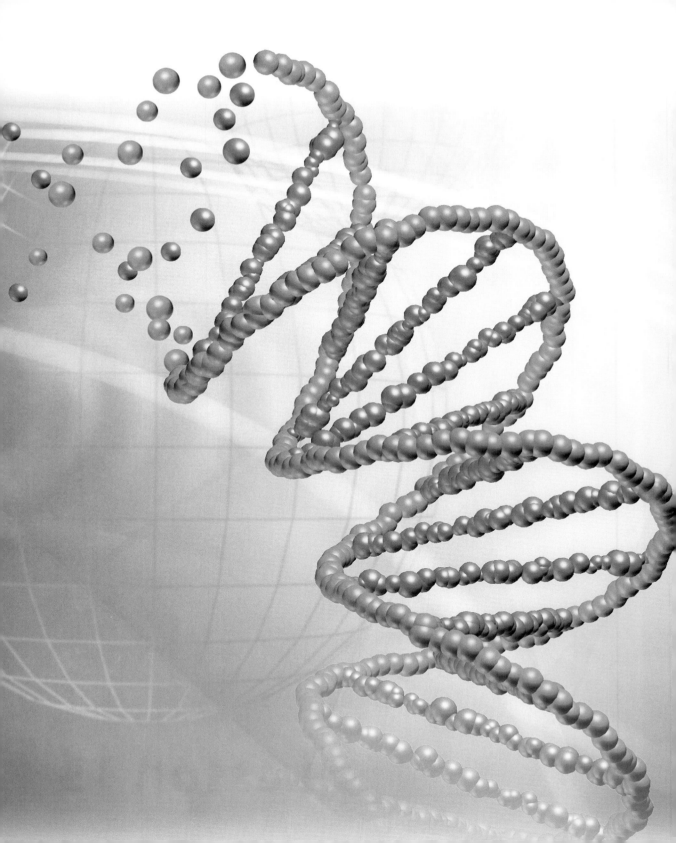

15 | HTML and Web Publishing

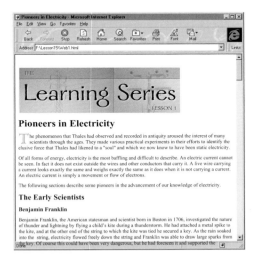

FrameMaker 7.0 documents easily convert to Hypertext Markup Language (HTML) for delivery on the World Wide Web or your company's intranet. You can convert single documents or books, split documents into multiple Web pages, and include image maps and links to other Web sites. FrameMaker 7.0 creates an HTML stylesheet along with the HTML document so that much of your text formatting is preserved when viewed with a Web browser that supports stylesheets.

In this lesson, you'll save a FrameMaker 7.0 document as Hypertext Markup Language (HTML) and view the resulting file in a Web browser. Then you'll refine your document by adding links and dividing the original document into a series of Web pages. You'll learn how to do the following:

- Save a document as HTML.

- Refine the automatic mapping of FrameMaker 7.0 formats to HTML elements.

- Add links to other Web pages.

- Create an image map.

- Split a long document into multiple Web pages.

- Add navigation buttons to a series of Web pages.

Note: The more advanced exercises require at least a little knowledge of HTML. If you don't have any familiarity with HTML, you can skip those sections.

For best results, you should view your HTML files in a Web browser that supports HTML stylesheets (.css files). Netscape Navigator 4.7 or later and Microsoft Internet Explorer 5.0 or later both support stylesheets.

Viewing the finished document

A copy of the final FrameMaker 7.0 document, called Finished.fm, is in the Lesson15 folder.

1 In the Lesson15 folder, open Finished.fm.

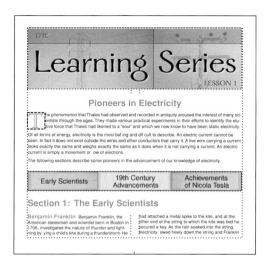

2 Take a few moments to explore it. Notice the following:

• The basic layout of this document is two columns, except for the first few paragraphs and the table at the end.

• On the first page, the graphic at the top of the page, the drop cap at the start of the first body paragraph, and the graphic describing the three main sections of the chapter are each in anchored frames.

• The document has three levels of headings. If you click in the title, *Pioneers in Electricity*, you'll see in the status bar that the paragraph tag is Heading1. The heading *Section 1: The Early Scientists* is tagged Heading2. The Heading2 format includes an autonumber (*Section 1:*). The run-in heading (*Benjamin Franklin*) is the third level of heading in the document, format Heading3.

• On page 3, at the end of the section about Thomas Alva Edison, you'll see a cross-reference to another section of the document: *see "The Achievements of Nicola Tesla" on page 4.*

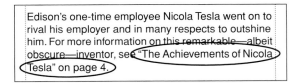

• On page 6, you'll see both numbered and bulleted lists, a table with ruling and shading.

3 Close Finished.fm.

Now that you're familiar with how the document will look, you're ready to start.

Saving as HTML

When you save a document as HTML for the first time, FrameMaker 7.0 automatically maps FrameMaker 7.0 formats to HTML elements and then converts the document. As you'll see later, you can adjust the automatic mappings if they don't meet your needs.

1 In the Lesson15 folder, open Web.fm.

2 Choose File > Save As, enter the filename **Web1.fm**, and click Save.

Now you're ready to convert to HTML, a process that can be as simple as saving the file.

3 Choose File > Save As.

4 Enter the filename **Web1.html**, making sure to include the file extension .html.

5 Choose HTML from the Save as type pop-up menu and click Save.

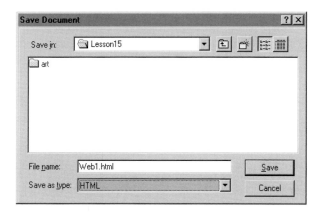

That's it. You've converted the document to an HTML file. In the few moments after you clicked Save, FrameMaker 7.0 set up mappings for formats to HTML elements, used those mappings to create a new HTML file, converted graphics in anchored frames to GIF format, and created an HTML stylesheet (more on stylesheets in a moment).

6 Minimize or hide FrameMaker 7.0 (but don't exit).

7 In your operating system, navigate to the Lesson15 folder. You will see the following files that FrameMaker 7.0 created (in Windows, you may need to show file extensions to differentiate these files):

- Web1.html, which is the new HTML file containing the original FrameMaker 7.0 text.

- Web1-1.gif and Web1-2.gif, which are graphics files.

- Web1.css, which contains HTML formatting information (the HTML stylesheet).

Viewing the results in a Web browser

Before you open the HTML file in your Web browser, you'll rename the Web1.css file. This way you'll see how your Web browser displays the HTML file without the effect of a stylesheet.

As you view the converted HTML file, remember that many factors affect how the Web page looks. Different Web browsers format text differently. Also, you may have customized the default settings of your browser.

Keep the FrameMaker 7.0 document handy as you look at the HTML file so you can compare the conversion.

1 In your operating system, rename the file Web1.css to xWeb1.css. Changing its name prevents it from being used when you view the HTML file in your browser.

2 Open the file Web1.html in your Web browser.

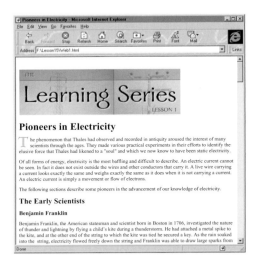

3 Notice the following:

• The entire Web page is one column even though the original document was two columns in FrameMaker 7.0. (HTML doesn't support multiple text columns, but a workaround exists. You could have created the FrameMaker 7.0 document by entering your text in tables. FrameMaker 7.0 converts tables without ruling lines to HTML tables with invisible borders, thereby simulating multiple columns of text.)

• The top banner graphic, and the drop cap at the start of the first body paragraph converted with the text. These graphics were originally TIF images. FrameMaker 7.0 converted them to GIF. (The Web doesn't support TIF.) Later you'll see how to convert graphics to other graphic formats that the Web supports.

• The section heading *The Early Scientists* no longer has its autonumber (*Section 1:*).

• The third-level heading *Benjamin Franklin* is no longer a run-in head.

• At the end of the second paragraph about Thomas Edison, the cross-reference converted to a link and the page number is gone.

• Near the end of the Web page, the numbered questions and the bulleted list converted to HTML numbered and bulleted lists.

• The table lost its shading and its rotated cells because HTML table formatting is more limited than that of FrameMaker 7.0.

4 Rename xWeb1.css back to Web1.css, and then click Reload (or Refresh) in your Web browser window.

As the page reloads, you will see the difference a stylesheet makes. (But if you're using a browser that doesn't support stylesheets, such as Navigator 3.0, there will be no difference.) The text size, weight, and color now more closely match the original document. The difference will be most obvious in the heading paragraphs.

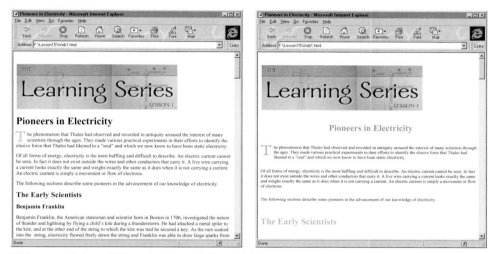

Without a stylesheet (left), and with a stylesheet (right)

5 Close your Web browser or minimize its window.

Refining the mappings

When you save a document as HTML or open the HTML Setup dialog box for the first time, FrameMaker 7.0 automatically maps paragraph and character formats to standard HTML elements and cross-reference formats to special conversion macros.

You can change these automatic mappings in the HTML Setup dialog box.

Looking at and changing paragraph mappings

The easiest way to inspect or change mappings is to use the HTML Setup dialog box.

1 In FrameMaker 7.0, go to the first page of Web1.fm, click in the first body paragraph, and then choose File > Utilities > HTML Setup.

This dialog box contains the following three pop-up menus:

• The Map pop-up menu determines the type of mappings. It is initially set to Paragraph Formats. If you wanted to remap a Character format, you'd choose Character Formats from that pop-up.

• The From pop-up menu lists the formats that are in the document's catalog.

• The To pop-up menu lists the HTML elements that can be mapped to paragraphs.

The mapping for the current paragraph is displayed in the HTML Setup dialog box: The paragraph format 1stParagraph is mapped to the *Paragraph* HTML element. You can view the mappings for other paragraphs simply by clicking in them.

2 Click in the paragraph under the heading Benjamin Franklin. You'll see that this paragraph, tagged Body, is also mapped to the *Paragraph* HTML element. (On the Mac OS, you may have to resize the document window so that both the window and the dialog box are showing.)

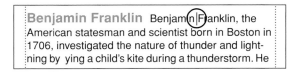

This mapping is what you normally want, so you won't change it.

You can also see what the mappings are that FrameMaker 7.0 set up by choosing a format from the From pop-up menu. You'll do this next.

3 Choose Heading1 in the From pop-up menu. Notice that Heading1 maps to *Heading (Auto Level)*. This mapping means that FrameMaker 7.0 will determine which of the six HTML heading elements is most appropriate. If you wanted to map a paragraph format to a *specific* HTML heading element, you would have to edit the special tables in the document's reference pages. You'll examine the reference pages later.

Again, this mapping is what you want in most cases, so you won't change it. There is, however, a format whose mapping in this document could be improved. The decorative divider dots used between the sections about the individual scientists in the original FrameMaker 7.0 document are less effective in the HTML document. Next, you'll remap them so that they won't appear in the HTML document.

The divider dots in the FrameMaker 7.0 document

The divider dots in the converted HTML document

4 Choose Paragraph Divider in the From pop-up menu. This format is currently mapped to the HTML *Paragraph* format.

5 Choose Throw Away from the To pop-up menu and then click Change.

The next time you save as HTML, any text formatted as Paragraph Divider will be omitted in the conversion.

Looking at cross-reference mappings

Cross-reference formats don't map directly to HTML elements. FrameMaker 7.0 uses a conversion macro to change cross-references to HTML.

1 Choose Cross-Reference Formats from the Map pop-up menu.

2 Click the From pop-up menu to display its contents. The From pop-up menu lists the document's cross-reference formats.

3 Click the To pop-up menu to display its contents. The To pop-up menu lists the currently defined cross-reference conversion macros. (Later you'll see where to add new macros in the HTML reference pages.)

The See Also macro is the default mapping for all cross-references in a document, and you won't need to change it in this document. However, if you wanted to keep the original format of a cross-reference, you would choose Original Cross-Reference Format from the To pop-up menu. If you wanted to delete the cross-reference from the HTML file, you'd choose Throw Away from the To pop-up menu.

Specifying a graphic format

FrameMaker 7.0 automatically copies and converts graphics in anchored frames to a specified Web image format. If the graphic was imported by copy, FrameMaker 7.0 creates a GIF (or JPEG, or Portable Network Graphics (PNG)) version of the graphic and places it in the folder in which you save the HTML file. If the graphic was imported by reference, FrameMaker 7.0 creates a new file if the original format is not the Web format that you specified.

You'll see how to set the image format for conversion.

1 In the HTML Setup dialog box, click Options. GIF is selected.

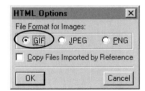

2 Click JPEG, click OK, then close the HTML Setup dialog box. The next time you save this document as HTML, the graphics will convert to JPEG format instead of GIF.

3 Save Web1.fm.

Adding hypertext links

You've seen that cross-references in the original FrameMaker 7.0 document automatically convert to HTML links, but you may also want to include other types of links in your Web pages. First you'll add a link to another Web site, and then you'll make an image map.

Adding a link to another Web site

A uniform resource locator (URL) defines the location of a Web page on the Internet. You'll insert a special marker into the document that will become a link to a URL when you save as HTML.

1 In the last paragraph of the document, below the table, select the text *Adobe Systems, Inc.*

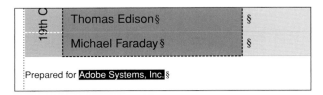

2 Press Control+8, press l (lowercase *L*), and then press Return to apply the Link character format to the selected text. (Actually, any character format would work, but the Link format has already been defined for you.) The text becomes underlined and purple.

3 Click between the words *Adobe* and *Systems,* and then choose Special > Hypertext.

4 Choose Message Client from the Command pop-up menu and enter **URL http://www.adobe.com** in the text box after *message*.

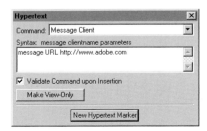

5 Click New Hypertext Marker, then close the Hypertext dialog box.

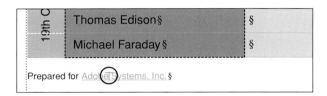

The next time you save as HTML, FrameMaker 7.0 converts this marker to a link to www.adobe.com. The active area of the link will be defined by the character format you applied (the Link format).

Creating an image map

An *image map* on a Web page is a graphic in which different areas of the image are defined as links to other locations. You'll import a graphic into the FrameMaker 7.0 document and set it up so that it converts to an image map when you save as HTML.

1 Go to the first page of the document and click at the end of the third body paragraph (the sentence ending with *our knowledge of electricity*).

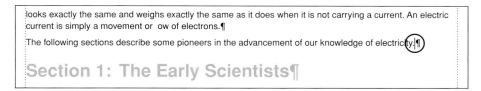

2 Choose File > Import > File, navigate to the art folder within the Lesson15 folder, and click Imagemap.tif.

3 Be sure that Import by Reference is selected and click Import.

4 In the Imported Graphic Scaling dialog box, click 72 dpi and click Set.

5 Click the Tools button (◢) on the right side of the document window to open the Tools palette.

6 Use the text frame tool (▤) to draw a text frame over each of the three panels of the graphic, as shown, clicking Set in the Create New Text Frame dialog box that appears after each drag. (If you can't easily make the frame the right size, choose Graphics > Snap to turn the snap grid off.) The placement of each text frame will determine a "hot spot" (a clickable rectangular area) of the image map. When you're finished, close the Tools palette.

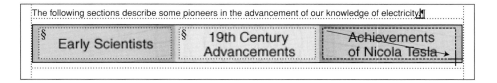

Now you'll add hypertext markers to the text frames. The markers can be links to other locations in your document, to other documents that you'll be converting as part of a book, or to a URL, such as the link you added in the previous section.

You'll create links to three headings in the current document. You need destination hypertext markers (called *newlink markers*) in the three heading paragraphs. These will convert into HTML anchors. You'll add a newlink marker next.

7 Click in the heading *Section 1: The Early Scientists*, and then choose Special > Hypertext.

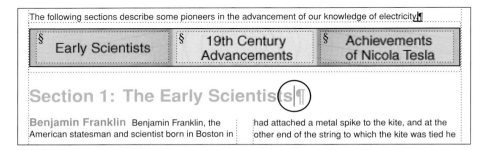

8 Choose Specify Named Destination from the Command pop-up menu, click in the text box, and enter **scientists** after *newlink*. Then, click New Hypertext Marker. This adds the newlink marker you'll need when you create a link in the image map.

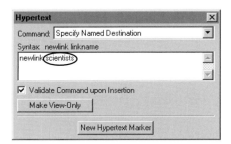

The other newlink markers in the other two section headings are already in place, so you won't have to insert those. Now you'll insert the hypertext markers in the image map that will jump to the locations of these newlink markers.

9 Click in the left text frame that you drew over *Early Scientists*. In the Hypertext dialog box, choose Jump to Named Destination from the Command pop-up menu.

10 Click in the text box after *gotolink* and enter **scientists**. Then, click New Hypertext Marker. (If you need to redraw the document display, press Control+l (lowercase L).)

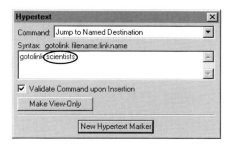

11 Click in the middle text frame that you drew over *19th Century Advancements*.

12 In the Hypertext dialog box, choose Jump to Named Destination from the Command pop-up menu, click in the text box after *gotolink*, and enter **19century**. Then, click New Hypertext Marker.

13 Click in the right text frame that you drew over *Achievements of Nicola Tesla*.

14 In the Hypertext dialog box, choose Jump to Named Destination from the Command pop-up menu, click in the text box after *gotolink*, and enter **tesla** (making sure to use the correct spelling). Then, click New Hypertext Marker.

15 Close the Hypertext dialog box.

The next time you save as HTML, the new graphic will function as an image map in the HTML document, with each area of the graphic being a link to each of the three sections.

Splitting the document into multiple Web pages

Accessing documents on the World Wide Web is more efficient when the documents are small. For this reason, you'll often want to have FrameMaker 7.0 split your document into several Web pages. Later you'll add links and buttons that readers can use to return to the main page and move between pages in the series.

To divide the document, you'll specify a heading format that will signify the start of a new Web page. Every paragraph tagged with the format you choose will appear as an H1 HTML element at the top of a Web page. Subheads in the document will be promoted and retain their relative head level to the new H1. On the main (first) Web page, you'll see the document's introductory paragraphs, followed by HTML links to the new files that FrameMaker 7.0 automatically split off. The result looks and works like a table of contents.

FrameMaker 7.0 names the new files by adding -1, -2, and so on, to the original filename.

1 Choose File > Utilities > HTML Setup.

2 In the HTML Setup dialog box, choose Paragraph Formats from the Map pop-up menu and choose Heading2 in the From pop-up menu.

3 Select Start New, Linked Web Page, and click Change.

4 Close the HTML Setup dialog box, then save the document.

Later, you'll save the document as HTML and see the results.

Seeing the results in HTML

You're now ready to save the Web1.fm document as HTML again to see the results of the work you've done so far.

1 Choose File > Save As and navigate to the Lesson15 folder.

2 Enter the filename **Web1.html**—make sure to include the file extension .html—and choose HTML from the Save as type pop-up menu.

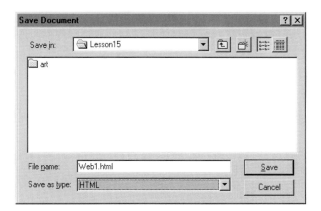

3 Click Save, then click OK (Replace on the Mac OS) to overwrite the existing Web1.html file.

4 Minimize or hide the FrameMaker 7.0 window.

5 In your operating system, open the Lesson15 folder. You'll see the following files that FrameMaker 7.0 has created:

• The main HTML document, Web1.html.

• The subdocuments that are linked to the main HTML document, Web1-1.html, Web1-2.html, Web1-3.html, and Web1-4.html.

• The HTML stylesheet, Web1.css.

• The converted graphics files, Web-1.jpg, Web1-2.jpg, and Web1-3.jpg.

6 Open Web1.html in your Web browser.

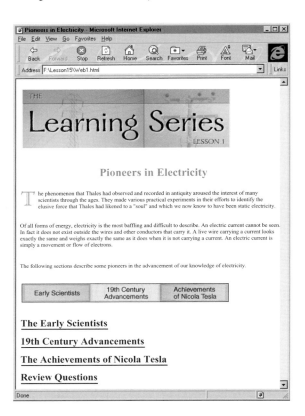

This is the main document. It contains the image map graphic and under it, hypertext links to the four subdocuments. Now is a good time to test the several types of links you entered.

7 Explore the linked files, noticing the following:

• The image map you created (see page 381) now works. You can click it to jump to the specified section. (Click the Back button in your browser to return to the main page.)

• The single FrameMaker 7.0 document has been automatically split up into linked HTML subdocuments, just as you specified (see the previous section) at each Heading2. You can click the links to jump to the specified sections. (Click the Back button in your browser to return to the main page.)

• The divider dots that you remapped to Throw Away (see page 378) no longer appear in the HTML subdocuments.

• Graphic files in the HTML document are now in JPEG format instead of GIF, as you specified (see page 379).

• Clicking the URL link you created (see page 380) at the bottom of the last subdocument opens the main page of the Adobe Web site (www.adobe.com) in your browser.

Advanced topics

The following sections deal with advanced topics that require some familiarity with HTML code and concepts. You don't need to go through these exercises unless you want to work with HTML macros or learn more about how FrameMaker 7.0 stores and keeps track of mappings.

If you decide to skip these advanced topics, you're finished with this lesson. To review what you've learned, see "Review questions" on page 394.

Examining the reference pages

FrameMaker 7.0 stores information about format mapping on reference pages. All the settings that you make in the HTML Setup dialog box are reflected on these pages—plus many more options.

This is where you set up conversion macros for cross-references or embed Java applets.

1 Minimize or hide your browser window and return to the FrameMaker 7.0 window.

2 If the HTML Setup dialog box is still open, close it.

3 Choose View > Reference Pages.

4 Go to the third reference page, called HTML. (You'll see the page name in the status bar.) This reference page contains several tables and spans several pages.

HTML Mapping Table§					
FrameMaker Source Item§	HTML Item§		Include Auto#§	Comments§	
	Element§	New Web Page?§			
P:1stParagraph§	P§ N§		N§	§	
P:Body§	P§ N§		N§	§	
P:Bullet§	LI¶ Parent = UL¶ Depth = 1§	N§	N§	§	
P:CellBody§	P§ N§		N§	§	
P:CellBodyRotate§	H*§ N§		N§	§	
P:CellHeading§	P§ N§		N§	§	
P:credit§	P§ N§		N§	§	
P:Heading1§	H*§ N§		N§	§	
P:Heading2§	H*§ Y§		N§	§	
P:Heading3§	H*§ N§		N§	§	
P:Mapping Table Cell§	P§ N§		N§	§	
P:Mapping Table Title§	P§ N§		N§	§	
P:MessageBody§	P§ N§		N§	§	
P:Numbered§	LI¶ Parent = OL¶ Depth = 0§	N§	N§	§	
P:Numbered-2ndlevel§	LI¶ Parent = OL¶ Depth = 0§	N§	N§	§	
P:Numbered1§	LI¶ Parent = OL¶ Depth = 0§	N§	N§	§	
P:Paragraph Divide§	THROW AWAY§	N§	N§	§	
P:Quote§	P§ N§		N§	§	
P:TableTitle§	LI¶ Parent = OL¶ Depth = 0§	N§	N§	§	
C:Emphasis§	EM§ N§		N§	§	

5 Scroll through the tables in the reference pages and note the following:

• The first table on the page is called the HTML Mapping Table. It sets up the mappings of FrameMaker 7.0 formats to HTML elements. The left column lists all the formats in the FrameMaker 7.0 document. In the first body row you see P:1stParagraph. The *P:* indicates that the item is a paragraph format. (*C:* indicates a character format and *X:* indicates a cross-reference format.) *1stParagraph* is the paragraph tag. The second column indicates the HTML element that this paragraph format maps to.

HTML Mapping Table§				
FrameMaker Source Item§	HTML Item§		Include Auto#§	Comments§
	Element§	New Web Page?§		
P:1stParagraph§	P§	N§	N§	§
P:Body§	P§	N§	N§	§
P:Bullet§	LI¶ Parent = UL¶ Depth = 1§	N§	N§	§

C:Emphasis§	EM§	N§	N§	§
C:Link§	EM§	N§	N§	§
X:Heading & Page§	See Also§	N§	N§	§
X:Page§	See Also§	N§	N§	§

• The third column indicates (with *Yes* or *No*) whether FrameMaker 7.0 starts a new Web page. Look at this setting for P:Heading2. You see a *Y* because this is the heading you changed earlier in the HTML Setup dialog box.

P:Heading1§	H*§	N§	N§	§
P:Heading2§	H*§	Y§	N§	§
P:Heading3§	H*§	N§	N§	§
P:Mapping Table Cell§	P§	N§	N§	§

• The Include Auto# column indicates (with *Yes* or *No*) whether to include a FrameMaker 7.0 autonumber in the paragraph. FrameMaker 7.0 automatically converts paragraphs that start with a number or a bullet to HTML ordered and unordered lists—so normally, you won't want the FrameMaker 7.0 autonumber also included.

6 Scroll to the System Macros table. This table contains predefined macros you can use to add items to the start and end of your Web pages. You'll edit this table in a minute.

7 Scroll to the last reference page, the Headings reference page. The only table here is the Headings table. This is where the settings for the autolevel headings are stored.

Headings Table§

Heading Level§	Paragraph Format§	Comments§
1§	Heading1§	§
2§	Heading2§	§
3§	Heading3§	§
4§	CellBodyRotate§	§

Now that you've had a brief tour of the mappings on the HTML and Headings reference pages, you'll edit a table.

Including return links to the main page

When you divide a document into several Web pages, FrameMaker 7.0 automatically creates a linked "table of contents" so that your readers can navigate to the other pages in the series. But to return to the main contents page, a reader must click the Back button in the browser window. You can provide a more elegant way to get back to the main document by having FrameMaker 7.0 insert a hypertext return link at the end of each subdocument. To provide the return links, you need to edit the System Macros table on the HTML reference page.

1 Scroll to the System Macros table on the HTML reference page.

HTML Mapping Table§				
FrameMaker Source Item§	HTML Item§		Include Auto#§	Comments§
	Element§	New Web Page?§		
P:TableTitle§	LI¶ Parent = OL¶ Depth = 0§	N§	N§	§ew
C:Emphasis§	EM§ N§		N§	§
C:Link§	EM§ N§		N§	§
X:Heading & Page§	See Also§	N§	N§	§
X:Page§	See Also§	N§	N§	§
X:See Heading & Page§	See Also§	N§	N§	§
X:Table All§	See Also§	N§	N§	§
X:Table Number & Pag§	See Also§	N§	N§	§

HTML Options Table§		
Control§	Value§	Comments§
Image Format§	0001IMAGJPEGMACP0001JPEG§	§
Copy Files Imported by Reference§	N§	§

System Macros§				
Macro Name§	Replace With§	Head§	Comments§	
StartOfDoc§	§	<TITLE> <$defaulttitle></TITLE>§		§
EndOfDoc§	§		§	§
StartOfSubDoc§	§	<TITLE> <$defaulttitle></TITLE>§		§
EndOfSubDoc§	§		§	§
StartOfFirstSubDoc§	§	<TITLE> <$defaulttitle></TITLE>§		§
EndOfFirstSubDoc§	§		§	§
StartOfLastSubDoc§	§	<TITLE> <$defaulttitle></TITLE>§		§
EndOfLastSubDoc§	§		§	§

2 In the Replace With column of the EndOfSubDoc row, enter the following HTML code to add a link to the subpages, but not to the main page or the last page in the series:

<P><A HREF="<$parentdoc>"> Return to main page </A></P>

Note: *Don't be concerned about how this HTML code wraps or hyphenates in the table cell. FrameMaker 7.0 will read the code as if it were one unbroken line.*

Here is an analysis of the parts of this code:

<P> ... </P>	<A> ... </A>	HREF="<$parentdoc>"	Return to main page

Start and end of the paragraph element	Start and end of the linking (anchor) element	The hypertext reference for the link: in this case, the FrameMaker 7.0 building block for the parent document (the document from which this document was split)	The text that will be the link (it will be clickable)

3 Copy the HTML code you just entered and paste it in the Replace With column of the EndOf LastSubDoc row. This takes care of the return link for the last page.

System Macros§				
Macro Name§	Replace With§		Head§	Com
StartOfDoc§	§		<TITLE> <$defaulttitle></TITLE>§	§
EndOfDoc§	§		§	§
StartOfSubDoc§	§		<TITLE> <$defaulttitle></TITLE>§	§
EndOfSubDoc§	<P><A HREF="<$parentdoc>">Return to main page </A></P>§		§	§
StartOfFirstSubDoc§	§		<TITLE> <$defaulttitle></TITLE>§	§
EndOfFirstSubDoc§	§		§	§
StartOfLastSubDoc§	§		<TITLE> <$defaulttitle></TITLE>§	§
EndOfLastSubDoc§	<P><A HREF="<$parentdoc>">Return to main page </A></P>§		§	

Adding navigation buttons to individual pages

You've added a way to return to the main page, but it would also be nice to be able to move to the next and previous subdocument without having to go back to the main page first. You'll add links to do that next, and enhance the links with graphics that work as buttons.

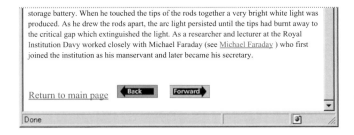

The button graphics are in the Lesson15 art folder. You'll reference these graphics and add the code to make them active.

Once again you'll edit the System Macros table on the HTML reference page.

1 In the System Macros table on the HTML reference page, click between *</A>* and *</P>* in the Replace With column of the EndOfSubDoc row.

System Macros§			
Macro Name§	Replace With§	Head§	Com
StartOfDoc§	§	<TITLE> <$defaulttitle></TITLE>§	§
EndOfDoc§	§	§	§
StartOfSubDoc§	§	<TITLE> <$defaulttitle></TITLE>§	§
EndOfSubDoc§	<P><A HREF="<$parentdoc>">Return to main page </A>|</P>§	§	§
StartOfFirstSubDoc§	§	<TITLE> <$defaulttitle></TITLE>§	§
EndOfFirstSubDoc§	§	§	§
StartOfLastSubDoc§	§	<TITLE> <$defaulttitle></TITLE>§	§
EndOfLastSubDoc§	<P><A HREF="<$parentdoc>">Return to main page </A></P>§	§	

2 Enter the following text:

<A HREF="<$prevsubdoc>"><IMG SRC="Art/back.gif" Border=0></A>
<A HREF="<$nextsubdoc>"><IMG SRC="Art/forward.gif" Border=0></A>

Note: Type the HTML exactly as you see it here. FrameMaker 7.0 cannot check the HTML code for errors. The links won't work if you make a typing error.

The buttons will appear in every Web page after the first—except for the last page. On the last page you'll want to add only a back button; you'll do that next.

3 In the Replace With column of the EndOf LastSubDoc row, enter the following text between *</A>* and *</P>*:

<A HREF="<$prevsubdoc>"><IMG SRC="Art/back.gif" Border=0></A>

The completed table looks like this:

System Macros§			
Macro Name§	Replace With§	Head§	Con
StartOfDoc§	§	<TITLE> <$defaulttitle></TITLE>§	§
EndOfDoc§	§	§	§
StartOfSubDoc§	§	<TITLE> <$defaulttitle></TITLE>§	§
EndOfSubDoc§	<P><A HREF="<$parentdoc>">Return to main page </A><A HREF="<$prevsubdoc>"><IMG SRC="Art/back.gif" Border=0></A> <A HREF="<$nextsubdoc>"><IMG SRC="art/forward.gif" Border=0></A></P>	§	§
StartOfFirstSubDoc§	§	<TITLE> <$defaulttitle></TITLE>§	§
EndOfFirstSubDoc§	§	§	§
StartOfLastSubDoc§	§	<TITLE> <$defaulttitle></TITLE>§	§
EndOfLastSubDoc§	<P><A HREF="<$parentdoc>">Return to main page </A><A HREF="<$prevsubdoc>"><IMG SRC="Art/back.gif" Border=0></A></P>	§	§

4 Choose View > Body Pages, and choose File >Save.

Viewing the navigation links in a Web browser

You've made all your adjustments, and now you're ready to save your document as HTML one last time.

1 Choose File > Save As and navigate to the Lesson15 folder.

2 Enter the filename **Web1.html**—make sure to include the file extension .html—and choose HTML from the Save as type pop-up menu.

3 Click Save, then click OK (Replace on Mac OS) to overwrite the existing Web1.html file.

4 Open Web1.html in your Web browser to test the new navigation links.

5 Click *Early Scientists* in the image map, scroll to the end of the Early Scientists page, and click Return to Main Page.

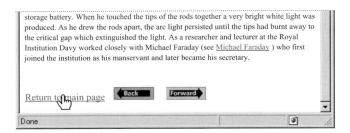

6 Now click the hypertext links on the main page, then use the Back and Forward buttons to move among the subdocuments.

7 When you're finished testing the links, close the browser, then return to FrameMaker 7.0 and save and close Web1.fm.

Moving on

You've completed this lesson. For in-depth information about converting FrameMaker 7.0 documents to HTML, see Chapter 20, "HTML and PDF Conversion," in the *Adobe FrameMaker 7.0 User Guide*.

Review questions

1 How do you make FrameMaker 7.0 automatically set up mappings to HTML elements?

2 What is the purpose of an HTML stylesheet? What are some of its limitations?

3 How can you change the default mappings that FrameMaker 7.0 sets up?

4 What is an image map and how does it work?

5 Why would you want to split up a document into separate HTML files?

6 What kinds of advanced formatting can you do by editing the tables on reference pages?

Answers

1 FrameMaker 7.0 sets up mappings when you save as HTML or when you choose File > Utilities > HTML Setup.

2 An HTML stylesheet instructs a Web browser to format the page and text to match the original more closely. For example, text size, weight, and color are retained. Stylesheets do not work with all versions of browsers (they don't work with Navigator 3.0, for example). Also, they do not retain many aspects of page layout, such as number of columns.

3 You can change a mapping in the HTML Setup dialog box. Advanced users can also change mappings by editing the special tables on the reference pages.

4 An image map is a graphic that has clickable areas (called hot spots). Each hot spot is an HTML hypertext link. To define a hot spot in FrameMaker 7.0, draw a transparent text frame over each area and then insert a FrameMaker 7.0 hypertext command in it. When you save as HTML, the graphic is converted to a fully functioning HTML image map.

5 Splitting up a document makes sense if the original FrameMaker 7.0 document is long or contains many graphics. That way, users won't have to wait as long to view a file. Also, splitting up a document lets you create a linked contents page, which lets users quickly skim and locate the information of interest to them.

6 Editing the reference pages lets you, for example, define buttons and links that appear at the start or end of each subdocument.

Part Two:

Structured FrameMaker 7.0

Getting Started with Structure

Extensible Markup Language (XML) was developed by a group of the World Wide Web Consortium (W3C), which included Adobe and other experts from Internet technology companies, business and publishing industry representatives, and information technology professionals. Their goal was to make SGML (Standard Generalized Markup Language) more flexible and useful to the Web and to expand the audience of users. The result is XML.

The first draft of XML was published in 1996, on the 10th anniversary of SGML, and today it has expanded the usefulness of the Web and gone beyond that to video and wireless devices. And it is proliferating.

Today there are hundreds of users developing XML-specific content applications. Every field is finding that markup languages can organize huge volumes of data into usable forms in short enough time to be useful. XML documents can flow directly into Chemical Mark Up Language, Mathematical Mark Up Language, Web Interface Definition Language, and Synchronized Multimedia Interface Language.

New markup dialects, such as chemistry, biology, math, astronomy, and commerce are being developed for industries all over the world. Scientists in China can exchange with scientists in the USA, formulas and molecular structures drawn from the same data via XML.

XML integrated into FrameMaker 7.0

Structured FrameMaker 7.0 and its handling of XML is a simplified but descriptive and powerful application for handling data transfers from one channel to another. It takes data beyond word processing and desk-top publishing, which are no longer adequate. It grew out of the need to structure documents beyond style sheet considerations.

Because FrameMaker has long been a comprehensive tool for working with large documents, it was logical to move into this burgeoning field of information handling with XML, HTML, and other applications. It is a valuable tool for anyone who needs to analyze information and make decisions based on it. This is needed not only for distribution within large companies and on the Web, but for a whole spectrum of other destinations like video and wireless devices.

Single document, multiple uses

Finding a format that can be used for transfer of data between databases of different vendors has always been difficult. One of the major advantages of XML is that it provides a backbone for data that can be searched and sorted for accomplishing any number of objectives.

A standard FrameMaker document is flexible to a degree, but short of that obtained in one created with Structured FrameMaker 7.0. In standard mode, the data component is nonexistent because it lacks that backbone of structure.

You can create a standard document, save it in many word-processing formats, as well as in HTML or Adobe Acrobat PDF. You can print it. But its utility diminishes when the use of the document is simultaneously important to information technology, engineering, marketing, public relations, inventory control, technical documentation, and warehouse distribution—a whole enterprise with many divergent requirements for the same data. If one person is using the data, there is no problem; when many users need to review data with different uses in mind, a structure gives consistency.

XML was developed to allow documents to be created once, but distributed to multiple users in multiple channels. HTML is for Web display. XML is for data. Structured FrameMaker 7.0 is an enterprise-ready application. It combines the simplicity of word processing with the power of XML data handling. It is WYSIWYG authoring in style-tagging mode, a structured environment for creating valid XML.

XML behaves the same no matter what platform or software you are using to output the data, so each new use of the data is created without time-consuming reconstruction. Every application understands what the data is, because it is tagged. A Web page uses it one way, a database in another. An individual does not have to redo a spreadsheet to create a database, a Web page editor to format a home page, nor an HTML editor to set up financial data on an Internet site.

Why XML is useful

Markup languages use structured data. You define a framework or schema to structure the data and then add the data. If you can represent data in a structured format, you can create markup language files. A structured file can be used to create HTML files for different browsers, a consistent starting point without recreating the wheel for each site. Structured FrameMaker documents let you turn your data into HTML, XML, or SGML efficiently, without having to be a programmer.

FrameMaker's structured authoring identifies (wraps) text as elements, represented by tags, which are in turn contained (wrapped) within other elements. This establishes a document hierarchy. Beyond formatting of paragraphs, structured elements provide information such as specific word meaning and importance.

Classroom in a Book exercises in structured mode

The XML exercises in this Classroom in a Book give you a chance to use the basic menu to export a Structured FrameMaker 7.0 file to XML for use in these new, information-heavy arenas. What's more, you can bring them back into Structured FrameMaker 7.0, revise them, and return them once again to their source.

Almost all documents have an implicit structure, logical units that appear in a consistent order with a specific hierarchy (in school we were taught we had to have an introduction-body-conclusion). FrameMaker allows you to work with a document's structure by organizing the contents–sections, headings, tables, and so on into logical units called elements. Elements can be further described by their attributes.

Markup languages with the text marked with tags, like sales tags on items in a store, provide information about the objects they're attached to. Nesting tags give a hierarchal structure. The FrameMaker 7.0 Structure View window displays the typical tree branching structure, showing the hierarchy of elements of information flow.

WebWorks Publisher

In addition to using the Save As command to export FrameMaker 7.0 documents to advanced structured formats, FrameMaker 7.0 includes Quadralay WebWorks Publisher Standard Edition, which provides robust features for creating HTML, Dynamic HTML, and XML output. You can use WebWorks Publisher Standard Edition to do the following:

- Map FrameMaker 7.0 elements (such as paragraph tags, character tags, and graphics) to online styles.

- Convert text, graphics, and tables to HTML, Dynamic HTML—HTML with cascading style sheets (CSS)—and XML.

- Determine how a FrameMaker 7.0 document is divided into one or more HTML files.

- Convert any images to online formats.

- Specify how navigation bars appear at the top and bottom of a page.

- Create an HTML FrameSet.

You can install WebWorks Publisher Standard from the CD in your FrameMaker 7.0 product package. For more information on setting up and using WebWorks Publisher Standard, see the *WebWorks Publisher Standard Edition User Guide*.

Well-formed XML

Start tags must be matched with end tags, attribute values must have start and end quotes, and elements must be properly nested inside each other to create well-formed XML. Structured FrameMaker 7.0 automates this process for you, so if the phone rings and you forget to enter an end quote, FrameMaker doesn't forget.

Structured FrameMaker 7.0 lets you create documents in a familiar word-processing mode but with the ability to be automatically hyperlinked for PDF, HTML, XML, and other electronic formats. Structure provides navigation ability. You can publish to multiple channels using a variety of formats. You can create a single document and publish it to a variety of formats. The program gives you tools for XML authoring and publishing Web pages and PDFs. Content management systems that handle industry databases such as product catalogs, annual reports, and stock market reports can reuse the content repeatedly.

XML enables communications

XML also allows one computer talk to another. As computer capabilities continue to evolve, more applications may be able to read an XML file. Currently, word processors cannot, and desktop publishing programs cannot. With tags, programs are able to talk to each other. Microsoft Excel with tags is easy to move to another form.

The gaming community uses XML in games, newsletters, and Web sites. Some sites publish news stories, that are never typed in by hand. Instead, the computer reads an XML file and parses the data out.

Understanding the principle behind structure

To help you contemplate why structure might be important, consider this. Your company wants to mass distribute a document by e-mail and conventional postal service. Your shipping department has been instructed not to send one by postal service to anyone who has received it by e-mail. There is a mix-up in the database related to the entry defined as "*Johnson.*" It is revealed that there are several families by the name of "*Johnson*" who live on a street called "*Johnson Blvd.*" in the town of "*Johnson City, Texas.*"

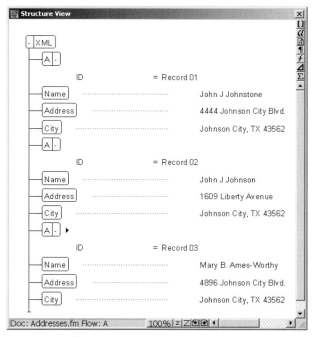

*An internet or database search for the element [Address]
containing the text: "Johnson" would find Records 01 and 03 but
not Record 02 in a structured file. Using an unstructured file would
find all 3 records, which in this example would be incorrect.*

In a structured database, with tagged elements, you would be able to search for all the Johnson entries that are tagged as [address].

You would thereby eliminate any errors that might come from people's names or from city names.

In databases that can be searched on the Internet, you can pinpoint searches with tags, as described in the example. Where there are trillions upon trillions of computations, precision and consistency are paramount.

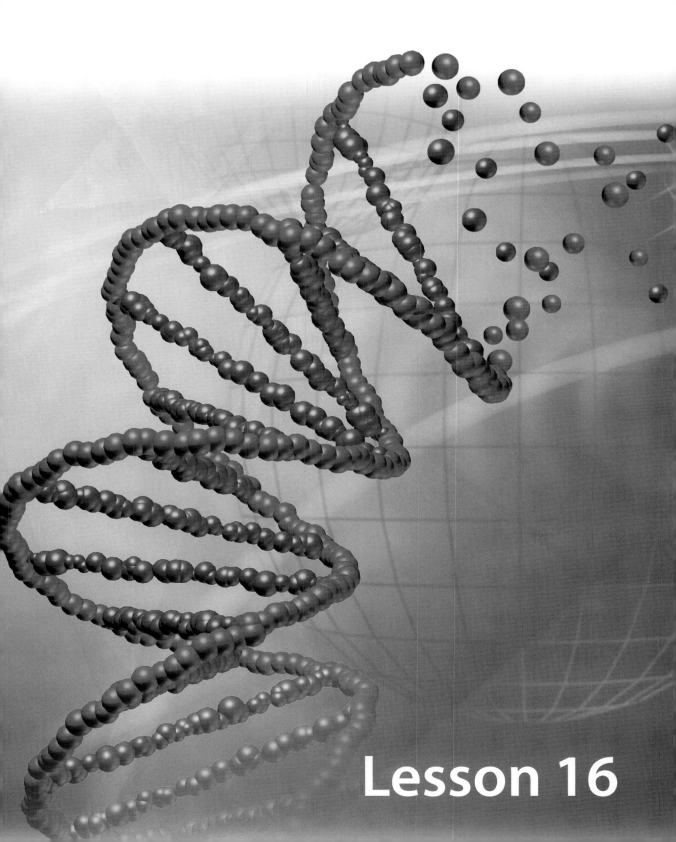

Lesson 16

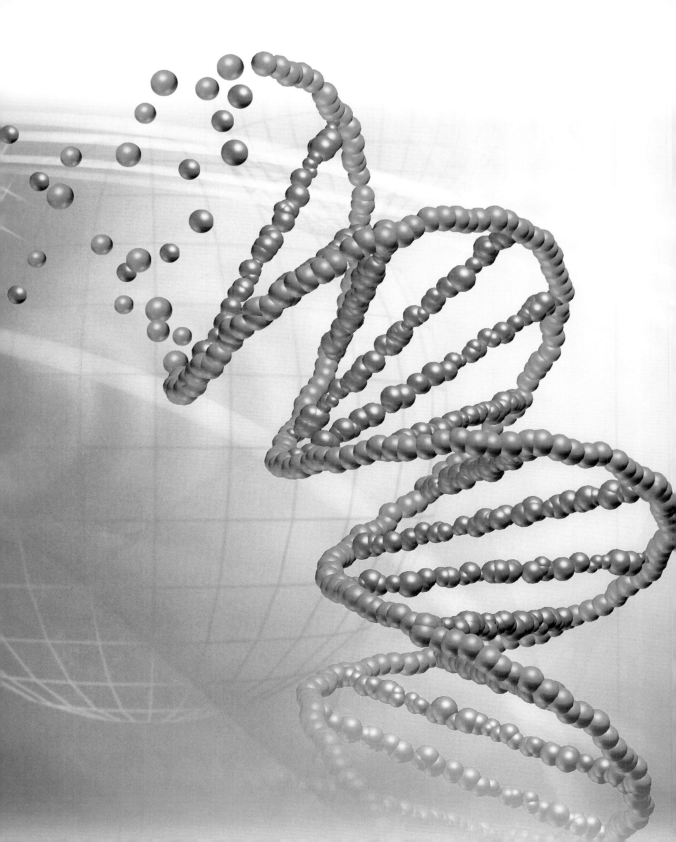

16 | Structured Documents

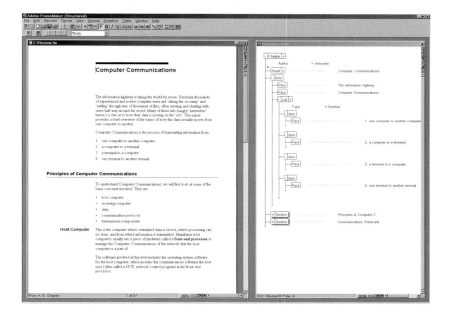

FrameMaker 7.0 documents easily convert to valid Extensible Markup Language (XML) and back again, addressing broad distribution requirements over servers, networks, wireless devices, and the Internet. You can create or convert single documents or books; split documents into multiple pages; and include elements, tags, image maps, and links that will be universally searchable across platforms, browsers, and databases.

Structured FrameMaker 7.0 documents let you turn your data into HTML, XML, or SGML efficiently, without having to be a programmer. Structured FrameMaker 7.0 provides the framework, using objects (or elements) and their properties (or attributes). In this lesson, you will be introduced to Structured FrameMaker 7.0. You'll learn how to do the following:

• Navigate the Structured FrameMaker 7.0 window and menu.

• Work in the Structured FrameMaker 7.0 window.

• Use the Element Catalog.

Structured FrameMaker 7.0 provides a WYSIWYG interface that users can employ to create structured documents not only for printing, but for the Web, for databases, or for hand-held devices. This lesson covers essential features of Structured FrameMaker 7.0 to get you up and running.

FrameMaker 7.0 for structured authoring

XML can take a long time to master. Structured FrameMaker 7.0 hides the XML syntax from the author and provides a graphical user interface to manipulate your document. It shows your document and its hierarchy.

Structured features

FrameMaker 7.0 is a complete, structured publishing system that you can use to produce documents ranging from simple one-page unstructured memos to complex multiple-chapter structured books with imported graphics.

From the Structured FrameMaker 7.0 window, you can use the Element catalog to define content, add specific attributes (properties), and organize the elements for any document. The Validation tool checks procedures, finds invalid structures, and fixes them.

This section illustrates setting up the Structured FrameMaker 7.0 work space, moving around in document and Structure View, expanding and collapsing elements, and using the Element Catalog to create a custom element list.

Structured FrameMaker 7.0 window and menu

The Structured FrameMaker 7.0 environment closely resembles standard FrameMaker, but there are some differences.

An additional menu item called Element has been added to the Main menu.

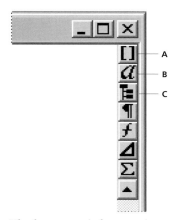

The document window contains
three additional control buttons:
A. *Element Catalog* ***B.*** *Attribute window*
C. *Structure View.*

Setting up Structured FrameMaker 7.0 work space

1 Open Studoc.fm from the Lesson16 folder.

2 Choose File > Save As, enter the filename **Review.fm**, and click Save.

3 Go to page 1 and zoom the document to 140%.

4 In the upper right corner of the document window, click the Structure View button (⌗). The Structure View appears.

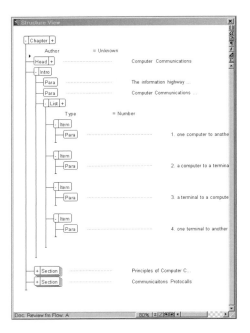

5 Arrange the document and structure view to resemble the work space seen here.

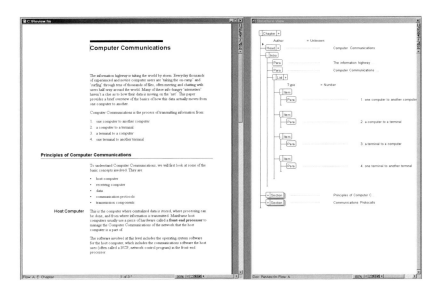

Under View in the Menu Bar, you have the standard options such as Text symbols, Borders, and Rulers. Plus you have two additional options:

• Element Boundaries surrounds each element with square brackets.

• Element Boundaries (as Tags) displays the element's name in bubbles at the beginning and end of the element.

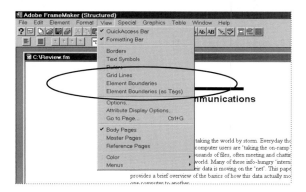

Elements can be inside of other elements. The boundaries *nest* to show the hierarchy of elements. Try both Element Boundaries and Element Boundaries (as Tags) to see the differences. "As Tags" can be helpful when editing.

Leave the document set for Element Boundaries (square brackets).

Working in the Structure window

Selecting elements

1 Click on the first Head element bubble. Make sure you are in Structure View.

The element is shown selected in both the Structure View and the document window.

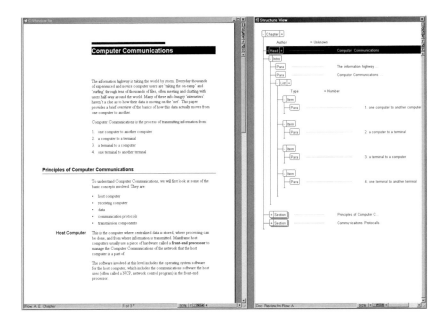

2 From the Structure View, select the List element.

The List element (parent), and elements within the List (children) are selected.

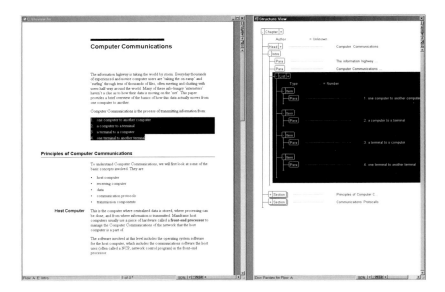

3 From Structure View, select the Chapter element.

All elements in the document are now selected because the Chapter element is the document's highest level (root) element.

4 In Structure View, select the first Head element.

5 Hold down the shift key, and click on the Intro element (below it).

Note: *Holding down the shift key allows you to select more than one element.*

Moving the insertion point in document view

1 In Structure View, click between the Chapter and Head elements.

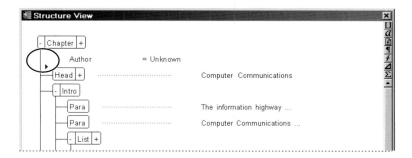

In the document window, the insertion point is positioned between the two opening brackets, in front of the word Computer. The outer bracket represents the opening tag of the Chapter element. The inner bracket represents the opening tag for the Head element.

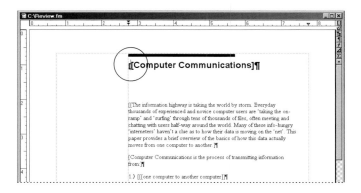

The status bar at the bottom of the document page displays the current element name. (In an unstructured FrameMaker document, the current paragraph format is displayed).

2 Press the Down Arrow key. Notice the insertion point moves down one line at a time in the document window.

3 Press the Up Arrow key. In the document window, the insertion point moves up one line at a time.

4 In the document window, click anywhere in the heading Computer Communications.

In the document window, the insertion point is inside the Head element. In Structure View, the insertion point is to the right of the Head element bubble.

In Structure View, the insertion point is shaped like a triangle. Depending on its location, the triangle appears as follows:

A. Beginning of element
B. Within the element
C. End of element

5 Press the Right Arrow key to move the cursor, one character at a time, to the end of the Head element.

The arrow in the Structure View changes to reflect the end of the element.

6 In the Document window, place the insertion point at the beginning of the C in Computer Communications element.

The arrow in the Structure View changes to reflect the beginning of the element.

7 Use the Left Arrow key to move the cursor one key stroke to the left, outside of the Head element.

The first bracket is the start of the Chapter element and the second bracket is the start of the Head element. You are now inside the Chapter element and before the Head element.

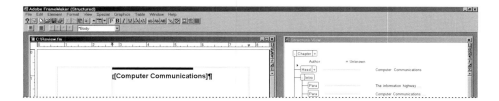

Moving the insertion point in Structure View

• (Windows) Press and hold Control + Alt, and then press the Down Arrow several times. The insertion point moves from element to element.

• (Mac OS) Press the Down Arrow to move from element to element.

Experiment moving between elements.

Collapsing and expanding elements

Collapsing elements in Structure View keeps the view compact, making it quicker to scroll through long structures. You can expand elements as needed. When an element is collapsed, all of its children are hidden but available. An element's content in the document window is not lost. You can expand the view when you want to see details.

Elements can be collapsed and expanded. In the element's bubble, to the left of the element name, click on the plus (+) symbol to expand or click on the minus (-) symbol to collapse.

1 In Structure View, locate the Intro element at the beginning of the structure.

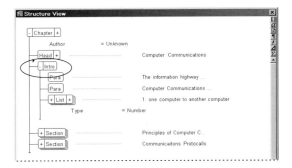

2 With the Intro element collapsed, click once on this element's plus (+) symbol to expand the view.

3 Inside the Intro element, locate the List element, and expand its view to show the four Item elements within.

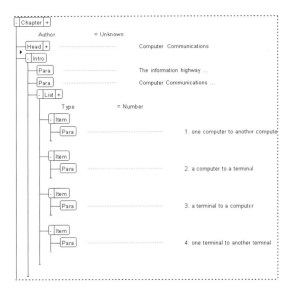

4 Press and hold the Shift key. Then click (or press the - symbol) on any of the four Item elements.

Viewing attributes

Attributes provide a way to store nonprinting descriptive information with an element. For example, a chapter can store the author's name even if it isn't shown. A list element can contain an attribute to switch the list from using bullets to using numbers.

An element can contain several attributes, which are displayed in Structure View directly beneath the element bubble. To reveal or hide attributes, click in the element bubble, on the + symbol (to the right of the element name), or use Attribute Display Options.

1 Choose View > Attribute Display Options. The Attribute Display Option dialog box appears.

2 Select the All Attributes option and click Set.

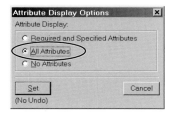

The Structure View displays all attributes.

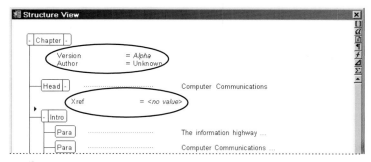

Attributes

This won't necessarily expand child elements to reveal their attributes. However, as lower elements are expanded, the attributes are displayed.

3 Click the minus symbol (-) next to the element to hide or reveal attribute information.

Note: *When expanding the Chapter element, notice that it takes two clicks to review all of the attribute information.*

Attributes fall into two categories: Required and Optional. When expanding attributes, the first click reveals Required attributes, the second reveals Optional attributes.

4 To hide attributes, choose View > Attribute Display Options. The Attribute Display Option dialog box appears.

5 Select the No Attributes option and click Set.

Using the Element Catalog

The Element Catalog is a context-sensitive list of elements in a document. The elements change according to the location of the insertion point or the current selection. The catalog also contains commands to insert, wrap, or change elements.

Using the Element Catalog to insert elements is called *Guided Editing* because the catalog guides the writer by helping choose valid elements. A valid element has a special symbol next to its name in the catalog.

A. *Valid element at the current location.* **B.** *Included elements, valid anywhere in the parent element.* **C.** *Incomplete, but valid in the current element.* **D.** *Valid in the current element, but inserting it makes subsequent elements invalid.*

Note: *If there is no symbol, then the element is not valid at the current location.*

Display options

1 In the first Head element of the document window, in front of the word Computer, click between the two opening brackets.

2 Click the Element Catalog button located in the upper right corner of either window.

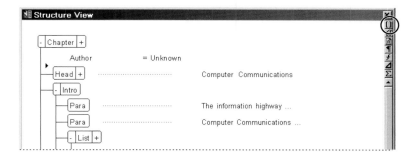

The Element Catalog appears, displaying elements valid at the insertion point.

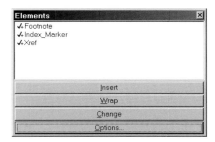

3 In Structure View, in the first Section element, click below the first Para element.

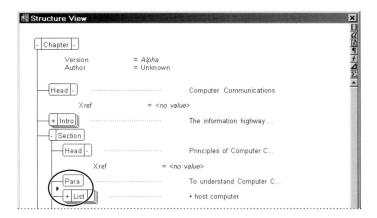

The Element Catalog changes to reflect elements valid at the insertion point.

Note: *The list of elements varies, depending on the location of the insertion point.*

4 Place the insertion point in other elements and view the valid elements displayed.

Changing display options

At present, the Element Catalog is set to display a list of valid elements at the insertion point. The Set Available Elements command lets you set which elements to display.

1 In Structure View at the beginning of the document, click after the Chapter element.

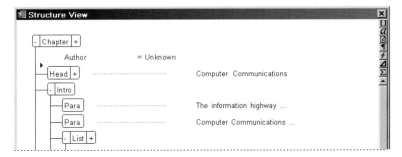

2 Choose Element > Set Available Elements (or click Options on the Element Catalog).

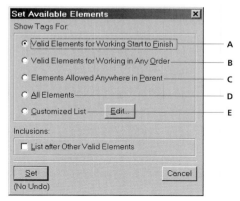

A. Use this option to work through a document from start to finish and to enter elements in their correct order. **B.** Use this option to build a valid document, not necessarily from start to finish. This is helpful when you do not have all the required information to complete an element. **C.** This option gives greater flexibility when inserting elements; it allows you to insert invalid elements and correct them later. **D.** Use this option when you're not building a valid document, but are wrapping elements around text.

3 Select All Elements and click Set.

4 If necessary, click the Element Catalog button in the upper right corner of the window to show the element list.

The Element Catalog now displays all elements available in the document. The elements are sorted into groups according to their validity at the insertion point.

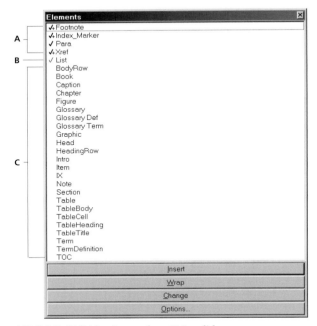

A. Valid *B.* Valid but incomplete *C.* Invalid

Creating a custom element list

A customized list is useful if your document has many elements.

1 Choose Element > Set Available Options (or click Options on the Element Catalog).

2 Select Customized List.

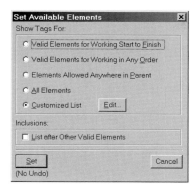

3 Click Edit.

The Customize List of Available Elements dialog box appears. All of the document elements are on the Don't Show scroll list.

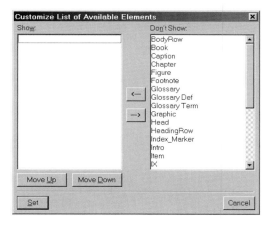

4 Select the Chapter element, and click on the Left Arrow button (or double-click the element to move it into the Show scroll list).

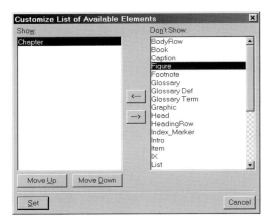

5 Repeat step 3 for the following elements: Intro, List, Para, Section, Term, Item, and Head. The Show list should look like the one shown below.

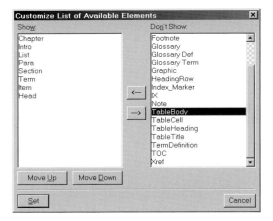

6 In the Show list, select the Section element.

7 Click the Move Up button twice to move the Section element just below the Intro element.

8 Use the Move Up and Move Down buttons to arrange the elements in the Show list in the following order: Chapter, Intro, Section, Head, Para, List, Term, and Item.

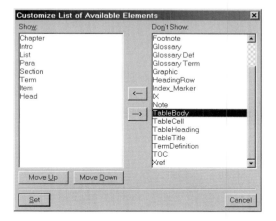

9 In the Customize List of Available Elements dialog box, click Set.

10 The Set Available Elements dialog box appears. Click Set.

The Element Catalog now displays your customized list.

11 Save and close the file.

Moving on

You've completed this lesson. For in-depth information about structured documents, see Chapter 3, "Working with Structured Documents," in the *Adobe FrameMaker 7.0 User Guide*.

Review questions

1 What buttons have been added to the sidebar in structured FrameMaker?

2 How can you make the hierarchy structure of the document appear?

3 What are the 2 new choices in the structured FrameMaker menu bar?

4 Do you have to move the insertion point separately in Structure View and document view?

5 What symbol beside an element indicates it has more content and can be expanded?

6 How do you collapse elements?

7 How do you call up the Element Catalog?

8 Why does the Element Catalog display different elements at different times?

9 How can you display all the elements available in an entire document?

10 How can you create a customized set of elements for your document?

Answers

1 The three new buttons display are the Element Catalog, attributes, and Structure View.

2 Click on the button for Structure View on the sidebar of FrameMaker.

3 From View in the menu bar, two new additions are: Element Boundaries and Element Boundaries (as Tags).

4 No, it moves in both views at the same time.

5 The (+) plus symbol shows you can expand an element.

6 Click on the (-) minus symbol to collapse elements.

7 Click on the sidebar button (at the top right) with square brackets.

8 Elements vary according to what structure is at the insertion point.

9 Click to bring up the Element Catalog, and choose Options at the bottom of the dialog box. The Set Available Elements dialog box appears, and you can click the radio button for "All Elements."

10 From the Set Available Elements dialog box as in answer 9 above, click the radio button for Customized List.

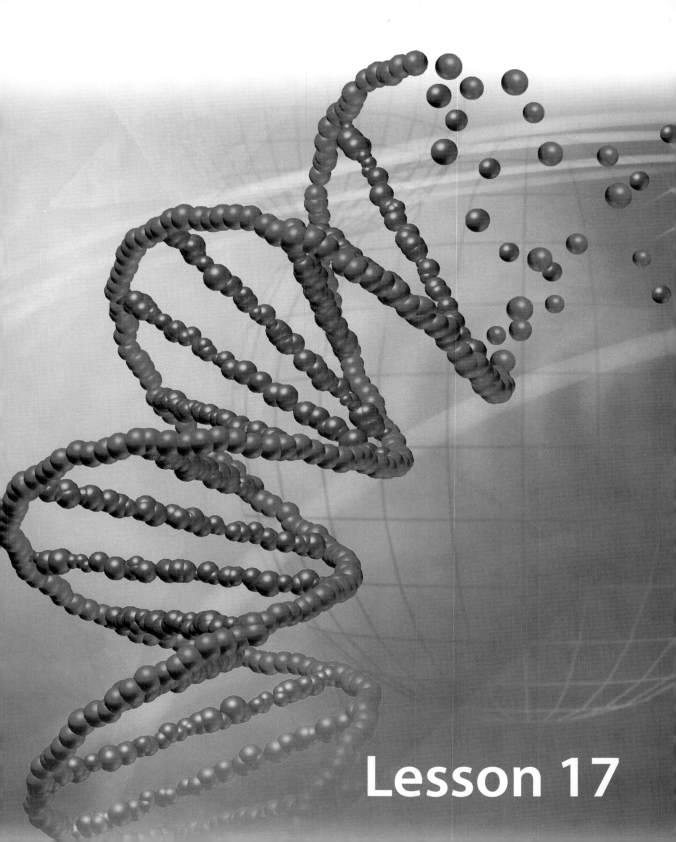

Lesson 17

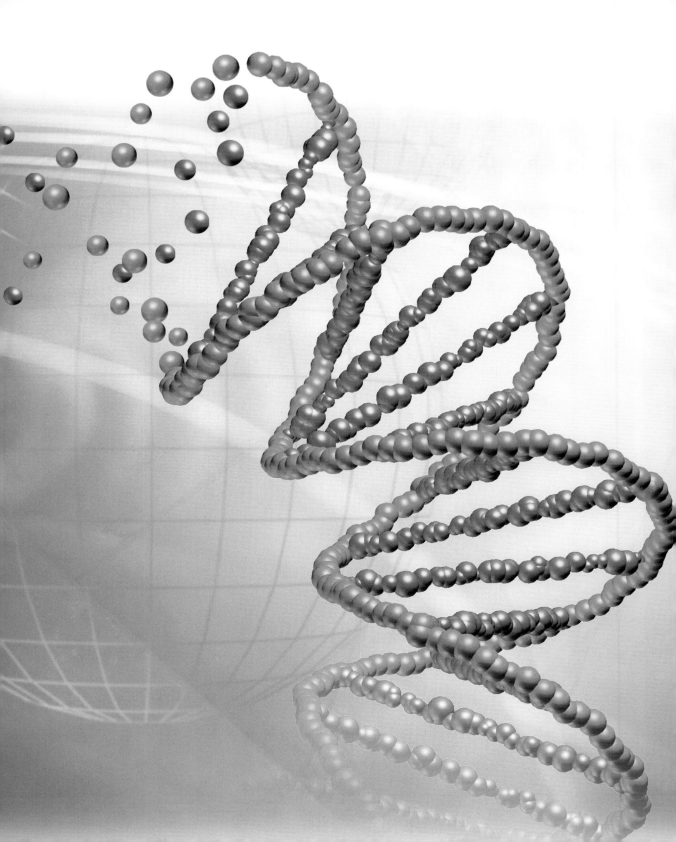

17 | Authoring XML

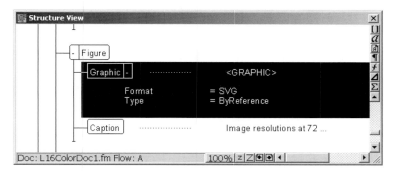

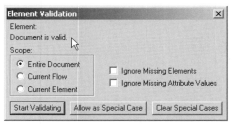

When the templates, tools, and applications required to author WYSIWYG-structured documents are assembled, guided editing is provided by the Element Catalog, and the Structured View window in Structured FrameMaker 7.0. Files are optimized for editing. The production of valid XML offers benefits expanded beyond standard authoring to organizations that need to customize information for a variety of audiences and users.

Structured FrameMaker 7.0 documents let you turn your data into XML efficiently, without having to be a programmer. This portion of the program provides you a framework for using objects (known as *Elements*) and their properties (known as *Attributes*). In this lesson, you will work with and edit a file in Structured FrameMaker 7.0. You'll learn how to do the following:

• Use the Element Catalog.

• Import an XML section into FrameMaker 7.0.

• Import an SVG graphic.

• Employ supporting files to guide your authoring: the EDD, DTD, Read/Write Rules, and Stylesheets.

• Validate a structured file.

• Reconstruct elements or their attributes for validation.

• Build interactive topics.

  Appendix A contains a Glossary of Structured Terms.

FrameMaker 7.0 for structured authoring

XML can take a long time to master. Structured FrameMaker 7.0 hides the XML syntax from the author and provides a graphical user interface to manipulate your document. It delineates your document and its hierarchy. FrameMaker 7.0 is a complete, structured publishing system that you can use to produce documents ranging from simple one-page unstructured memos to complex, multiple-chapter structured books with imported graphics. The basic parts are:

• The Element Catalog, which guides you through the insertion of elements into complex structures and shows you how to change elements at a location. Use the Element Catalog to define content and add specific attributes (an element's properties and options).

• The Structure View.

• A validation tool, which locates invalid elements and assists you in correcting errors.

A brief XML tutorial

It is straightforward to author XML from Structured FrameMaker 7.0 documents. One key feature to understand is that XML authoring is template-driven. Several interdependent support files act like templates and master pages to control the behaviors for authoring, importing, and exporting your projects. Although FrameMaker 7.0 documents are not XML documents, the FrameMaker 7.0 program can export valid Structured FrameMaker 7.0 documents in the XML format, and it can import an XML document back into FrameMaker 7.0 for re-editing and updating, a process called a round trip.

To start Structured Authoring, you need a Structured Template. Before you save your first document to XML markup, set up an XML application file, reference your XML DTD (Document Type Definition), and create XML read/write rules. The FrameMaker 7.0 Structured View enables you to look at the hierarchy of your structure. The Element Catalog guides you through complex structures.

You might think of these necessary files working in the background like the internal systems of the human body. The Structure View tree is like the spinal column, with its branches the nerve center and bones of the file. The elements and attributes of the structure are the vertebrae and nerves branching out. The files working in the background, like other systems of the body, are the DTD, Read/Write Rules, Stylesheet designations, and pointers needed to validate the document. A valid XML file is then useful on the Web, as a PDF, in catalogs, in print, and on wireless devices. Without the inner structure, however, the whole thing would fall apart. A valid XML document, therefore, is a system of vitally important files working together in the background behind the fluent face of the finished work.

Using *XML Cookbook* to author XML documents

The *XML Cookbook* is a FrameMaker tutorial that lets users practice using the details of Structured FrameMaker 7.0 to create XML.

The methodology from the Cookbook is adapted here as an opportunity for you to become familiar with an XML file, edit its content, and save it. In the next lesson, you will view the results in a browser, as a PDF, and import it back into Structured FrameMaker 7.0. You can use the *XML Cookbook*, included with your original FrameMaker 7.0 CD, to amplify what is covered in this lesson.

Another resource provided with the program disk, is the directory entitled *OnlineManuals*. Be sure to explore the contents of that directory for helpful information about XML and structure.

Creating an application

To set up an XML application, you need to identify the locations of all its necessary files and define its properties and preferences. This is called "creating an application" and is accomplished using a specific type of FrameMaker file with the name of structapps.fm. To create a structured XML application, you edit the structapps.fm file.

The EDD (Element Definition Document) controls use of the elements and establishes the architecture of the final file, describing interpretation of fonts, formats, tables, and graphics. It is like a flowchart, outline, or schema but is expressed in Structured FrameMaker 7.0 definitions, using elements as its components.

To create and edit in Structured FrameMaker 7.0, use the Structure View to navigate and manage your document, and draw from the Element Catalog when inserting, changing, or moving elements.

When an element does not conform to the rules, Structure View identifies the error in red; it can be a missing, undefined, or misplaced element. A file that does not conform to the rules will not validate; then it will not export into XML.

XML uses tags. Tags indicate data content, not style. Formatting is handled separately in the Read/Write Rules. XML documents have to follow rules. XML separates data from style and content. In this way, a document can be interpreted with any one or a combination of these building blocks for multiple purposes. For instance, the data can be extracted or analyzed without changing the style or the content.

For more information about structure, elements, rules and definition files, structured applications, stylesheets, and other essentials of authoring valid XML documents, see "Getting Started with Structure" on page 399 of this book and Chapter *3*, "*Working with Structured Documents*," in the *Adobe FrameMaker 7.0 User Guide*.

Setting up files for the conversion to XML

In this exercise, you'll update and expand a validated Structured FrameMaker 7.0 document into XML. You need an XML or SGML application file. You'll use one composed for this purpose called TechDocs.

You'll take a Structured FrameMaker 7.0 document and in the next lesson create an XML file. You would follow similar steps to create an SGML file.

GRAPHICS FORMATS: SVG and PNG You'll be encountering two graphics file formats that were developed for the Internet and for other uses where resolution needs to be sharp while file size must be small. Both the SVG (Scalable Vector Graphics) and the PNG (Portable Network Graphics) fulfill these requirements in their own ways. When first introduced, browsers could not take advantage of them. Recently, both formats have become more prevalent. As XML has taken hold, browsers have been formulated to use and display them properly.

• SVG are used when the source of the graphic is in an outlined illustration format like AI or EPS. They have a feature that permits interactivity. Experiment by double-clicking on an SVG graphic in the Art folder of Lesson 17. The graphic will open in your browser. Try changing the colored circles by moving the sliders. One of the most significant features of SVG is that because they are vector images, they are infinitely scalable, while they retain their sharpness at any size.

• PNG are used when the source of the graphic is in a bitmap format like TIFF or PICT. They can be compressed very small without losing image quality, yet allow for the use of an alpha (mask) channel, which permits the creation of transparent backgrounds in PNG images. The overall image quality equates to TIFF, usually superior to JPEG and much superior to GIF.

CIBColorDoc1.fm to CIBColorFinal.fm

These exercises utilize a FrameMaker file you have worked with in earlier lessons and guide you through the steps of adding structure and validating so that you can create an XML file that can then be used in other forms of documents. Begin by opening the structapps.fm file and setting template applications. Then use the structure tools to read them in order to make them the active templates for a particular session. These two basic steps direct FrameMaker 7.0 to set up the files for conversion, while either importing for authoring or exporting for output.

Note: Elements will be indicated in the text of the exercises in lessons 17 and 18 in square brackets. For example, a Head element would be read as [Head].

Begin by locating the Lesson17 folder on your hard drive. It is organized into 3 sub-folders.

1 In the L17XML folder, open the structapps.fm file.

2 Choose File > Structure Tools > Read Application Definitions.

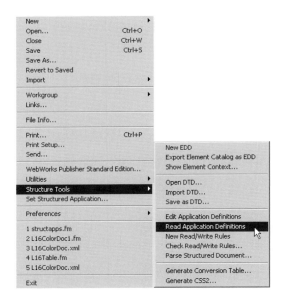

3 In the dialog box, click OK.

4 Choose File > Set Structured Application.

5 In the Set Structured Application box, select TechPubs from the pop-up menu, and click Set.

6 Choose File > Open > CIBColorDoc1.fm.

7 Choose View > Element Boundaries (as Tags).

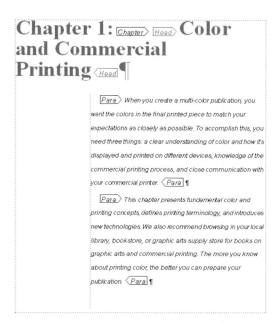

You can scroll through the document to the end, observing differences from the earlier standard FrameMaker lessons that used this material. Explore the tags and graphics.

Be sure that text symbols are turned on for viewing, and refresh the screen periodically.

Importing an XML section

1 With CIBColorDoc1.fm active, place the cursor at the end of the document before the [Chapter] tag at the last paragraph text symbol.

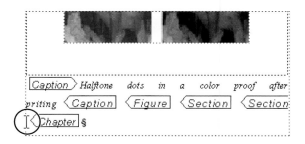

2 Choose File > Import > File > CIBColorDoc2.xml, and Import by Reference.

3 The Unknown File Type dialog box appears (Windows and Unix). Choose XML and click Convert. Mac OS users should skip step 3.

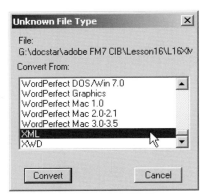

4 In the Import Structured Text by Reference dialog box choose Automatic and click Import.

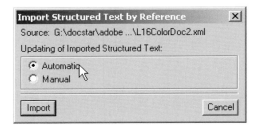

The *Bitmap image and output resolution* section appears at the end of the document.

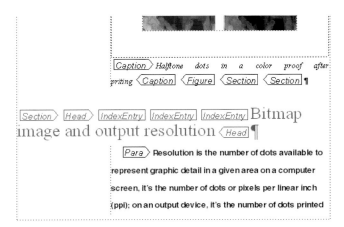

5 Save the document.

Converting the XML section to editable text

1 Place the cursor anywhere in the newly imported XML section.

2 Double-click in the section.

The whole section is selected, and the Text Insert Properties box appears.

3 Select Convert to Text.

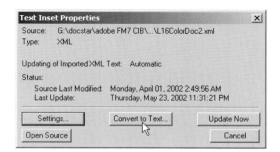

The Convert Text Insets to Text dialog box appears.

4 Choose Selected Text Inset and click Convert. The new section is now editable.

5 Save the document.

Reformatting the XML section

Reformat the new section on bitmaps and resolution by placing the cursor in the [Head] element text beginning with the word *Bitmap*.

1 In the Paragraph Designer, change the paragraph Default Font Family to:

• (Windows) AGaramond-Semibold.

• (Mac OS and UNIX) Adobe Garamond, Weight: Semibold.

2 Click Apply.

3 Select the remaining three paragraphs of the newly imported section.

4 In the Paragraph Designer, change the Default Font Family to Myriad-Roman (Windows) or Myriad (Mac OS and Unix).

5 Click Apply.

6 Save the document.

Importing an SVG graphic into a [Figure] element

1 At the end of the new section's second paragraph, select the Paragraph Text Symbol to the right of the word *detail*.

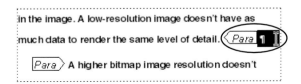

2 Choose Element > Element Catalog, and the Element Catalog appears.

3 In the Element Catalog, click once on Figure and then click Insert.

The Anchored Frame box appears.

4 Make sure the Width is 246 pt, and the Height is 144 pt.

5 Click New Frame.

A new anchored frame is inserted at the end of the paragraph. Notice the structure tags.

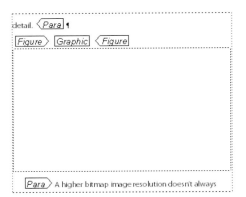

Notice also that the Element Catalog reveals which new elements can be inserted at this place in the logical flow of the structure. Here it shows only Caption as an available next step.

6 In the Element Catalog, click Caption.

7 Click Insert.

[Caption] tags appear.

8 Between the [Caption] tags, type **Image resolutions at 72 ppi and 300 ppi**.

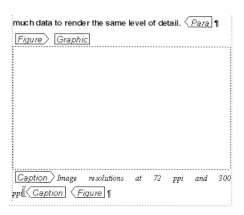

9 Select the blank anchored frame above the caption.

10 Choose > File > Import > File.

11 Go to the Art folder within the Lesson17 folder.

12 Select Import by Reference.

13 In the Art folder, locate and select Resolution.svg, and click Import.

14 In the Unknown File Type box, be sure SVG is selected, and click Convert. The Import SVG box appears.

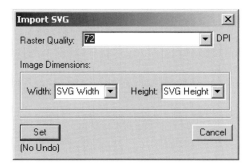

15 Click Set.

16 Resolution.svg is imported into the anchored frame.

💡 *Try double-clicking on Resolution.svg. It will appear in a browser window. Move the magnifiers around.*

17 Save the document.

Validating the document

To output an error-free structured document, you need to validate its structure.

1 To validate the document in its current state, choose Element > Validate.

The Element Validation box appears.

2 Be sure that the Entire Document radio button is selected, and click Start Validating.

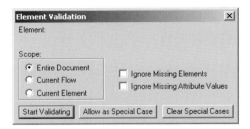

The graphic element you inserted containing Resolution.svg will be selected. The Element Validation dialog box reports the Element Graphic is invalid and a Value is required for attribute [Type].

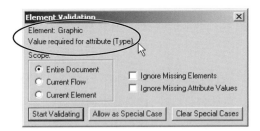

Resolving Element Validation issues

Next, you will resolve the Element Validation issue related to the Figure's attributes.

1 In the upper right corner of the document window, open the Structure View by clicking the Display the Structure View button (⌸).

The Structure View appears with the validation issue indicated by being selected.

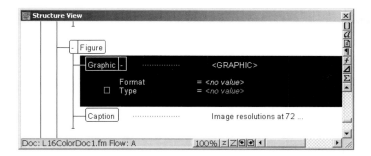

2 In the Structured View, double-click the words *<no value>*.

The Attributes box appears, indicating <no value> for Type.

3 Select Type under Attribute Name.

4 Click and hold the pop-up menu button to the right of the area called Attribute Value.

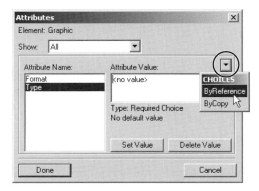

5 From the Choices pop-up menu, choose ByReference.

ByReference appears in the Attribute Value area of the Attributes box as the Type value.

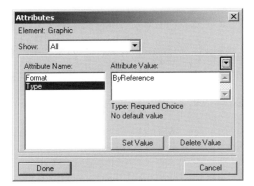

6 Click Set Value to keep the ByReference choice.

7 Under Attribute Name, click Format.

8 The Attribute Value pop-up menu now contains graphic formats. Choose > SVG.

9 Click Set Value to keep the SVG choice.

10 Click Done.

The attributes structured for Resolution.svg have been corrected.

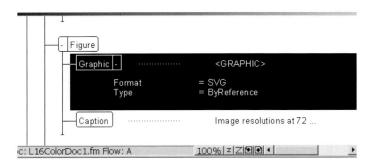

11 Now return to the Element Validation box and click Start Validating again.

The document is reported to be valid.

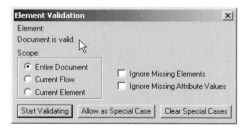

12 Save the document.

Inserting a [Table] element

1 Scroll to the end of the document, and place the cursor at the end of the last paragraph ending with the words *be poor.*

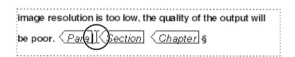

2 In the Element Catalog, select Table.

3 Click on Insert.

The Insert Table dialog box appears.

4 Choose Standard Table. Make sure it will insert 4 columns, 3 body rows, 1 Heading row, and 0 Footer rows.

5 Click Insert.

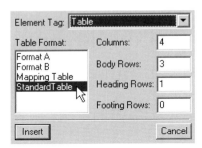

An empty table appears at the end of the document.

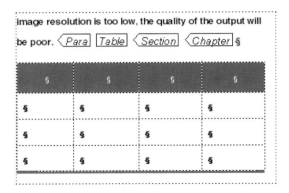

6 To gain quick access for the text to insert into the table cells, choose File > Open.

7 Go to the L17XML folder within the Lesson17 folder.

8 Open the FrameMaker file called Table.fm.

The Table.fm file appears as a separate document.

9 In the Table.fm file, select the entire Heading row.

Image Size§	Publicatio n§	Resolutio n (ppi)§	Line Screen (lpi)§
§	Newspa-per§	160§	80§
5 x 5 in.§	Magazine§	266§	133§
§	Art book§	350§	175§

Text source file Table.fm for completing [Table] element in CIBColorDoc1.fm.

10 Choose Edit > Copy.

11 In the main document, drag to select the entire Heading row.

12 Choose Edit > Paste. The Paste Rows box appears.

13 Select Replace Current Rows, and click Paste. The Heading Row has been inserted into CIBColorDoc1.fm.

14 In the file Table.fm, drag to select the remainder of the cells in the table body.

15 Choose Edit > Copy.

16 Drag to select all the body cells in the CIBColorDoc1.fm table.

17 Repeat the paste process you used for the Heading Row.

Image Size§	Publication§	Resolution (ppi)§	Line Screen (lpi)§
§	Newspaper§	160§	80§
5 x 5 in.§	Magazine§	266§	133§
§	Art book§	350§	175§

18 Close the Table.fm document. Leave the main document open and save it.

Adding [Topic] elements

At this point, you've imported and changed the fonts of a valid XML section; imported and corrected attributes of a [Figure] element to make them valid; and inserted a [Table] element as well as its text. The final exercise in this lesson is to finish authoring your XML document by adding interactive Topic Paragraph elements. Topics are created as cross-references, which make them linkable within PDF and HTML files upon export to those and other types of documents.

1 Scroll to the beginning of CIBColorDoc1.fm.

2 Place the cursor at the end of the second paragraph that ends with the words, *your publication. [Para]*.

3 Select the Paragraph Text Symbol after the [Para] element.

4 In the Element Catalog, click once on TopicsList.

5 Click Insert.

6 The cursor appears between two [TopicsList] elements in a new paragraph.

7 In the Element Catalog, click on TopicHead.

8 Click Insert.

9 Between the new [TopicHead] elements, type, **Chapter Topics:**

10 In the Paragraph Designer, change the [head] paragraph Default Font Family to:

• (Windows) AGaramond-Semibold;

• (Mac OS and UNIX) Adobe Garamond, Weight: Semibold.

11 Click Apply.

12 Move the cursor to the end of the paragraph between the last two element boundary markers: [TopicHead] and [TopicsList].

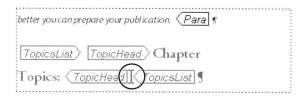

13 In the Element Catalog, click once on TopicPara.

14 Click Insert.

15 The Cross-Reference dialog box appears.

Adding [Topic] paragraphs

In the Cross-Reference dialog box, proceed exactly in the same way as you did in Lesson 10.

1 Choose HeadLevel(2) if it is not already selected in the Element Tags area.

2 In the Elements area, choose *The Properties of Color*.

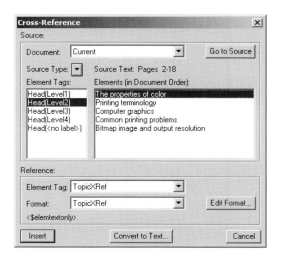

3 Click Insert.

4 *The Properties of Color* becomes the first topic in the list. It will be formatted in blue text.

5 Move the cursor between the last occurrence of the [TopicPara] and [TopicsList] elements.

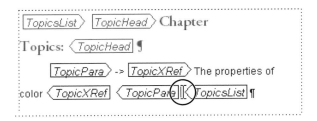

6 Now repeat the steps for adding topics to the document until all five HeadLevel(2) elements are done.

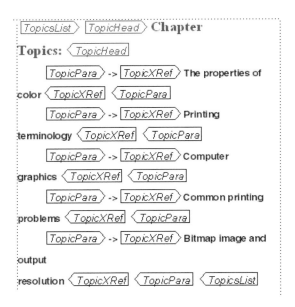

7 Select the five topics that appear in blue type.

8 In the Paragraph Designer, change the [head] paragraph Default Font Family to:

• (Windows) Myriad-Roman, Weight: Bold.

• (Mac OS and UNIX) Myriad, Weight: Bold.

9 Click Apply.

Completing the valid XML document

To make sure everything is in order for future uses of the document, you'll do two final checks. You have affected the document in many ways, so some reconfirmation can be helpful.

1 Make structapps.fm the active document.

2 Read the underlying template applications again through File > Structure Tools > Read Application Definitions.

3 Reconfirm that TechPubs is the active application through File > Set Structured Application.

4 Make CIBColorDoc1.fm the active document.

5 Validate the document.

6 Save the document.

7 Finally, choose File > Save As.

8 Save the document as CIBColorFinal.fm in the L17XML folder within the Lesson17 folder.

9 Also, save the document as CIBColorFinal.fm in the L18XML folder within the Lesson18 folder. You will use it in the next lesson.

Congratulations, you've made a valid Structured FrameMaker 7.0 document that can become an XML document and be read back into Structured FrameMaker 7.0 to complete a round trip.

Moving on

For in-depth information about authoring XML using FrameMaker documents, see Chapter 3, "Working with Structured Documents," and Chapter 21, "Elements in Structured Documents," in the *Adobe FrameMaker 7.0 User Guide*.

Review questions

1 What three errors might Structure View identify?

2 Do tags indicate formatting?

3 What are in square brackets in FrameMaker 7.0?

4 Can XML be converted to editable text?

5 Why does the Element Catalog list different elements at different times?

6 How do you get an error-free structured document? (short answer)

7 Why do you view text symbols in working with FrameMaker 7.0 to author XML?

8 Can FrameMaker 7.0 contain tables?

Answers

1 A missing element, an undefined element, or a misplaced element are three errors that Structure View might identify.

2 No, the element tags in Structured FrameMaker 7.0 indicate data or content, not formatting.

3 Elements are within the square brackets in Structured FrameMaker 7.0.

4 Yes, XML can be converted to editable text.

5 The insertion point may be at a variety of different locations in the document, so that the elements that are valid at those different places may be different.

6 Validate the document to get an error-free structured document.

7 Viewing text symbols enables you to precisely select a paragraph ending symbol, so that it will be recognized and used in putting together the structured document.

8 Yes, tables can be included in Structured FrameMaker 7.0.

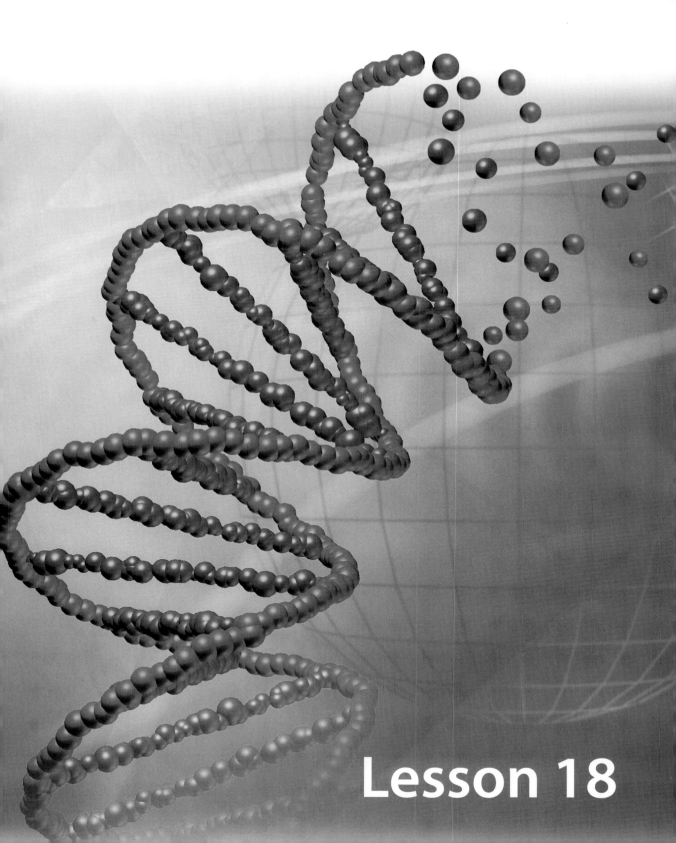

Lesson 18

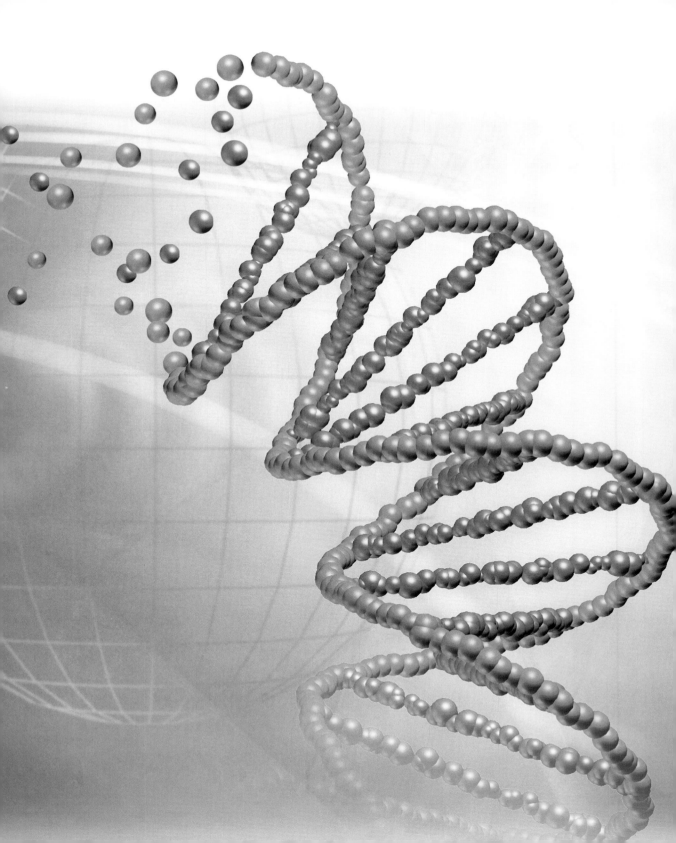

18 | Exporting and Importing Structured Files

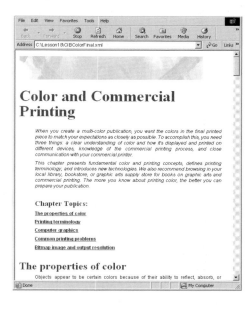

Valid Structured FrameMaker 7.0 documents are useful in multiple formats outside of the program. Because the data is treated separately from the formatted contents, it can be mined in searches or used for databases. Saved as an XML file, the document looks similar when viewed on a Web browser or when read back into Structured FrameMaker 7.0, a process called a round trip.

Once you have authored a valid Structured FrameMaker 7.0 file, you have the flexibility to output it in many ways. In the previous two lessons, you learned what a structured document looks like and built CIBColorDoc1.fm into one. Then you saved it as CIBColorFinal.fm for use in this lesson. The key factor to keep in mind is that the files you'll make here will look reasonably similar to the original FrameMaker file but will not be identical. Achieving a perfectly articulated file which is identical in distributed multiple formats such as XML, HTML, SGML, XHTML, and PDF is a subject for advanced study and experience beyond this Classroom in a Book.

In this lesson you'll:

• Export a valid structured document to PDF and to XML.

• In a browser, view the XML document after it is transformed into an HTML file.

• View the PDF document in Adobe Acrobat.

• Complete a round trip by importing the XML file back into Structured FrameMaker 7.0.

• Learn about WebWorks Publisher for creating and manipulating XML, HTML or other structured files.

Exporting to XML

You'll be opening the document you created in Lesson17, CIBColorFinal.fm, and reusing it. Then you will explore the way in which different applications reflect the files' structured data.

1 Go to the L18XML folder within the Lesson18 folder and open the structapps.fm file.

2 Choose File > Structure Tools > Read Application Definitions.

3 In the dialog box, click OK.

4 Choose File > Set Structured Applications.

5 In the Set Structured Application box, select TechPubs from the pop-up menu.

6 Click Set.

7 Go to the L18XML folder within the Lesson18 folder and open CIBColorFinal.fm.

8 Choose File > Set Structured Application.

9 In the Set Structured Application box, select TechPubs from the pop-up menu and click Set.

10 Choose Element > Validate.

The Element Validation box appears.

11 Make sure the Entire Document is selected and click Start Validating. This ensures the document is valid and ready for export.

12 Choose File > Save As.

13 In the File Name area of your file management system, change the *.fm* suffix to **.xml,** so the file name becomes **CIBColorFinal.xml**.

14 In the Save As Type area pop-up menu select XML.

15 Be sure the destination is the L18XML folder within the Lesson18 folder, and click Save.

You'll view the resulting file later in this lesson.

Exporting to PDF

The procedures for saving structured documents as PDF are the same as for unstructured documents, with the exception of setting bookmarks. In structured documents, you create bookmarks from element tags, rather than from paragraph tags. Elements add an extended level of searchable data and bookmark links.

Remember that Adobe Acrobat Distiller 5.05 is required for this process. To set Acrobat bookmarks in structured documents:

1 With CIBColorFinal.fm active, choose File > Save As.

2 For File Name, change the suffix to **.pdf** in the Save as Type pop-up menu (making the file name: **CIBColorFinal.pdf**).

3 Be sure the destination is the L18XML folder within the Lesson18, and click Save.

4 In the PDF Setup dialog box, choose Bookmarks from the pop-up menu, or click the Bookmarks tab (Windows).

5 Select Generate PDF Bookmarks.

6 To specify at which level bookmarks appear expanded in the exported PDF, select an option from the Bookmarks Expanded through Level pop-up menu. Type 2 to specify that you want the top two levels expanded.

7 From the Bookmark Source pop-up menu, choose Elements.

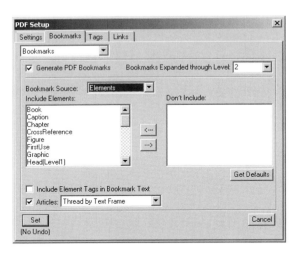

8 Move all entries from the Include Elements area into the Don't Include area. Hold the shift-key and click on the right direction arrow between the columns of entries.

The Include Element area is now clear.

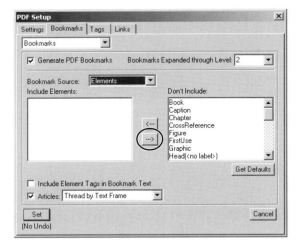

9 For this lesson, move the following elements into the Include Elements list by double-clicking the element or selecting the element and then clicking on the left direction arrow:

• Chapter.

- Head(Level1), Head(Level2).

- Section.

- TopicHead, TopicPara, TopicsList, and TopicXRef.

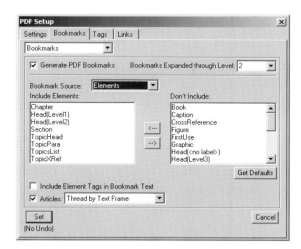

Note: To include element tags along with text in the bookmarks, select Include Element Tags in Bookmark Text. Use this option to see the levels of bookmarks in a draft PDF file. Deselect it to clear the page for conventional printing.

10 Click Set.

Note: If a Warning dialog box appears regarding Element boundaries, click OK.

To set other PDF options, see "Saving documents and books as Adobe PDF," in Chapter 20, "HTML and PDF Conversion," of the *Adobe FrameMaker 7.0 User Guide*.

Viewing the XML file in a browser

XML is a powerful tool for information users. In a large document, the ability to locate key pieces of information without having to read through the entire document saves time and provides organized information quickly to those who need it. These users might be restaurant managers, airline schedulers, product catalog ordering people, and ordinary users of the World Wide Web searching for information.

1 Launch your Internet browser.

2 From the L18XML folder within the Lesson18 folder, open your valid structured document for viewing by:

• (Windows) dragging CIBColorFinal.*xml* onto an Internet browser window. With Microsoft® Internet Explorer® 5.5 or greater you will get immediate and pleasing results. The pages are transformed into Web-friendly HTML through a process called XSLT.

• (Mac OS) The Macintosh requires an external XSLT application, written either in Java, or PERL or other scripting language. For this lesson, a free open source Java application has been downloaded from The Apache Software Foundation (*www.apache.org*). The XML file has been converted into HTML as *CIBColorFinal.html*.

Drag *CIBColorFinal.html* onto an Internet browser window. You will get immediate and pleasing results.

• (Unix) If you get uneven or unsatisfactory results with the XML file, use the HTML version of the file included in your Lesson 18 folder, *CIBColorFinal.html*. It has been made with a free open source Java application, that was downloaded from The Apache Software Foundation (*www.apache.org*). Drag *CIBColorFinal.xml* (or *.html*) onto an Internet browser window.

Note: You can also type the directory path name into the browser's URL navigation box.

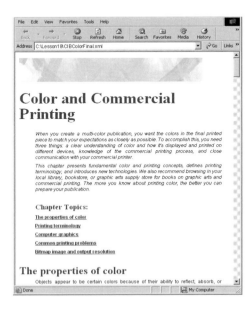

The computer has used its XSLT coding to translate the XML file with the use of the key template applications: *Chapter.xsl* (Extensible Stylesheet Language) and *Chapter.css* (Cascading Style Sheets) and *Chapter.dtd* (Document Type Definition) in your lesson folder.

3 Notice similarities and differences between CIBColorFinal.fm and CIBColorFinal.xml:

• A linked index has been added to the end of the XML file in your browser. Click the page numbers to go to an indexed topic.

• The interactive SVG graphic "Image resolutions at 72 ppi and 300 ppi" has two circles of magnification that can be moved to display authentic magnified images.

• The five Chapter Topics formatted in blue are linked and will take you to the appropriate place in the document; the browser's Back button returns you to the list of topics.

• The table looks similar in both the FrameMaker and XML files.

• The headings in FrameMaker are side-heads, whereas in the XML-into-HTML version in the browser, the headings extend across all columns over the paragraph text.

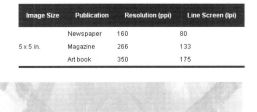

Image Size	Publication	Resolution (ppi)	Line Screen (lpi)
	Newspaper	160	80
5 x 5 in.	Magazine	266	133
	Art book	350	175

Index

Viewing the PDF file in Adobe Acrobat

1 From your Lesson18 folder, double-click CIBColorFinal.pdf.

2 Explore the bookmarks by expanding and collapsing. Click on bookmarks to observe different sections of the PDF. Notice that in the PDF, the SVG graphics are not interactive.

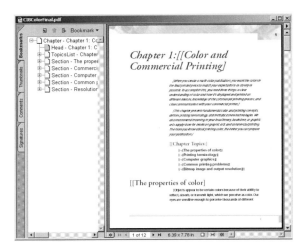

The XML Round trip

When all the support template applications are working in a coordinated manner, the results are encouraging. Now you'll get to see the structured file you created earlier in this lesson, which you reviewed in a browser and as a separate file in Adobe Acrobat. Here the translation is done with the Read/Write Rules and the formatting operations dictated by the EDD (Element Definition Document).

1 In order to complete a round trip, restore Structured FrameMaker 7.0 as your active program again.

2 Make Structapps.fm the active document.

3 Choose File > Structure Tools > Read Application Definitions.

4 In the FrameMaker box, click OK.

5 Choose File > Set Structured Applications

6 From the pop-up menu choose TechPubs and click Set.

7 Choose File > Open CIBColorFinal.xml.

8 Choose TechPubs to set the structured application.

You will see that the .xml file has been converted to an .fm file.

Exploring the XML file in Structured FrameMaker 7.0

You've arrived at the completion of the circle. The round trip of converting a Structured FrameMaker 7.0 file to an XML file and the XML file back into FrameMaker as a Structured FrameMaker 7.0 file again is what extends FrameMaker's capabilities to the Web and beyond. You can compare the two versions and observe:

• The structured file in FrameMaker 7.0 shows almost the same colors as appear on the HTML and Acrobat versions.

• The five cross-reference-type linked chapter topics at the beginning of the chapter behave in standard FrameMaker fashion. With:

(Windows) Control-Alt-Click the paragraph text.

(Mac OS) Control-Option-Click the paragraph text.

(Windows) Control-right-Click the paragraph text.

The cursor changes to a pointing hand and jumps to the linked topic. To return to the list, press Page Up on the keyboard.

• Tables in Structured FrameMaker 7.0 look substantially similar to their corresponding tables in the XML file displayed as HTML on the Web.

• The linked index of the Web version from the XML file is derived from the structure of the FrameMaker file. You can generate the index in Structured FrameMaker 7.0, as you learned in Lesson 12, "Indexes".

• The SVG and PNG graphics display well in printed materials and offer added interactivity in the Web version generated by the XML file.

WebWorks Publisher

Another way to convert documents to HTML or XML is to use WebWorks Publisher. Formerly, WWP was sold as a stand-alone program for HTML Web development. Now, Quadralay, the maker of WWP, has teamed with the staff of Adobe FrameMaker, and these two powerful programs are bundled with FrameMaker 7.0.

WWP converts FrameMaker 7.0 documents to HTML documents using templates, a set of macros that reads MIF files and writes HTML or XML files. If you want to stay within FrameMaker to create files from authoring to the Web, you can do that with Structured FrameMaker 7.0. If you want to create your FrameMaker 7.0 files and then convert them separately, WWP is there for you. A WWP User's Guide is included in the FrameMaker 7.0 directory. A WWP Training CD is packaged with the FrameMaker 7.0 materials.

WebWorks Publisher gives you the ability to reuse content from your print documentation in online deliverables. You start with tagged content, a valid Structured FrameMaker 7.0 file. Your content might contain paragraph tags, character tags, markers, tables, conditional text. You set up mappings in WWP so that, for example, a Chapter Title paragraph tag becomes HTML <H1> output. WWP can also automatically map several styles to their corresponding FrameMaker styles.

A WWP project consists of a list of the FrameMaker source documents to be converted and a list of FrameMaker components (tags) and how they will be converted, and support files used during the conversion (a .css file), and the output generated (HTML, XML files).

Note: In order to use WebWorks Publisher, install WebWorks Publisher Standard Edition from your FrameMaker 7.0 program disk.

Creating a WWP project file for HTML conversion

WebWorks helps you to create multiple outputs from one set of FrameMaker 7.0 files.

The New Project wizard takes you through the steps specifying what you need. As in Structured FrameMaker 7.0, you have two views; in WWP there is the application window, the shell of the application, and the project window, which displays the project's hierarchy.

To create a WebWorks Publisher project, you associate your FrameMaker book with a template.

1 Choose File > WebWorks Publisher Standard Edition.

The project launcher window is displayed.

2 From the Template pop-up menu, select the Portable HTML Standard Edition.

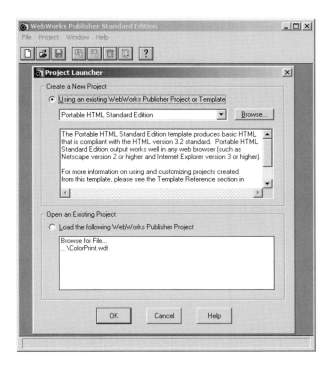

3 Click OK.

The New Project Wizard is displayed.

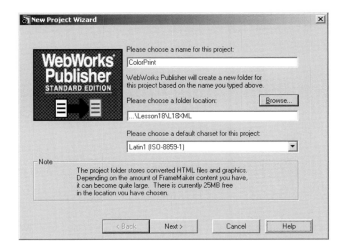

4 Give your project a name. For this exercise, type **ColorPrint**.

5 Specify the directory where you want to keep the project by typing in the directory path or by selecting the Browse button and navigating to your L18XML folder within the Lesson18 folder. Leave the default charset (character set). Click Next.

6 Select the FrameMaker book file to be converted.

7 Use the Browse button to locate and select CIBColorFinal.fm in the L18XML folder within the Lesson18 folder. Click Next.

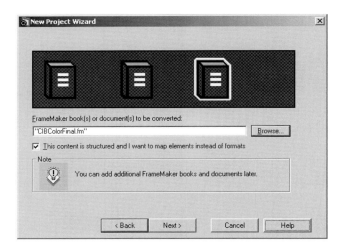

WWP scans the files in CIBColorFinal.fm and builds a list of element, paragraph, and character tags used in the book. WWP performs some automatic mapping

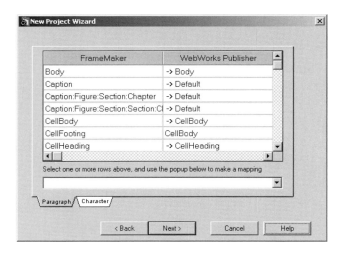

8 Click Next.

You now have the option of converting immediately or postponing conversion and experimenting with mappings.

9 Select > Yes, go ahead and convert the content.

10 Click Finish.

Your new ColorPrint project is displayed along with the support files that WebWorks generates.

11 Save the project. Select File > Save.

The project window lists all the files in the project. The FrameMaker and Generated Files folder shows you the source FrameMaker files.

12 Click on the plus signs (+) or triangle ◀ (Mac OS) in the FrameMaker and Generated Files directory to see the HTML and GIF output files.

13 View the HTML output in your Web browser as you did with CIBColorFinal.xml.

14 To see the HTML output of the document in a browser, double-click CIBColorFinal.html.

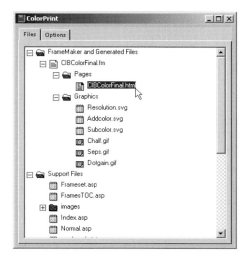

Your Internet browser is launched.

Note: As before, you can also drag the file onto an Internet browser window, or you can type your directory path name into the browser's URL navigation box.

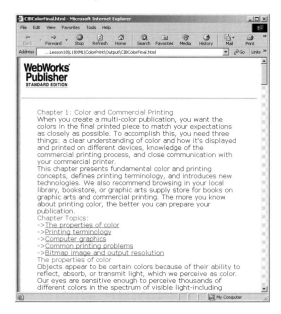

15 Compare the formatting with other outputs you have done in this lesson.

The results you see are based on default interpretations of the elements and paragraph tags in CIBColorFinal.fm. Read User's Guide.pdf, provided in the WebWorks Publisher Standard Edition folder called "pdfs."

Moving on

Congratulations! You've now completed lesson 18 and the *Adobe FrameMaker 7.0 Classroom in a Book*.

For in-depth information about exporting and importing structure, see Chapter 18 "Importing, Linking, and Exporting" in the *Adobe FrameMaker 7.0 User Guide*.

Review questions

1 To create bookmarks for a PDF in Structured FrameMaker 7.0, what do you use instead of paragraph tags?

2 In the Bookmark Source pop-up menu, what do you choose?

3 What are two ways to get your XML file into a browser to view it?

4 Can an .xml file be converted to a .fm file?

5 What are the four parts of a WebWorks Publisher project for converting FrameMaker files into XML files?

Answers

1 Element tags are used instead of paragraph tags.

2 Elements should be chosen in the pop-up menu.

3 Drag the XML file to the open browser window and drop it on the page, or type the XML file's directory path into the browser's URL navigation box.

4 Yes, an .xml file can be converted to a .fm file. A round trip is the conversion of a .fm file to an .xml file and then back again from an .xml file to a .fm file.

5 A WebWorks Publisher projects consists of:

• A list of FrameMaker source documents; a list of FrameMaker tags (and how they will be converted); support files (.css file); output files (.xml and .html).

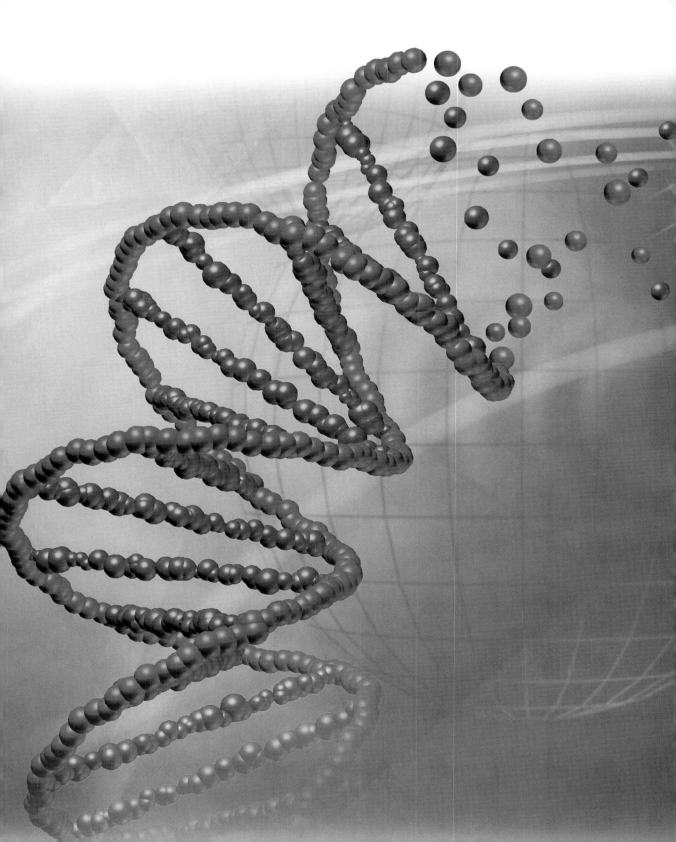

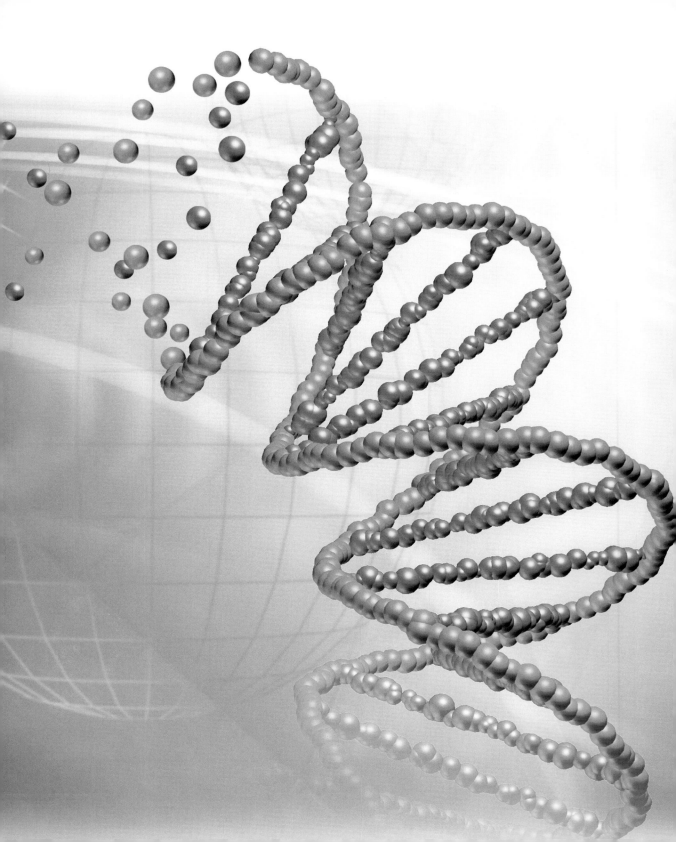

Appendix A
Glossary of Structured Terms

Ancestors	In the element hierarchy, all elements that are above
Attributes	Additional information used to describe an element such as a list or graphic reference number
Child elements	Elements that are containing by or subordinate to a higher element.
CSS	An abbreviation for cascading style sheet.
Descendants	In the element hierarchy, all elements that are subordinate to a parent element
DTD	An abbreviation for Document Type Definition, which defines the markup rules used for a given type of structured document.
EDD	An abbreviation for Element Definition Document, a document that contains element definitions.
Element	A structural unit of a document
Element boundaries	Square brackets in the document window that mark where each element begins and ends.
Element boundaries as tags	Arrow heads with element names in the document that mark where each element begins and ends.
Element bubbles	Rectangular "bubble" shapes in the Structure View that contain the name of an element. The vertical and horizontal connecting lines show how bubbles are related
Element Catalog	A collection of element types defined for a document. As you enter elements, the Element Catalog lists the element you can use at the current location.

Element hierarchy	The structure that defines which elements are above, subordinate to, or equal to others.
ELement Catalog display	Using the Set Available Elements display option to control the elements that appear and can be used depending on the location of the insertion point
HTML	An abbreviation for Hypertext Markup Language. HTML is an encoding system used to describe the content and organization of an electronic document published on the World Wide Web.
Invalid document	A document that has one or more areas in which correct structuring procedures have not been followed
Nesting	When elements are inside other elements they are said to be nested.
Parent element	An element that contains other subordinate elements.
Root element	The highest level element in a document, in which all other elements are contained
SGML	An abbreviation for Standard Generalized Markup Language, an internationally recognized encoding system used to describe the content and organization of an electronic document, independent of platforms and applications.
Sibling elements	Elements that are at the same hierarchical level.
Text snippet	The beginning text of a text-containing element, located in the Structure View to the right of the element bubble.
Valid document	A document in which all elements conform to their defined content requirements (conforms to FrameMaker's EDD or in SGML/XML a DTD.
Validation	Using the Element Validation tool to locate and fix invalid and incomplete elements.
XML	An abbreviation for Extensible Markup Language developed ten years ago.

Appendix B

Importing Microsoft Word® into FrameMaker 7.0

With FrameMaker 7.0, you can easily import documents from other applications, such as the latest versions of Microsoft Office®, for which there is an installed filter. You can now import Word 97/98/2000 files into FrameMaker in just a few simple steps. You can choose to retain the Word document's formatting or reformat the text using the current FrameMaker document's catalog.

Importing the latest versions of Microsoft Excel® files is also easy and takes just a few simple steps. You must select the Excel 97/98/2000 filter upon importing. For example, if you saved your Office 97 Excel document as a Microsoft Excel 5.0/95 Workbook file, you must import it using the Excel 5.0 filter because the Excel 97/98/2000 filter will not open it.

The intent here is to address the migrating Word user, who may have concerns about the complexities of FrameMaker. This would be a page of specifics about the Word and Office-related filters.

To import a Word file:

1 Click in your document where you want to insert the Word file and choose File > Import > File.

2 Scroll through the list of names until you find the file name of your Word document.

3 Click Import.

4 Choose Microsoft Word 97/98/2000 in the Unknown File Type dialog box.

5 Click Convert.

To import an Excel file:

1 Click in your document where you want to insert the Excel file and choose File > Import > File.

2 Scroll through the list of names until you find the file name of your Excel file.

3 Click Import.

4 Choose Microsoft Excel 97/98/2000 in the Unknown File Type dialog box.

5 Click Convert.

To import an RTF file

FrameMaker 7.0 now supports RTF 1.6 import and export.

To import a MIF file

You can import the text of a specified flow of a MIF file as you do any FrameMaker file. When you import by copying, all reference and master pages are imported as well as the body pages, and the body text appears on a disconnected page. To connect pages and flows, see the section on "Connecting text frames," in Chapter 12 of the *Adobe FrameMaker 7.0 User Guide*.

Appendix C
Keyboard Shortcuts

Windows

- Character Designer/open: Escape + Shift + f(lowercase F) + i(lowercase I) + c(lowercase C).
- Document display/redraw: Control + l(lowercase L).
- End of document: Alt + pgdn.
- Find/Change: Control +f(lowercase F).
- Paragraph Designer/open: Escape + Shift + f(lowercase F) + i(lowercase I) + p(lowercase P).
- QuickAccess Bar/display: Command + 8.
- Spelling Checker: Escape + e(lowercase E) + s(lowercase S).
- Structure view: Escape + f(lowercase F) + i(lowercase I) + v(lowercase V).
- Table Designer/open: Escape + Shift + f(lowercase F) + i(lowercase I) + t(lowercase T).
- Thesaurus/open: Escape + e(lowercase E) + t(lowercase T).
- Undo: Control + z(lowercase Z).

Mac OS

- Anchored frame/resize/shrink-wrap the object: Escape + m(lowercase M) + p(lowercase P).
- Body Pages/view: Command + Option + b(lowercase B).
- Character Designer/open: Command + d(lowercase D).
- Document display/redraw: Control + l(lowercase L).
- Find/Change: Command +f(lowercase F).
- Master Pages/view: Command + Option + m(lowercase M).
- Page/go to: Command + t(lowercase T).
- Paragraph Designer/open: Command + m(lowercase M).
- QuickAccess Bar/display: Command + 8.

- Reference Pages/view: Command + Option + r(lowercase R).

- Rulers/display: Command + u(lowercase U).

- Spelling Checker: Command + l(lowercase L).

- Table Designer/open: Command + Option + t(lowercase T).

- Text Symbols/turn on/off: Command + y(lowercase Y).

- Thesaurus/open: Command + Shift + t(lowercase T).

- Tools palette/display: Command + 3.

UNIX

- Document Display/redraw: Control + l(lowercase L).

Appendix D
Copying the Sample Files (UNIX)

The Classroom in a Book CD-ROM contains all the lesson files you need to complete the exercises in this book. These instructions describe how to check whether the CD-ROM drive is mounted, how to mount the CD-ROM drive (if necessary), and how to copy the sample files from the CD-ROM.

The process is different depending on whether the CD-ROM drive is local or remote:

Local CD-ROM drive If you have a CD-ROM drive connected to your UNIX workstation, you can mount the CD locally. (To mount a CD-ROM drive, you must know your system's root password.) You can then copy the sample files to your machine's hard disk or to your home directory. This appendix contains instructions for doing this.

Remote CD-ROM drive If you don't have a local CD-ROM (or if you don't know your system's root password or don't want to mount the CD yourself), you can give the CD to your system administrator. The system administrator would then mount the CD and copy the lesson files to a directory that you have access to. This appendix does not contain instructions for mounting a CD-ROM drive remotely. System administrators may refer to the *Installing Adobe FrameMaker Products* manual (included with the FrameMaker 7.0 product) for more information.

Copying the sample files from a local CD-ROM drive

If you have a UNIX workstation with a CD-ROM drive, follow these steps to mount the drive and copy the lesson files. These instructions describe how to do the following:

• Determine whether the CD-ROM drive is mounted.

• Mount the CD-ROM drive, if necessary (some SGI Indy and Sun Solaris systems mount the CD-ROM drive automatically).

• Copy the sample files.

To determine if the CD-ROM drive is already mounted:

1 Insert the CD-ROM into your disk drive.

2 Check for /cdrom or /CD-ROM on your system.

If you find a CD-ROM directory, check whether the drive is mounted as described in the following step.

3 Determine if the CD-ROM drive has already been mounted by entering one of the following commands:

- On an HP or Solaris system, **/sbin/mount.**

- On an IBM system, **/usr/sbin/mount.**

- On a SunOS system, **/etc/mount.**

4 Scan the on-screen list of mounted file systems. If the CD-ROM drive has already been mounted on your local system, a line similar to one of the following lines appears in the list (where the value of *device_name* depends on your system):

- On an HP system, `/cdrom on` *device_name* `readonly on date`.

- On an IBM system, `/dev/cd0 /cdrom`.

- On a Solaris or SunOS system, `/dev/sr0 on /cdrom`.

5 Do one of the following:

- If the drive is already mounted, you can begin copying the sample files (see step 1 on page 481).

- If the drive has not been mounted, see the following section.

To mount the CD-ROM drive:

1 Log in as the root user by entering **su root**.

You will be prompted for the root password for your computer. If you don't know the root password, ask your system administrator for help.

2 Create the CD-ROM directory by entering one of the following commands (if the directory already exists, skip this step):

- On any system, **mkdir /cdrom.**

3 Mount the drive by entering one of the following commands:

- On an HP system, **/sbin/mount** *device_name* **/cdrom –r –t cdfs.**

- On an IBM system, **/usr/sbin/mount –v cdrfs –r /dev/cd0 /cdrom.**

- On a Solaris system, **/sbin/mount -F hsfs –r /dev/sr0 /cdrom.**

- On a SunOS system, **/etc/mount –r –t hsfs /dev/sr0 /cdrom.**

The value of *device_name* depends on your system. The –r option mounts the drive as read-only. Use this option to prevent media error messages from appearing. The –t option specifies the CD-ROM type.

4 Verify that the drive was mounted correctly by entering one of the following commands:

- On an HP or Solaris system, **/sbin/mount.**

- On an IBM system, **/usr/sbin/mount.**

- On a SunOS system, **/etc/mount.**

You should see a list of mounted file systems, including the name of the drive you just mounted.

5 Log off as root user by entering **exit.**

To copy the sample files:

1 Enter **whoami** to make sure you're no longer logged in as root user.

2 Make sure the CD-ROM is still inserted in your disk drive.

3 Move to your computer's hard disk or to your home directory.

4 Extract the sample files from the archive on the CD-ROM by entering:
tar xvf */device_name/***unix/unixcib.tar** where device_name is the name of your CD-ROM device. This will create a directory called FM7_0CIB.

5 When the files have finished copying, log in as root user again.

6 Unmount the CD-ROM by entering **/etc/umount**.

7 Remove the disk and log out as root user by entering **exit.**

Index